ETERNITY

Conversations with

Hemitra

Suzanne King

For information contact
Suzanne King
suzanneking@verizon.net

ISBN
9798542634579

Cover by Mia Bosna

Self-Published in conjunction with
Ronni Sanlo Literary
www.ronnisanlo.com
Sequim, WA 98382

Printed in the United States of America

ETERNITY

Conversations with

Hemitre

Suzanne King

To Hemitra
and the
Return of Gaia

Acknowledgements

To my beautiful family. If I had to pick again, I'd pick all of you.

Linda Hallowell, the shamanic passage you embarked on with me will forever be remembered with the deepest love and gratitude. You're one in a million, and I'm honored to call you my eternal friend. Thank you for the accurate and amazing messages from Hemitra, as she demanded that I learn the rules of eternity.

Much gratitude to Danielle Schwartz for the unique journey we took together, which began with grief and pain and evolved to awareness and new life. It cannot be described in words. Thank you for your clarity translating Hemitra from the next dimension. I learned volumes of the essentials, as I moved through the dark and into the light remembering that life on Earth is a great gift and so are you.

Love and gratitude to Michele Lanham for the hours of her time, as we traveled a sometimes difficult, healing journey together. I so appreciate your patient kindness and keen intuition. I'm also really grateful that you're funny.

Ellen Youngdahl, thank you for your healing presence, wisdom, and years of friendship, as you added to the story line of memories here and there in time.

Monique Brown and Teresa Souders. Thank you for entering and enriching our lives at the perfect moment. Many thanks for your gifts, and the joy we shared in our short time together.

Damini Celebre and Anna Marie Noble. How I appreciate your loving kindness and watching over me in those beginning months! As the years go by, we're still there for each other in all kinds of weather. We are proof that fun and laughter is not reserved for when times are perfect. No one could ask for better friends.

To Pat Salvitti, I'm grateful for your exquisite healing skills, vital information and friendship.

To my lovely long- time friend Virginia McKinnie, thank you for your support and for the kind words of introduction.

Joan Menapace and Connie Keener, thank you for so many things!

Jacqui McDonald, gratitude always for giving your heart at Heart of the Goddess.

Renee Welde, performance artist extraordinaire, thank you for your love and support. Rave on!!

Thank you, Lynn Mitchell for your friendship and carrying on the role of Bee Priestess.

Barbara Reid, my gratitude to you for helping Hemitra make her smooth transition.

Debbie Goldberg, bless you for your many hours of editing, as you started with my very rough draft. Thank you for your friendship and loving support.

Mia Bosna, what an exquisitely beautiful cover! Thank you for that and for all the years of   magnificent artist creations for our catalog covers and designs. You were and are an essential part of Heart of the Goddess.

Ronni Sanlo, thank you for your guidance, patience and kindness in publishing this book.

Thank you to Martin Gray for your generosity in allowing me to use the information from your beautiful website.

Adelle Garrod, I'm so grateful for your open heart, intuitive wisdom, and skill that you bring to the work.

To all the women over the years, who joined us as we took the journey of remembering together. It was a joy!

Introduction

Most of our fairy tales begin with the words, 'Once upon a time'. However, this is not a fairy tale in the traditional sense. It really happened and continues to happen. This story is about the lives of two women brought together by fate to live a life of time, magic and of course love. It is a story about what happens when one beloved is separated from another through the realm of death. Most people see death as the end of this life, yet death is a character in this story that begins a magical and loving new relationship.

Around the turn of the last century, I walked into a small boutique in a suburb of Philadelphia. The shop was filled with carefully curated jewelry, clothing, books, crystals, Goddess statues, candles and a variety of other feminine-focused items. My gaze became transfixed by the two striking and beautiful women behind the counter display of jewelry. Sue and Hemitra, the founders of *Heart of the Goddess* and co-creators of *Woman's Wisdom*, would soon become my teachers and dear friends. Their loving and expansive hearts made a place at the *Heart of the Goddess* for all women, with classroom space for workshops, ceremony, creativity and a multitude of healing modalities. Their offerings focused on honoring women, the sacred feminine and the Earth. They sent me and a host of other women on a journey of self-discovery teaching us to trust the inherent feminine wisdom within us and all women.

What struck me most about Sue and Hemitra at our first meeting is exactly what still draws me and continues to draw me to Sue's book about her ongoing communication with her partner. These two women still break all the rules. Their life together encompassed remembering and exploring past lives and bringing those lessons and wisdom to their present community, devoting their careers and talents to honoring the sacred feminine and enlivening that wisdom in all women. Lifetime after lifetime, they incarnated into partnerships, and together they explored and fulfilled their souls' lessons. Sue (and Hemitra as well, because she certainly is having a say in this book!) has written about breaking down the barriers of even death and opening a channel of communication. They remind us of how love transcends our preconceived notions when it comes to what is "supposed" to happen. Sue's telling of their ongoing relationship between dimensions creates a map for us concerning what does happen in the afterlife. Their experiences break through the conventional and take us on a journey that goes beyond traditional models and belief systems. It's an ongoing process, because love and life are ongoing, even when it feels like everything has ended in pain and heartbreak. No one we love is ever lost to us. Hemitra and Sue teach us that love, and yes, humor open the door to all eternity.

And so, they continue to live the magic that is available to everyone.

Virginia McKinnie

Chapter 1

I woke from a coma-like sleep, 3:10 a.m., the insistent knocking forced me awake, and my heart pounded violently. God, please no! But I knew, I just knew.

Body shaking, I bolted out of bed and stumbled to the window. Two police cars were in the drive. "I'm coming," I called from the upstairs bedroom window.

In seconds, I found shorts and a top and somehow got into them. My body trembled, and I wondered if I could walk. Sleepless for three weeks now, I leaned on the stair banister to stay upright and stumbled downstairs. Please no!

I turned on the outside light, unlocked and opened the front door. Two uniformed police stood outside. "Ma'am, I'm sorry to wake you. She's taken a turn for the worse. The hospital's been trying to reach you."

I grabbed my bag and keys that lay on the wooden table by the door. In a daze, I stepped out on the front flagstone terrace into the oppressive heat of the late July night, and it felt like a heavy damp towel. "Are you ok?" asked the officer in navy blue.

My answer, "I'm going."

"They want you to go in through emergency."

Hurry, just move, I thought. I jumped into my car and watched the two police cars maneuver down the drive.

A turn for the worse…at 10 last night, I had kissed her good night. "I love you. Stay sleeping." The sedative worked, and Hemitra never responded. That night she had been suffering from anxiety, had trouble breathing, and was in unusual pain. I asked the nurses to knock her out.

Blinking lights and no traffic, so I hit the gas pedal. No, slow down. You're not awake. I tried to calm the mounting terror and fill the dark space in my head with rational thoughts, reality, the way it should be.

Today, later this morning, Hemitra was supposed to have a minor surgical procedure. Something the docs had diagnosed about air pressing against her lungs post extensive abdominal surgery, 16 days before. She was home getting better, getting her appetite back, but suddenly the night before last, she had trouble breathing and pain more intense than ever before. I stayed with her for hours. Her temperature dropped to 94 degrees, and she broke into a cold sweat.

"Let me take you to the ER," I pleaded. She insisted on waiting until morning to call the surgeon. As I held her cool damp body, an inner knowing tore at my insides. Before light the next morning, I called for help. She went to the ER by ambulance and was readmitted. After more tests, the conclusion was that a simple procedure would relieve the air pressure from the previous surgery. The pressure was causing her shortness of breath. The MD said she would come home again in a day. I wanted to believe that.

After checking on Hemitra only hours ago last night, I staggered home from the hospital and collapsed. Because of so little sleep and Hemitra out cold, I didn't take the phone upstairs. The hospital tried to reach me for two hours and finally called the police.

I turned right into the parking lot and was able to park directly in front. I bolted to the door that opened automatically, and I landed in the cool sterile ER. Adrenaline rushed through my body, heartbeats one explosion after another.

The ER was quiet with one staff member at the desk. Was she waiting for me? "Suzanne?"

"Yes, which way?" The woman pressed a button to open the double doors and gave instructions to the 4th floor. Inside the elevator, it took forever to move upward. I watched—1, 2, 3, the numbers flashing—finally 4. I gasped for a breath, sprinted to the end of a short hall, and turned left.

The next stretch of endless hallway looked to be the length of the entire hospital. There were no patients, only closed doors at regular intervals. It was cold, stark and eerie. The dim lighting highlighted the institutional gray walls. Every closed door led to another empty silent room. No matter how hard I ran, I didn't seem to be getting to my destination. My feet hit the floor and echoed a strange reality, as I ran toward the nightmare I was to face.

I turned right and saw two lit rooms, one across from the other. A doctor opened the door to one of the rooms and walked toward me. "Suzanne?"

"Yes, where is she?" My voice was quiet, strong and desperate.

"Come with me." The young man in the white coat guided me to a room and opened the door. This small room had a desk with an open laptop, some file cabinets, and machines.

"Where is she? Take me to her."

The white coat spoke, "She coded at midnight, and we resuscitated her. She coded again shortly after that. She's brain dead and on life support. We were waiting for you."

The words *brain dead* and *coded* swam in my head. Stop talking I thought! "Where is she? Take me to her!" I witnessed my voice as it gained intensity.

In mid-sentence, the young man cut his words and led me to the room across the hall and opened the door. The woman I loved was no longer there. A breathing apparatus filled her mouth, everything taped in place, monitors beeping and beeping with the green lines running up and down on the screen. The once beautiful symmetrical face distorted by whatever process her body chose to shut down. Then I understood *coded* and *brain dead*. The decision to execute her living will and free her took only seconds. "Take it all off her now!" I demanded.

"Do you want...?"

I didn't let the nurse finish. "Take it all out."

One by one, the nurses removed the gadgets from Hemitra's nose and mouth. The beeps of the monitors slowed. I stood by my wife's bed holding her hand. My hand touched her warm shoulder under the hospital gown as the last signs of earthly life slipped from her body. In under five minutes after the life support removal after the life support was removed, only silence. I kissed her face and turned away. A strange numbness set in, nothingness.

A hand touched my arm, and a nurse said, "I'm so sorry. Can I get you anything?"

"A bullet."

"You answered that too quickly." The nurse grimaced.

The nurses began to move around, do things with the machines, no talking, only silence.

Another nurse asked, "What do you want us to do with her body?"

"She wanted to donate it to science." I knew that answer.

Someone gave me a paper to sign and handed me two plastic bags with drawstrings, which included all that Hemitra had with her in the hospital: iPod, phone, clothes, and a watch.

I staggered back down the stark and endless corridor. Hospital engraved plastic bag in each hand and my bag over my shoulder, I fell through dark space spiraling in emptiness. Everything suddenly gone.

****

I turned into the driveway with no memory of how I got there. Like a robot, I exited the car with two white plastic bags and walked to our house, the place where we loved to live together. Inside, I threw the bags on a chair and took the first step upstairs, but the waiting Sunami of pain hit, and I sobbed—racking, choking sobs and collapsed at the bottom of the carpeted stairs. I screamed, as my body twisted in agony and my nails dug into my palms.

"Noooooo!" The protest repeatedly echoed through the house. There would be no relief, no escaping the horror, no way to squirm or twist away from what was now and what lay ahead.

Energy spent, I got up and climbed the stairs to the bedroom. No one to call—not at 4 a.m. I wouldn't do that to my family or hers. There was plenty of harsh endless time to come. I lay in bed suspended in a dark emptiness and horrifying unreality, shocked and stunned.

Suddenly, Hemitra was there. I saw her vividly in my mind looking like she had 22 years ago when we first met; her hair was big and wild and her body tan and lean. She moved toward me and seemed to dissolve into me. I automatically brushed my cheek as if her hair had tickled my face, as it had many times before. Though this moment represented one of the most unusual happenings of my life, I understood completely. The vivid image lasted only seconds, yet there was no mistaking this powerful message that announced her successful transition to the next realm.

My brain felt dull and listless, as if it was injected with a kind of padding that numbed my thinking and froze my heart. Pieces of me were shattered and separated, some running down the sterile hospital corridor, others watching the monitor slow to silence. She was out of pain and gone from this world. Right now, the barrier of unimaginable grief prevented me from fully celebrating this moment with her.

However, the image of a young and vibrant Hemitra seared itself forever in my memory. It was the most hopeful and believable event of the last hideous 90 minutes. Little did I know that this visit from beyond, and many more to come, would change my world and my perception of reality forever.

From that moment, and for the second time this lifetime, she and I would break through the barriers of cultural conditioning and the way we were told it was to realize the way it really is.

Ten percent of the time, I questioned my sanity. Ninety percent of the time, I accepted the gift of my perception, our on-going loving relationship, and universal truth from my new guide. It did not happen easily.

Chapter 2

At 6 a.m., my daughter Meg sat on the living room couch on one side of me and my daughter Amy flanked the other side. This is not how we usually do things. When we're together, we put food on the table for family dinners. We clean up and deal with kids. Today, we just sat. I related the last hours, talked, and cried. It was odd to have the three of us be still and take time in the moment.

"Shouldn't you be getting ready for work?" I asked them.

"No, Mom, not today," Amy answered, realizing I was not in my right mind because my perspective had been numbed by shock.

Years ago, when Hemitra and I first fell in love, the girls hated me, hated her, hated us. How could I? The family broke into pieces as this unexpected event concluded with my painful decision to leave a 20-year marriage.

I grieved for and with my girls and our mutual pain at that time. I couldn't imagine what they must have gone through. They had their own journey of acceptance, as their dad and I battled through my decision to divorce, and we all lived with the consequences. How complex for them; they had no reference point or signs that something like this might possibly happen. The kids' sense of right and stable living changed to fear, anger, uncertainty, grief, despair, and loss.

Amy, my younger daughter, reacted by leaving college and getting pregnant with her high school sweetheart. She married and had a baby at 18, making family life even more challenging. My relationship with my daughter began again after a beautiful granddaughter arrived. After all, a reliable grandmother was needed.

Megan was angry, but her own marriage, pregnancy and baby brought a newness to our family roles with each other. We all lived in close proximity and the family gradually adjusted as best they could as we changed to a new dynamic and stayed connected by the love between us.

Jack, my ex-husband, arrived shortly after the kids the day of Hemitra's passing. He kindly offered condolences and concern. The divorce, years before, hurt him the most. His disbelief and despair were crushing. Besides the ensuing battle, the anger, the strategy for survival and territory that a divorce brings, we suffered together as our marriage came apart. No one deserves more credit than Jack for his eventual gracious acceptance of what he felt was an unacceptable situation.

In the midst of our divorce, after Amy and Tom's wedding in our back yard, Jack and I parted that day. We said, "I love you" to each other. The proceedings of the divorce were bitter and long. However, we spoke the truth that day. We did and always will love each other.

In short order, Jack began a 20-year relationship with a younger woman in the neighborhood. He never married.

Through the years, Hemitra joined the family for special occasions such as Christmas, holidays, and big family events. I can't say we all achieved complete comfort, and most of the time, I would see the family on my own. However, I will be forever grateful for my family's difficult adjustment to a huge change in their lives.

Now my daughters surrounded me on the worst day of my life and months to follow. They protected me as best they could by making sure my shattered pieces didn't escape, as they brought food, made me drink water, took calls, accepted flowers, and handled endless details. They knew I had taken the big blow.

Tribal mourning and an unraveling of the last 13 months began. Many didn't know about Hemitra's surgery and hospital stay. She wanted no visitors. She said she would tell everyone when she was home and recovered. It had been her wish to treat the cancer with alternative methods. That world was familiar to me since I treated all my health issues with holistic care whenever possible. I knew several people who had successfully recovered from different stages of cancer by using the best of natural cures.

Heartbreak by heartbreak, the necessary calls began. The first was our dear friend Renee. "No, I don't believe it," she sobbed. "How can someone who seemed so alive be dead?"

Renee cried as I related the details. "Oh, thank you, thank you for taking the path you did and for honoring what she wanted. Now I understand how right it was." I received great comfort from Renee's words.

Renee and our friend Joan had supported Hemitra's and my choice to avoid harsh medical treatment. Eighteen months ago, we were making wedding plans, beginning to write a book about the unusual events that fused us together, and launching new classes that excited our friends. Five months later, Hemitra received a diagnosis of breast cancer.

In a hazy stupor, we listened to the recommendations of a reputable surgeon. Hemitra held a three-inch notebook for breast cancer patients in her lap. We asked questions but the answers were not what we hoped to hear.

"Can you do a lumpectomy in the breast and remove the hard lymph node under her arm?"

"No," the surgeon's reply. "We must do chemotherapy first to shrink the tumor. The next step is a breast biopsy."

The real nightmare began. The first breast biopsy didn't work, and the anesthesia didn't numb the pain. Because of Hemitra's high blood pressure and sensitivity to the anesthesia, they had to use a lesser numbing technique. The medical team held her down as she screamed. The second biopsy was the same. The horror and trauma had started.

Next, the results needed to be sent to an oncologist who would read the report, stage the cancer, and determine a plan of treatment. In the oncology office, Hemitra's blood pressure rocketed to 252 over 111.

The oncologist appeared with a not too pleasant manner and told Hemitra she should be taken to the ER. My body was already in fight or flight mode as I stood with my left side next to the exit, wondering how to position myself as my mind searched for an escape. Hemitra stepped up and firmly stated that it was her body, and she would make that decision. We immediately knew she wouldn't withstand the assault of chemo or radiation and the harsh plan from this doctor. We walked away quickly, as if we were in a scene from a movie and on the run from the law. Conventional medicine was out. We would find other treatment options.

That moment, our absolute certainty gave us the precious gift of the next year and created memories that would last forever. Some of our friends and family were angry and afraid. They thought we were crazy to take such a path, and we retreated into our own world to deal with the cancer by alternative healing, continued to plan a wedding, and learned ballroom dancing. I shielded my mate as much as possible from fear, criticism and unwanted advice.

Thankfully, we never followed through with the oncologist to receive the staging of the cancer. We shared a magical and final year together, and she remained strong and as positive as possible. Now I know the last tests would have uncovered metastasized 4th stage cancer. How could we have held any hope?

One morning, as we staggered through the shock of the initial news, Hemitra reported a dream she'd had. In the dream, she was in a hospital and passed the oncology department where they gave radiation and chemo. An X marked the door, and she knew that showed her that she didn't need to be there. In meditation, close to the same time, I saw her in a beautiful garden. She looked radiant and in perfect health. Our dreams and visions comforted us. Looking back, I wasn't in that garden with her, and now I knew it lay in another dimension. The dream was correct. She didn't need to endure the cancer treatments.

By the following spring, Hemitra suffered worsening digestion problems and other symptoms, but she and I tried to remain positive and hopeful. I was her support and it took everything I had to stay in a hopeful space. At that time, I felt deep inside what I never wanted to know; possible metastasized breast cancer could win and shatter the future we planned.

****

The one thing I had to do for my survival on that first day was contact our friend Linda and have her reconnect me with Hemitra. Linda, a longtime friend, had been with Hemitra and me from the beginning of our relationship. Linda worked as a gifted intuitive at our former holistic learning center and gallery.

Linda's first words after the tears were "She's right here." Instantly Hemitra made her appearance and began a stream of dialogue through Linda. She said, "I'm sorry. I tried to stay, but I was so tired. I feel great now. I don't have any pain. I love you. I wanted to be with you, and I am with you. It's beautiful here. It's like our wedding. Stay there. It's not your time. I love you now and always."

Standing outside on the flagstone terrace, I felt my partner's presence. As if the end of the flagstone marked the boundaries between us, and I saw an image of a split part of me bang my shoulder against an invisible wall, as if I wanted to break down the door that stood between us. Another part of me held the phone and stood with feet on the ground.

"I'm going to call you tomorrow. I know you have too much to handle now," said Linda as a sea of flowers poured in and more painful calls beckoned. "Know she's with you. She keeps showing me the eternity symbol. I'll call you tomorrow," Linda promised. The eternity or infinity symbol means forever. This encounter with Hemitra through Linda felt normal; the other part of the day wasn't real.

****

Day one became night one. Waking at 1 a.m., I heard a noise. Where is she? What day is it? Is she in her room? I must check on her. Is she in the hospital? When can I go? The same final reality—the woman I loved wasn't any place I could go. Waking each hour at 2 a.m., 3 a.m., 4 a.m., brought the same renewal of pain and loss over and over. My screams and sobs filled the house.

At 5 a.m. the second day, I felt unable to wake up and reenter the trauma each hour. I crawled out of the covers and wandered through the house. I straightened up, stayed in motion, and tried to move through the agony.

I heard in my head, "The cancer was destroying us." It was a message from Hemitra. It had been a year and six weeks from the diagnosis, but much of that time she remained relatively well. After the wedding, her strength deteriorated quickly. We didn't know the cancer had spread, but I woke often at night to help, offering homeopathic remedies, massage, and arms wrapped around her. Yes, we were both exhausted and afraid. How could we continue?

I grabbed the two plastic bags from the hospital that lay on the stair landing and took them upstairs. I pulled out the blue shirt that she last wore. It was close to my face, and an acrid blast hit my throat. At the same time, I heard, "Wash that." I held it in my hands and again heard the instruction, "Wash it!" The shirt must have been saturated in toxic residue from all the drugs in her body. She was with me.

Another load in the washer, I headed upstairs and the metal cane in the entrance way caught my eye. After Hemitra returned from her 13 days in the hospital, she needed it for support. "Put that away," the direction came clear and definite. "I don't need it."

I smiled. "No, you don't." A picture of her dancing filled my mind. She was a great dancer. I grabbed the cane and continued upstairs to store it in a closet and throw on clothes.

I moved through the cluttered neglected house. There had been no time for anything but her care over the last month. Just as I noticed the blood pressure cuff in the office, the voice in my head said, "I don't need that. My blood pressure's fine."

Why did she say her blood pressure was fine? Did she have blood pressure? Am I going crazy? Of course, we both wanted the illness out of site and mind. Thinking of the cancer, how it had spread, or what more we could have done wasn't where either of us wanted to linger. That was clear, but "my blood pressure's fine" threw me beyond known reality.

As I tucked the monitor in a drawer and closed it, a wave of euphoria swept through me. The seconds of bliss that flooded my body were as powerful as if I'd stuck my finger in a light socket. That was not my euphoria—it was hers. There was no capacity for joy in me. She sent me the tremendously expanded awareness to communicate the energy she now accessed. Seeing her, hearing her, and feeling her got me through the hours.

****

Hemitra's vivid communication thrilled me, and over the years, I had received other messages from the next dimension. I thought of when my mom passed suddenly and early from a massive heart attack. Right away, she gave me clear detailed instructions from the next dimension on how the memorial service and burial were to be conducted. I listened and repeated the instructions to my family as if it came from me. Absolutely no autopsy, she told me. My dad and brother agreed. She clearly picked the oak casket lined with pink satin. It was reasonably priced and practical. She liked her service filled with many loving friends and family. After that, it felt as though she would visit at times. I thought her spirit popped in on occasion from some distant realm.

How long would Hemitra be available? Was our communication temporary? I didn't want it to be. I wanted to know all that I could possibly know about what I now experienced.

Chapter 3

Day two at 9 am, the phone rang, and Dr. Sanders showed on the caller ID. She was Hemitra's primary care MD. "Sue, I'm so sorry. I'm devastated. There was nothing more you could do. The cancer was too advanced."

"You knew that when we came in." I choked on the words.

"Yes, and you knew too. I could tell by the way you looked at me."

"But I couldn't give up hope." I answered.

"I only saw the two of you together for 20 minutes but being around you and witnessing her upbeat attitude as I admitted her was astounding. You took such good care of her. You two had something special."

Three weeks ago, Hemitra couldn't keep food down. We rushed to Dr. Sanders, who admitted her to the ER. The MD was seeing her for the first time since we had abandoned all western medicine. She asked what treatments we had done for the cancer? Hemitra told her that she was under the care of an MD acupuncturist, using homeopathy, and doing the Bengston method. Dr. Sanders knew the capable acupuncture MD who treated Hemitra, and she was well versed in alternative medicine. She wanted to know about the Bengston method.

That day I told her, "It's different", not wanting to go into details.

The woman pressed on, "Different is good. I don't discount anything."

Hemitra and I briefly described William Bengston's method, as it was explained in the book, *"Energy Cures."* After 30 years, the technique had a 97 % cancer cure rate if the patient didn't use chemo or radiation, and anyone could learn it. The information about this method was a great gift from our friend and chiropractor, Pat. Right after Hemitra's diagnosis, Pat told us she and her sister would be attending a Bengston workshop in two weeks. Pat asked if we wanted to go? Yes.

****

A little more than a year ago, Hemitra and I drove 11 hours to a life changing workshop near Lake Erie. Bill Bengston, a brilliant, compassionate scientist, delivered information on how to apply his technique with a zany sense of humor, yet with the seriousness it deserved. In five days, he instilled hope in us, and showed us a positive direction to pursue. His treatment plan, which had cured many with cancer, along with the acupuncture, and homeopathy gave Hemitra the strength to enjoy a last beautiful year with me.

Again, Hemitra's doctor mentioned our alternative treatment. I was prepared to defend our choice and said that we'd made the decision a year ago.

My body stiffened with her response, "What did you get out of that year?" Not waiting for an answer, Dr. Sanders continued, "You got a whole year together to plan and execute that beautiful wedding. If you had gone the traditional route, she would have been sick and throwing up. You would have been running back and forth to the ER to treat her for dehydration. She would have lost her hair and her spirit. I don't know if you would have even had a wedding."

"Thank you. We felt we did the right thing, and yet how could we really know?"

After we hung up, I basked in the kindness and understanding of Hemitra's M.D., and Linda called. Immediately, I shared the doctors' words and her support regarding the way we treated the cancer.

Linda began speaking the messages from Hemitra, "She's here and she said thank you. What we did prolonged our good times and gave my soul peace."

I felt incredibly grateful for the affirmation that we had chosen a right and gentle path. The final word from Hemitra affirmed our decision. There could be no more truthful answer. This message was a beautiful gift that spared me a lifetime of questioning.

Linda added, "During the illness, she felt the tug of some who pulled on her."

"You mean those who were afraid and disapproved of the way we treated the cancer?"

"Yes," Linda confirmed.

At the same time, I asked a question that all who have lost loved ones most likely ask. "Please tell me Linda, is there anything more we could have done? Did it have to be this way?"

Again, Hemitra spoke through Linda. "We are forever," she said. Hemitra repeated, "I'm sorry. I really was tired and couldn't hang on. I didn't mean to leave. It was my time. There really is a time for people."

Linda continued, "It was her time, and if it hadn't been the cancer, it would have been something else. She showed me the infinity symbol again."

"I'm free, and I want you to experience the joy. You must stay there. I need you on Earth. You have your family. You must write the book. I'll help you. This is only the beginning," Hemitra continued.

The beginning of what, a lifetime of missing you, I thought? Linda continued translating Hemitra from another dimension.

"You will know when you're in a place of peace. We're in the same space just different energy fields. Pay attention to your dreams. I'm there. I really want you to take care of yourself because we must do the work. Now I can take care of you the way you took care of me."

How can she do that, I thought?

"She understands how powerful your love is to stay connected through eternity. Your marriage is for eternity. She's always with you and enjoying through you," Linda added.

Linda continued channeling Hemitra's words, "The two of us together are such perfection. We're on different sides of the coin. We are infinite. I'm in many different places, but I'm with you always. We are together in different forms."

I listened not able to fully understand.

Hemitra spoke again, "We are one, and we are together always and forever. Right now, you must have one foot in the etheric realm and one foot in the physical. I had to go first. You know I couldn't live without you. Everything happened the way it should have. I'll make it up to you. I promise we'll be together again."

From the next world, my partner jumped from thought to thought, and she seemed excited about the contact with me through Linda. "You were almost too much for me. I was jealous of you. You had all the people who loved you and your family," Hemitra confessed.

"Hey, you were a lot for me. You were larger than life," I countered.

"I know I am. I may be a bitch, but I'm awesome. You're the only one who could handle me. Why do you think I kept you? No one else could put up with me for two minutes." I laughed hard for the first time in a long time, and Linda joined me.

"Glad she's kept the attitude," I added.

Hemitra continued through Linda, "Nothing is more important than you. You are what I'm doing. You are my project. You're the work I'm doing here. I gotta be honest if I'm going to pass the test."

"I'm her project. Pass what test?"

"She's getting oriented and seems to be doing a review of her life here, and she's getting future assignments in the next dimension," Linda added.

"So, I'm her assignment?"

I'd read about a life review one had to experience after passing to the other side, and how one's entire lifetime flashed before them.

Hemitra came through Linda, "Now I'm your partner, and I'm your guide. Our mission together is forever."

Linda explained, "She will help you now from where she is. She really wants you to write the book."

Fair enough. We were always guides for each other on Earth, and now she's my guide from her clear Heavenly perspective, I reasoned.

I looked at the lined yellow tablet. The last thing on my mind now was writing a book. Getting through each hour proved a struggle. There were tests she had to pass. She had to come clean and be honest about her in depth feelings.

"We were ready to meet when we did," Hemitra's dialogue continued. "We had and have the perfect partnership. There's no other like it. Nothing else could fit like this. My star soul partnership forever. We are electricity exponential, and we encompass other realms. I'm getting this firsthand and I want you to remember."

I wrote as quickly as my fingers could move, and my heart raced pounding hard.

Hemitra read my body and mind, "Slow down, slow down, slow down. I'm right here. You don't even know how much help you have. We love each other. We have an infinite love affair. Once you have a plan, you will get support. I love you Honey, you hot broad."

Oh good, she's still flirting with me.

The messages continued, "Slow down. All will be ok. You have the support of others. Don't be so anxious on the Earth plane. I want to enjoy that with you from here. I didn't think the kind of magic we had could exist in the physical world. I want my ecstasy to be your ecstasy. We are one heart one love."

Hemitra was viewing the life we had together on Earth from her clear and lofty vantage point, as my heart continued to break, and my understanding of everything was being tested.

I wrote quickly on a yellow lined tablet on the coffee table. The messages ended, and Linda spoke as herself. "Just know how much she loves you, and that she's with you. I love you. Take care of yourself."

"You can't imagine how much this means to me. I love you too."

The call ended and I stared at the scribbled writing and the beautiful messages. The book…is the book in this tear-stained tablet? When we decided to write a book, Hemitra said nothing we'd ever done together thrilled her more. The year before she passed, we began an outline and notes for writing the pages that documented our amazing tumble through time, years ago.

Chapter 4

The next day, I sat on the couch in the living room, as the sun streamed in the window, and I remembered the beginning, 22 years ago and before and the unusual unveiling of former lives Hemitra and I shared.

Since my mom told me about reincarnation, or past lives, when I was a teenager, I'd always embraced the concept. Later, I belonged to an Edgar Cayce study group where we talked about and studied past life information from available books.

Four years before I met Hemitra, my best friend, Alexia, learned of a past life workshop in our area, and we signed up. A woman named Melanie was the leader, and Mea, Melanie's friend, was the hypnotherapist. Our instructions in the hypnosis; relax as Mea did a meditation, and we would go to former lives that were pleasant. If we encountered anything we didn't want to see, we could just pass it by.

It was easy to relax with Mea's guidance, and suddenly a vivid image appeared. I was swimming underwater with my arms outstretched and pointing upward. My skin was brown, and I wore gold bracelets up my arms. The light green water felt soothing, and I surfaced to see an Egyptian barge on what I knew was the Nile River; the woman I embodied felt happy and at home.

That image changed, and I saw a man in what looked like a tunic with an elaborate head dress. He entered a pyramid showing me another Egyptian life. Mea didn't have us stay long in one life, and the next frame of my movie that appeared was the back of a man paddling a gondola in what looked like Venice, Italy. The man wore a ragged brown jacket. That life didn't appeal to me, so I simply traveled to the next place in time with Mea's gentle guidance.

Next, I embodied a woman wearing a veil and a long dress. I saw a gold turret and a mosque in the background. Two children clung to my legs. I felt restricted and bound by my life under the dark veil. I wasn't unhappy, but I lived with the constraints of a woman in that time and culture, probably in the Middle East. That life dramatically contrasted to my life in Egypt as a woman who felt free and empowered, as she swam half naked in the Nile River.

This first experience remembering my past lives later stirred a memory from my childhood. I sat in fifth-grade history class not paying too much attention to my teacher, Mr. Werner. Then, I heard the words fertile crescent, and I instantly snapped to attention and hung on to every detail. The fertile crescent in the Middle East was an important rich agricultural land mass that bordered Egypt. It was also called the "Cradle of Modern Civilization." Whatever the historic details, the words conjured the deep feeling of peace and being at home that I experienced when I reconnected with the Egyptian woman, who swam in the pale green waters of the Nile. All of our many lives lay stored away in our unconscious minds. I liked that memory.

Melanie proved to be a great teacher, mentor and friend, and she expanded my world in many directions. The day of the past life regression group, I picked up her flyer. She was teaching a class on flower essences, so I decided to join the group and was the only person who showed up.

I learned that flower essences were made by taking flower petals and making an infusion by putting them in pure water and allowing them to steep in the sun. The water takes on the imprint of the qualities of each flower, and when one takes it, those positive qualities of the flower are healing. This modality is from ancient times and had been studied and revived by many today.

For the next two years, we studied three flower essences a week from the many that Melanie used. We took the prepared drops and meditated on the messages from the flowers. What a joyful experience we shared! We were both intuitively learned the flower's qualities. We received self-knowledge and healing at a deep level. The flowers flooded us with their positive wise vibes and showed us what we needed in life from their therapeutic properties. Soon, Melanie and I began to make our own essences of wildflowers. Later we did the same with crystals, which added to my knowledge of vibrational medicine, and complimented my work with homeopathy.

Melanie introduced me to color healing techniques and the book, *Let There Be Light* by an East Indian MD, Darius Dinshah. Spectra-Chrome therapy, or use of color for healing, had also been used by ancient civilizations in Egypt and India. In the 1930s, Dinshah successfully treated patients for 350 different aliments with specific color gels. Sunlight and it's many colors is the basis of all life on Earth. Medicine that was gentle effective from nature made the most sense to me. I gathered books and information on the properties of color.

Melanie studied monthly with a Seneca Elder in Buffalo, New York and shared the teachings with me. For the past several years, I had also studied native wisdom. For two years, we taught classes together on Native American wisdom, color and other Earth based traditions, and healing modalities. We also began celebrating the Solstices and Equinoxes, and we planned a Summer Solstice party at my house.

That night, over 60 people attended our unique and memorable party. Preparation started days before the event. Two of the husbands brought materials in a truck and built a Native American sweat lodge and fire pit, which was my introduction to this ancient tradition. Husband Jack was away on a business trip but said he didn't care if they put the lodge in the back of our secluded yard.

The sweat lodge was built by first digging a pit that would be the center of the lodge. The Earth from the three-foot diameter, one-foot deep pit, was piled directly outside the doorway of the lodge and considered sacred Earth. Next, the main trunks of twelve small young saplings were dug into the ground in a circle and bent over to form a dome like structure. They secured the saplings with duck-tape. Twelve rocks, each weighing 3-5 pounds, would be heated red hot in a wood fire close by. Before the ceremony, the hot rocks were to be brought into the lodge by pitchfork and placed in the center pit. Next, participants entered and sat silently on the grass around the pit of glowing hot rocks. This structure could hold ten people comfortably. Once in the lodge, the leader slowly poured a small amount of water on the rocks which created hot steam, and four rounds of prayers followed. The purpose of the intense heat and sweating was purification and spiritual growth. It was going to be a busy night, so I would have my sweat lodge initiation at another time.

A Swedish woman friend gave directions for constructing a maypole. Brightly colored ribbons hung from the top of the pole. She was going to teach the children and mothers the maypole dance. Plans were laid for other world dances and rituals to fill the evening festivities, and I had fun creating an entrance to the enchantment, which was a path strewn with a soft fragrant mix of pink and white Peony petals. I found a glass magic wand with glitter inside and ribbons on the end to shower a joyful blessing around all who arrived. The guests carried luscious baskets of food, flowers, musical instruments and blankets as they stepped into the realm that was surely filled with fairies and magic equal to Shakespeare's *Mid Summer's Night's Dream.*

Hemitra arrived around 8 p.m. that evening, invited by a friend of Melanie's. She wore a two- piece checked pink and white gauze top and skirt. She was medium height, slender and beautiful with lots of long dark hair and a perfect smile. Hemitra was dressed and made up to impress, with cleavage showing and a confident attitude.

We were introduced, and I must have said, "So glad to meet you," and maybe other polite nothings, now blurred because many people and details needed my attention.

By about 12:30 a.m., most of the families had gone home, and I witnessed this new woman in action. The remaining group filled the living room/dining room area. One of our unique guests was the chief of the Lenape nation, a Native American man who wore a full feathered headdress that went from head to foot. The chief lead the conversation, and the circle gave him full attention. The chief lingered on the subject of the white man taking over native lands.

Now, cleaning up in the kitchen with a couple women friends, I heard Hemitra interrupt the chief's sermon with an angry comment, "When will you ever forgive?"

The room fell silent. Outspoken? Yes. Angry? Yes. I glanced at my friend who raised her eyebrows and made no comment.

Twenty minutes later, Hemitra walked into the kitchen to thank me for a wonderful evening. "I live a few miles down the road. We should get together sometime."

"Yes," I said politely. No, I thought.

Chapter 5

Since we were part of the same crowd, Hemitra and I ran into each other at events, but for some reason, I continued to avoid her. She invited Jack and me to her 37th birthday party in January the following year. We were invited to another party the same night, and I was relieved to have the excuse to decline her offer.

I began to feel guilty about being rude and unsociable, and I always found excuses to turn down her gestures of friendship. I had learned shiatsu massage from a series of classes given by my friend Melanie. In February, I told Hemitra I would give her a massage as a belated birthday present.

Hemitra arrived wearing a loose-fitting white sweat suit. She cried during the treatment and revealed feeling a lot of loneliness since her divorce. After the session, we stood looking out the dining room window at the back yard and pool. She said, "I could spend the whole summer here." I silently winced at the thought of my privacy being invaded.

As she left, we hugged, and she lingered in my arms. We both felt comfortable, like old friends, and I knew she needed the nurturing. She thanked me enthusiastically and repeatedly expressed her gratitude for the healing gift.

It took me at least a year to tie together the details of that day—the white sweat suit, and the dream I'd had many months, or even a year, before I met Hemitra. I woke one morning questioning, who was that? I dreamt that I was up high in the clouds, standing in a small, pure white, dome like structure facing a woman. We had our arms around each other. The woman was dressed all in white. She was an inch taller than me and had red highlights in her hair. She felt familiar, yet we'd never met. We were lost in a long-locked embrace that gave me the most comforting, heart-warming feeling imaginable. We were one consciousness, as we shared a blissful moment in some cosmic space. The dream was profoundly real, but when I woke, I reasoned that the woman must have been a part of myself, a new self-acceptance. I'd just finished a book on the meaning of dreams. It would be impossible to feel that depth of understanding and grace with another human. I concluded the woman had to be a part of my own soul. However, the dream left me with a longing in my heart. How could I capture that feeling again?

Hemitra stood an inch taller than me, and her hair shone with red highlights in the sun, but I just didn't connect that day with the woman in white and my memorable dream. It was good that the realization was delayed.

In April of that year, I was happily covered with dirt and working in my organic garden, as I planted the first vegetables for the season—onions, broccoli, peas, and swiss chard. Hemitra arrived unannounced. She had just dropped over to invite me to a Goddess gathering, and she described the event with great exuberance! I didn't know where that so-called party fell between Tupperware and high tea, but I wasn't taking any chances and politely declined. "Sorry, I already have something else on the calendar," I said with a smile, still resisting her friendship. I didn't understand my own behavior, since I'm usually open to all kinds of new things and people.

In late May, I included Hemitra in a small dinner at the house. Jack traveled for that week, and five women friends joined me around the pool for the evening.

Paula, Hemitra's close friend, suggested we do a relaxation exercise and float each other in the water. Hemitra and I were in the hot tub and the other four in the pool, so we became partners. "Just close your eyes and let the other person support your body and gently swirl you around," Paula instructed.

Thirty seconds into the exercise, floating and comfortable, I had a strange vision. I felt the warm water and saw it as bright red blood that gushed from my middle. The water would be crimson if I opened my eyes. Dressed in a helmet and a vest of linked metal, I wore a large red cross on my chest. I was a soldier who was dying in the arms of a nun. In the vision, she wore a dark habit. She looked at me with kind eyes. It was Hemitra in a past life. I was comforted by the nurturing presence of this nun. My turn ended soon after that, and I opened my eyes. Hemitra's black and white bikini didn't look at all like a nun's habit, and I shared the details of the horrible vision.

"Oh, I've been a nun in so many lifetimes," she answered casually, as if I'd commented on the weather. "It sounds like you were a crusader in the Inquisition," she added.

"Yes, it's the worst memory I've ever had of other lives, and I'm seeing it for the second time. The thought of being in the holy wars and killing humans, including women and children in the name of Christ makes me sick."

My best friend, Melanie, was at the party. It was with her I'd first glimpsed this gruesome past life memory, a year before, when we studied flower essences. We took a red flower essence called Scarlet Monkey Flower. Melanie led the meditation, and I saw an image of myself in a dark cave full of spider webs. I wore the same uniform with the red cross of a crusader in the 11th or 12th century. I hated the scene. That day with Melanie was the first time I became aware of a past life spontaneously brought to my conscious awareness. I often thought the memory had something to do with the fact that I stayed clear of organized religion this lifetime. Some of my best friends were devout Christians, Jews or Buddhists. Many in my family exemplified true Christian love and I basked in their Light but chose a different path. I believed all sentient life to be sacred and love must be the foundation.

That late warm May evening, the storyline deepened to include Hemitra, and the awareness of our journey through time began. After the nun version of Hemitra, and her kind gesture ushering me, the crusading knight, into the next world, we saw each other more and began to get to know one another. I felt differently about her. Somehow, sharing that lifetime held significance that was yet to be explained.

We told our stories. Right after college, Hemitra began her search for knowing and spent a little time in Canada studying with Fritz Perles, the well-known German psychologist. Her spiritual quest also led her to Ram Dass, a famous teacher and author of the book *Be Here Now*. The transformational gem in Hemitra's life was her Transcendental Meditation practice. She'd been meditating twice a day since a few years after college, done advanced training in Switzerland, and became a TM teacher. The TM movement broadcast a radio show in Philadelphia with Hemitra hosting for two years. I would come to understand her as the most dedicated to and disciplined with her spiritual practice person I'd ever known. She exuded a quiet spiritual strength and wisdom from her training. She told me her first and middle name at birth was Jane Cary. The name Hemitra was channeled, and she described it as her soul name. The name Hemitra was Sanskrit and meant 'dear and glorious friend.' I would come to understand that soon.

After college, the same time Hemitra searched for meaning, I taught high school English and then stayed home with our girls. I studied everything I could find about natural health, how to raise kids, eat well and grow organic vegetables and fruit. Natural everything felt good and taught me how Earth worked. My world expanded in love, as I developed my intuition and learned to talk to the spirits of the plants and animals feeling ecstatic as they answered me. Some things I considered successes were coaching Meg's eight-year-old little league softball team to a championship or having fun each year with my teacher friend's first grade classes, when I read them a book I'd written called *Daisy the Skunk*. Daisy was Meg's pet skunk, and she got her about the same time that we adopted a tiny orphan raccoon that our big dog, Max, found in the woods. I developed nature programs for the local elementary schools. Life was good.

Chapter 6

As Hemitra and I spent more time together, I let go of all initial judgments. She had an edge for certain. Her recent divorce left her unhappy and sharp, but underneath the bravado, this unique woman searched for connection and fulfillment.

Hemitra began to call often with some ideas of what we should do. I wanted to get back to my routine. "I can't do anything. I have too much work to do." I tried reasoning to justify my life of constant work and projects. Her sales job had ended, and she would start another in September. No one had ever been allowed to break down my privacy barrier. She did. A great friendship began between us.

Hemitra had two brief, unsuccessful marriages, the second lasted five years. She remained good friends with her second husband, whom I got to know and liked very much. They simply weren't compatible. She told me that a friend, who was a channel, once read for her and reported that she would have three marriages. The first two would be difficult, and the third would be made in Heaven. She wanted to find the man who would provide the made in Heaven marriage.

Further conversations revealed that she had received a marriage proposal from a successful, caring man she dated for two years. She said they had much in common, and he adored her. Puzzled, I asked why she didn't marry him? "Looking back, I know it wouldn't have worked, "she answered. "I seriously considered it, but again, my friend and trusted intuitive told me,"

"A secret love awaits. One who will reflect you better."

I began to observe the man hunt and listened to her. One of her guys was jobless and bright with masterful manipulation skills. Another she talked about was a successful and charismatic man who would leave her for weeks with no explanation.

Why the problem finding a good man? Hemitra had majored in theater in college and spent two years in New York getting small parts, as she hung with a variety of prestigious people and made connections. When she gave up that world and returned to home territory, she taught Transcendental Meditation, did some modeling, and explored a variety of careers and creative ventures. She presented a blend of worldly sophistication and delightful naïveté—uniquely different than anyone I knew. This feisty intelligent woman had much to offer.

****

Paula announced to Hemitra one day in the spring, that she was getting married and moving to California. Although Hemitra felt happy for her friend, the news created envy, and she must have questioned where was her own mate?

"What would you think of Paula and Dave having their wedding in your backyard?" Hemitra called me with this idea, eager to plan a sensational party.

It sounded good to me. Paula was a well-liked part of our community, and good friends would mean many hands for details. This was a second marriage for Paula, and it would be a perfect casual wedding. Paula expressed excitement. There would be a small wedding shower for Paula, which meant planning and decorating the yard. I had to admire Hemitra's social genius. There were many ways this mysterious woman, that I once held at arms' length, found methods to engage me in her plots.

Hemitra and I planned Paula's shower. Everyone would share in the food prep, and we would eat outside around the pool. We anticipated missing Paula and wanted to make this a special time.

On a late afternoon in mid-June, with perfect blue-sky weather, six of us brought gifts and great food to Paula's bridal shower. We had all known each other for several years and reveled in joining together for the party. Ingrid, an artist, was a close friend of Melanie's. Tanya, was a long-time friend and associate of Paula's. Diane, drove two hours to join us. We celebrated around the pool with champagne toasts to Paula and ate the delicious offerings.

After dinner, I turned on the hot tub, where I would serve dessert. No one wore swimsuits to jump in the hot tub. Jack wasn't home, and the private back yard let us feel free. We had many women's sweat lodges at our place and always went into the lodge naked to spare the sweltering burden of clothing.

We talked and laughed for a few minutes, then I grabbed my towel and went to the kitchen. I'd made prunes in port for dessert, a recipe from the Alice B. Toklas cookbook. The prunes were soaked for two weeks in the sweet liquor. I spooned several into bowls, covered them with home-made whipped cream and sprinkled the mix with candied violets.

I loaded everything onto a tray with spoons and napkins and wrapped my towel around me to carry it outside. The wet towel fell to the ground, and I let it go to save the dessert from spilling, so I was naked with a tray hoisted on my shoulder. I didn't think anything of it, and the girls laughed. The dessert and party were a hit. Everyone enjoyed, as our free-spirited group celebrated the night.

We lingered in the hot, bubbling water, as we honored our friend and bride to be. I sat opposite Hemitra, and at one point, caught her looking at me with her dark eyes not breaking the gaze. She starred at me so intently, I looked away.

The next day, Hemitra called to thank me and rehash the celebration. She paused and said, "By the way, I must tell you, you have a beautiful body."

I laughed and said back, "Thanks." I was a little surprised but liked the compliment.

After the conversation ended, I thought about her comment. None of my other women friends would have said that. We might have said something about our weight or hair style, or any other thing women obsessed about. "Have you lost weight?" or "Your hair looks good." The intense look the night before, I didn't know.

After getting to know Hemitra, I felt that she wasn't consciously flirting with me, but that look was seductive, and it caught my interest. Unconsciously, the love between us was unveiling, and she simply blurted out whatever was on her mind.

Paula and Dave's rehearsal dinner happened at the home of one of Paula's friends. That beautiful summer evening, I met Nick. Dave's best man was in his fifties, a large framed, nice-looking guy with a great smile. No one he met got a handshake-all received a bear hug. Everyone at the party crowded around Nick. A former basketball coach at a university, he was now an astrologer by profession, and he added keen intuition to his readings. I was intensely drawn to him and felt immediately comfortable in his presence, as though I was reconnecting with an old friend. When he looked at me, I knew he saw much more than the surface me, and I wanted to know him better. Nick asked for everyone's birthdate and time, if we knew the time detail. He was going to do a short reading for those present.

Hemitra, our friends, and I had spent hours planning and decorating the yard. Paula and David had perfect weather for their June wedding. The sky was clear and deep blue with low humidity. The couple took their vows under a flower laden arch. We basked in the beauty of flowers blooming in the gardens and gracing all the tables. After the formal ceremony, Nick gave an eloquent toast to the bride and groom. We ate delicious food catered by a friend of Paula's, and a string quartet played. After the quartet, Jack turned on the outside speakers, and we played familiar songs and danced. We filled every inch of the space with joy and laughter, as we celebrated the couple and loved life. The day was a perfect gift.

Hemitra and I danced together, and it appeared as though our free form dancing had been choreographed and practiced for days. She danced beautifully, and I loved to dance. With unrestrained sensuality, in the spirit of the day, we improvised in uncanny sync and flow with one another. Some in the group watched us. When the piece of music ended, we hugged and exchanged a look that made my heart do cartwheels. One woman commented, "That was beautiful!"

When the bride and groom left, some of us sat around a table outside, continuing the fun by ordering pizza for dinner. I happily sat next to Nick. Apparently, he had done a few horoscopes for us and now gave mini readings. He looked at me with a knowing unnerving smile. "Your life's going to change." He paused then continued, "You've had some wild lifetimes, and you always come in as a rebel with a cause."

For some reason, I looked around the table to see if anyone heard Nick and felt a sense of relief that everyone was focused elsewhere. I knew my life would change. With Amy, our youngest, going to college in the fall, Jack and I would probably travel more. Secretly, I hoped that this change would be enough to fill the ever-growing void and yearning for that unnamed something. Rebel? Yes, always. Wild lifetimes, rebel with a cause...hmmm.

Chapter 7

I no longer resisted Hemitra's ideas about how we could be together and created my own suggestions. I'd always had good friends, but Hemitra and I had a connection in which we saw, heard and valued each other in a deeper way than I'd ever known. The attraction between us grew in intensity, yet we didn't openly talk about this impossible subject.

Once, when I was at Hemitra's place, she asked me to listen to a message from a man she had dated recently. "Arrogant, cold and potentially not nice," was my instant reply, when I heard his voice. "May I please ask, why do you put up with these unsuitable men? You're gorgeous, smart and talented? Why?"

She accepted the critique well, as I'd meant it in support. After naming the pros and cons of the owner of the voice, she looked at me and said, "Why do you put up with having such limited control and emotional absence in your marriage?"

As head on as she was, I liked her directness and sharp observation. Many looked at my marriage as perfect, and we were the hub of our large and loving family. Hemitra saw beneath the surface. Jack's control issues were intense, and there was an absence of emotional support. He and I had decided I would stay home to raise our girls. Homeroom mom, creating kids' programs, softball coach, organic gardener, hostess, taking care of Jack's grandparents, and making our place a haven for all kids happily filled my life. I also lived a separate existence with friends who shared my interests. The rest, I chose to put aside.

Jack and I were college sweethearts, and we married young; I was 21 and he was 23. At the wedding, the minister told us we were "doubly blessed," because we were so in love. We both had a sense of humor as well as great chemistry. In our many years of marriage, we grew up together, and our relationship deepened. However, Jack wanted to be the stand-alone authority in our decision making. When it was important, I stood my ground and didn't budge until he yielded. Movement forward sometimes proved slow and exhausting. I loved Jack. Control battles over money, or anything, weren't as much of an issue as not ever being heard or understood. I had girlfriends to talk to, but it would have been fulfilling to be truly known and heard in my marriage.

Sometimes with friends, I was the stronger one. I guess I'd been trained like that or thought emotional self-sufficiency offered some kind of bravery badge. As my friendship developed with Hemitra, I learned the complete balance of give and receive as equal partners, and the deep connection, respect and comfort between us blossomed into a radiant force field.

We laughed like teenagers, each finding the other funny. Hemitra was a tell-it-like-it-is girl, and that invited me to be my authentic self and drop the social masks. It felt comfortable to expose every weak place and vulnerability with this woman. We shared similar beliefs, and we matched in our spiritual quest and personality. We loved talking about our mystical experiences and the depth of who we were. We both lived a joyful wildness and played outside the box.

Change was a given with Amy leaving for college in the fall. Would I go back to the traditional classroom as an English teacher, finish my master's degree, become a psychotherapist, or create something? What would it be like without the kids? I didn't want anyone to get hurt with these changes and the independence I needed to create. A whisper of doubt threatened, yet my perfect life continued, eminent change thankfully stayed veiled for a time, as a category five hurricane slowly approached us.

One day, Hemitra looked at me and pointed to a barely visible scar on her upper lip. "See this?" she pointed to the spot. "When I was a kid, I ran into the edge of a wall. I told myself for years that I was happy to see my dad, and I went running to him when he got home. It wasn't true. I was running away from him because he was going to beat me with his belt."

Hemitra told me about a lifetime of these beatings. The abuse from her alcoholic father left deeper scarring than the slight mark on her lip. He tried to control and suppress this strong spirited woman. Nothing could justify cruelty like that. Now I understood Hemitra's sometimes volatile nature and the sadness deep in her eyes. My heart opened more to my friend.

****

One day early that summer, Hemitra and I sat together dangling our legs in the pool, as we sat close to the waterfall that fell from the raised hot tub next to us.

Out of nowhere I said, "It feels like ancient Greece."

"It does," agreed Hemitra, somehow thinking we knew how that should feel.

"I loved studying Ancient Greece in school."

"I did, too." And so the conversation went.

"Maybe we had a life together at that time."

"It feels that way."

Ancient Greece seemed to superimpose itself onto my secluded suburban backyard, even though a jet trailed a white stream far above us, and there were no marble columns on my two-story house. We felt protected, peaceful and blissfully happy. Being together acted as a catalyst that parted the veils of time. We had both done hypnotic regressions to past lives, so we accepted the experiences as unusual, yet somehow an exciting normal, unable to realize the meaning and full consequence of what was to come.

Chapter 8

The unusual summer proceeded and so did my memories. From ancient Greece, many fragments of shared past lives surfaced spontaneously. These glimpses brought us the realization of our timeless soul connection. The images appeared as clearly as if they had happened yesterday.

Next, camels and the desert appeared in my head. A vision of a young man surfaced, and he was riding one of those camels. His head was wrapped in a turban, and his mouth covered with a cloth, but I recognized the eyes. They were her eyes.

Nick and I became friends, and he would often call from his home near Seattle to ask how I was doing? I told him about the glimpses of lives and now the annoying camels. Nonchalantly, he reported that Hemitra and I had lived a few times in the Sahara to learn about survival. I didn't want to delve into the desert lives, and the camels moved on.

"We were Cathars." The words came out of my mouth one day as Hemitra and I sat together in my kitchen. I didn't know who the Cathars were, but the words slipped out. I learned they were a Christian sect in Southern France in the 12th and 13th century. They weren't accepted by the Catholic church, and they were persecuted and eradicated in a cruel inquisition.

Nick told me that Hemitra and I had many lifetimes in France. One was with what he called the 'White Robed Sisterhood.' We were renegades on the run in that French lifetime.

Nick began to refer to Hemitra and me as the Scandinavian Bohunk Babes, as he related a lifetime we shared living in Norway. He only gave sketchy information. We worshipped Oden and had something to do with running a small town. The man seemed to know us well. I didn't personally remember anything about that life.

Hemitra encouraged me to learn meditation, and that wove another thread in the bond between us. Sometimes, when I quieted my mind to meditate, more images of former lives came forth. The scenes changed with the weeks. One day at home, I began to meditate and felt a wave of sadness. I choked and smelled smoke. When I looked down in my vision, I saw fire and realized I was remembering being burned at the stake. The memory was unpleasant and added to the knowledge of a stream of Earth experiences. When I spoke to Nick, sometime after that, he laughed, "It's ok. That won't happen this time."

Very funny, I thought, but how close will I get to that?

Another memory came through when Hemitra and I spent time together sitting at my kitchen table about to drink a glass of wine. The scene changed in my mind, and another experience sprang from my unconscious.

"It feels like we're in a castle," I shared. Several hundred years peeled away and we sat together in a not so elegant, ancient castle. There was some sort of food on a table that we shared, and straw littered the floor. My skin was warm from the afternoon sun streaming in the windows, yet I felt the damp cold of the castle.

"Well," Hemitra pitched right in, "It's more like the basement of a castle." She frowned.

I laughed. "Yeah, it's a dark place" The feeling of an Earthy life at a lower level came to mind. I think we were two men somewhere in Europe.

Not only were we each as weird and over the acceptable edge as the other, but we time traveled. She didn't just listen and believe, she joined me in far off places and spaces, as she saw and sensed the same images adding to the details. The walls of time and space didn't contain us.

I fell behind in all the projects that needed to be done. I fed the family and worked on my usual routines, but my daily contact with my new friend consumed lots of hours. That wasn't the responsible, goal oriented me.

Hemitra and I shared the intrigue of our endless lifetimes together. We wanted to be close together every day. We hugged and laughed, as we experienced a joy that neither of us expected.

We plunged deeper into a realm that always fascinated me and now engulfed me. In one conversation with Nick, he brought forth a lifetime that Hemitra and I lived in the ancient lost civilization of Atlantis. According to his intuition, we saved each other's lives during an initiation, because we used the powerful psychic bond of telepathy between us.

I asked Nick what was going on with the endless memories which included Hemitra, as I tried to solve the mystery of my rapidly changing life? He said that Hemitra and I had made an agreement to be together at this time when we were between lifetimes.

I remember his words. "You two come together lifetime after lifetime to help each other when the Earth is spiritually evolving." My heart felt that statement. It implied purpose, destiny, and the feeling of trouble ahead. My secure existence was in the process of shattering to pieces as Hemitra and I grew closer.

Chapter 9

On a warm late July afternoon, Hemitra stopped over, and we decided to take a walk around the quarter mile cinder track in the large athletic field close to my house.

We started on the track with our arms around each other, and I watched the way our feet moved together in perfect harmony. Being close felt comfortable, and we stayed in sync all the way around the circle. We were different, yet compatible, like two pieces of a puzzle that fit together. The dry track surface kicked up a fine gray dust that lightly covered our sandals.

Hemitra told me she'd just had a phone conversation with an old boyfriend who lived on the west coast. This man had remained a loyal admirer and wrote her beautiful poetry. She ended the retelling of her conversation by telling me she made an announcement to the man. She told him, "I'm in love with a woman." Obviously, that woman would be me. My heart quickened at her words.

That statement was the first real mention of what had transpired between us. We had fallen in love. Time stopped in that moment, and there were many things I could have said in response. I didn't speak but pulled her closer to me and laughed softly, or perhaps I choked, and it sounded like a laugh. I had no words, because the wedding rings I wore on my left hand bound me to silence.

Hemitra shared with me, at some point, as we got acquainted, that in her high school yearbook, along with being voted best looking she was voted most tactless. The woman lacked a filter. Sometimes, in hindsight, she would confess to me, "I can't believe I said that." However, she spoke the truth for both of us on that hot summer day. The admiring poet never called again.

The details of that moment seared themselves into my heart and mind. As I played that memory, I could again feel the warmth of her skin through the soft cotton blouse she had worn.

****

Hemitra wanted to show me her favorite gift shop that summer and introduce me to her friends who owned the shop. I had to buy a present for an upcoming wedding that Jack and I would attend, and I agreed to go.

We met Linda, an attractive, 30 something, slender woman with long blond hair and an ankle length flowered skirt. Linda was talking to the owner of the shop when we walked in. Hemitra introduced me to Sarah, the owner, and Sarah connected us with Linda. Sarah mentioned that Linda did intuitive readings at the gift shop one day a week.

We talked to Linda while Sarah wrapped the pretty multicolor vase I'd found for a wedding present. We liked this unusual woman and looked knowingly at one another, as we shared the same thought. "We'd love a reading. Could you do one for us together?" Hemitra jumped right in.

"I only have a short time before my next client, but I could give you a mini reading."

In a room behind the shop, we sat opposite Linda at a wooden table. She handed us the gorgeous tarot deck that she'd created.

"You're a wonderful artist." I complimented her, and she made light of her obvious talent. She asked us both to cut the cards, then we handed them back to her. She turned several face up.

"You two have been together many times before." She smiled.

"No, we're not really together. I'm married. We're just here together." At that point we weren't lovers, but Linda must have easily seen the future that awaited us.

"Actually, the three of us have known each other in many lives. We were priestesses in Delphi long ago," Linda said.

I may have liked studying ancient Greece, but I didn't know anything about Delphi.

Linda continued, "Hemitra, you were brought to the temple as a young child because you had some experience that showed you were to be a priestess. It was something about a snake." Hemitra shuddered.

"Sue, you were also brought to the temple by your parents when you were eight. You resisted, kicking and screaming."

Spiritually reluctant or just ornery, I thought.

"At the time, Hemitra, you were twelve. You took Sue under your wing, and you became inseparable. When you were grown you became lovers and spent your lives in service to Gaia, the Earth mother. You were healers and were trained to become oracles. I see you breathing something from the Earth and telling the future."

Linda continued, "There were sacred caves in the mountains there where you performed ritual. I see you as part of a circle, and you wore animal masks as you did ceremony."

We sat in fascination as Linda read us. "You grew old and witnessed the beginning of a huge change. From a woman-centered temple, the men began to take over. It was the beginning of the end for Gaia, the Earth Goddess, and it happened all over the world. You were old women by then, and you didn't like the change, but you had lived a wonderful life."

At age 18, Linda told us she had remembered many details of the world of ancient Greece, and history verified her memories. She would become one of our most trusted friends and intuitive in the coming years. In this present moment, she faithfully called me every day to check in.

The old memories offered me comfort, but the spell broke, and I brought myself back from 22 years before and perhaps, 4000 years before that. I picked up the yellow tablet to reread Hemitra's lifegiving messages through Linda. "I didn't think that kind of magic could exist in the physical world." From her place in the next dimension, she was viewing the life we had together on Earth. No, there was nothing to compare it too. We had lived in a world of our own, a magical, mystical world.

"I want you to experience the joy." What joy? There's no joy in me. How would I ever experience joy again? And why did she say, "I want to enjoy the Earth from here with you?" I desperately needed an instruction manual.

A knock at the door completely jolted me back to August 2014, where I didn't want to be. The lawyer's office was delivering the papers to probate Hemitra's will.

Chapter 10

I climbed the wide, marble steps of the elegant, freestanding stairway to the second floor, Orphans Court, county courthouse. Two months ago, Hemitra and I beamed as we took the same steps to get a marriage license. My heart pounded wildly as I focused on keeping the agony at bay and my body functioning and upright.

Anita, our lawyer's young legal assistant, met me outside the door where we were to probate Hemitra's will. "Good morning, how are you?"

"Fine, how are you?" I lied.

"This won't take long - just a few papers to sign," the woman said casually.

On autopilot, I walked through the door to the same counter where marriage licenses were issued. Numb with pain, I tried not to sob when I saw the woman who issued our marriage license behind her desk. She remained focused on her work while another clerk put two papers in front of me. I signed the papers and swore an oath that I don't remember.

"What else do I do?" I asked.

"That's it for now. I'll get in touch with you step by step. Take care of yourself." Anita looked at me, and I hoped I didn't look the way I felt.

"Thank you, Anita." We shook hands.

As I drove home, I thought about two months ago and signing the 'other' papers. The clerk had smiled and handed us the intake form for our marriage license. "Sorry, she laughed, there are two questions I must ask you. First, are you two related in any way?"

"Not that we know of." We shook our heads like 10-year old girls.

With a big grin, the clerk asked, "Are both of you of sound mind?"

That question made us laugh out loud and look at each other with mischief in our eyes.

"Yes," we spit out the correct answer, though it was a perfect opportunity for play.

Driving home that day, Hemitra sat in the passenger seat holding the marriage certificate like it was a rare treasure. We glowed.

****

Falling in love surprised both of us. None of this had been in either of our conscious master plans, yet the knowing evolved that it was an agreement we conceived before this life began.

I'd never cared who loved whom or why. It was not an issue. Once Hemitra and I knew we must be together and remembered our many past lives of love in the bodies of both women and men, the truth that love existed between souls was all that mattered. To us, it was simply and ridiculously obvious. What was all the fuss about? However, I became a good actress and carefully guarded the truth of our relationship to most. We spent the majority of our years publicly referring to the other as housemate, business partner or friend, acutely aware that society at large did not share our 'obvious' truth.

I drove home with too many memories. "Help," I pleaded out loud, breaking under the unbearable pain.

Instantly, Hemitra appeared in my mind. "Come with me." We wore Greek dresses and stood by a spring with a mountain in the background. I was wounded and sat on the edge of a small rock pool with my feet in the water. Hemitra, the Greek version from several millennia ago, took a handful of water and caressed the top of my head. I felt the water trickle down my face and the back of my neck. She touched my shoulders, and a powerful, gentle healing vibe surged through me. The agony stopped, and I gasped for breath.

Red light! Slamming on the brake, I stopped the car. Please can you keep it together, I said to me. What just happened in my head? That was a potent vision, but how could it cause the physical and emotional relief? Self-suggestion? Crazy with grief? I was just transported to the waters of a healing spring used for thousands of years in ancient Greece—the sacred Castalian spring where the oracles would purify themselves before doing their prophecy? What was happening to me?

Home again, I called Linda. "Sorry to bother you, but I may be losing what's left of my mind."

"I doubt that. What's up?"

I described the healing that Hemitra delivered from the spring at ancient Delphi.

Linda reported, "Hemitra said, "Why do you question? Just see and believe."

I felt annoyed, my tone sarcastic, "If you were here, you would question things like that, wouldn't you?"

"Touché, but don't question, just believe." Hemitra responded, showing that she understood my hesitation trying to believe she had given me a healing from another time and place, yet she had done just that.

"Your intuition is opening up more and more. See it, feel it, and believe it," Linda added as she continued translating the messages from my partner.

"I'm more alive than ever. I'm living it, you're writing it. It's no accident that you are a channel, and there are others around you to help. Journal. I'm going to help you. There's so much joy feeling our love coming through."

"She's excited about that," Linda added.

Linda continued the stream of Hemitra's dialogue from beyond. "She says, I go to the temple at Delphi all the time. I wish you were here. I see you as a beautiful priestess with me. You are the most beautiful oracle Goddess. We loved each other then and now. I want you to continue to be that beautiful, strong, hunky Goddess for me. I'm traveling to all the places where we've been. That's what I'm doing. It's all about the book. That's my way of bringing it from where I am to you. From here, I can get better information. The life we had in Delphi and the culmination of all our lives; I feel like this was the plan all the time."

"She's showing me that she travels to all the places you two have been in other lives," Linda added.

"I will take you there in dreams," Hemitra continued. "In your dreams we will travel to Delphi. There are infinite possibilities. You will get exactly what you need at the right time. All will come to you. This is the beginning of the new work," Hemitra told me confidently from her broad perspective.

"Delphi, Greece, a past life together that we remembered years ago, still exists? What is she talking about?" My view of reality crumbled. "She goes to Delphi, to our lifetime?" I repeated the words in a daze.

"Time doesn't exist, and now your partner has a view of all eternity and existence. It's not that the Delphi you lived exists in the physical. It's hard for us to grasp," Linda tried to explain.

Linda continued to channel Hemitra. "We'll be together again, as long as you put up with me. There really is a time for people. You have to do the Goddess work. You couldn't have done any more than you did. I need you on Earth. I have work to do here. We're in the same space, but we're in different energy fields. I really want you to take care of yourself. I'm here, and I will help you. I want to take care of you now. I'm getting stronger. There's a bigger picture that you don't understand yet. I'll never leave you."

I realized that Hemitra repeated messages she knew were important. My taking care of myself became a theme. She also kept telling me that she stayed with me and would take care of me. Hemitra seemed to have a strong agenda, and the repetition of her words soothed my pain.

"I have it easier. I always did." Hemitra said.

"Are you referring to the fact that when we got together, I had to go through a divorce? Hard as that was, this is so much harder, and yes, you have it easier now for sure." I didn't want to, but I felt envious of her.

Linda continued, "Your twin soul will lead you to amazing things. This is just the beginning. Your house is a priestess place and is part of you two. It is the Heart of the Goddess, and there is divine feminine energy there in the place you both manifested and continue to manifest. It's your haven. You are helping to bring the Goddess light to the world from the infinite source. You were meant to be together. The book will be good for you and was part of the plan. It will help you heal your grief and bring light and hope to the grief of others who lose loved ones. Hemitra said, "Everything was perfect."

In the beginning of our friendship, Hemitra spoke often of the Goddess, and now in her messages from the other side, she referred to the fact that we had enthusiastically aligned with the rising movement that brought back the honoring of the sacred feminine in women and Mother Earth. Since recorded history, the pendulum had swung dangerously in the direction of a patriarchal social system that dominated, as they raped, ravaged and polluted the Earth. Now, at the end of this long and arduous era, all life on Earth and the feminine had suffered abuse beyond endurance. This sacred and charismatic life-giving force that naturally resided in men and women had been forgotten. All of life on Earth must come back to balance, if we were to survive. The forces of aggression and war over everything had raged out of control.

The Goddess and the lifegiving qualities of love, compassion, nurturance, heart, harmony and wisdom must return.

The Goddess concept spoke to the desperate need for global change. I had always loved and defended the Earth and spent my life forging a deep alignment with Her and Her emissaries and elementals. My passion centered on learning natural healing modalities and teaching Earth based spirituality—the conscious intelligence in all life. I heard, felt and sometimes saw the beautiful beings from another realm. Hemitra and I spoke the same language. It was somewhat early in that game for the east coast, but in a short time, we opened a holistic center and gallery called Heart of the Goddess. We taught classed that we created and invited wonderful authors and leaders to do workshops, as we happily rode the waves of change. We began by remembering who we were and why we were here together again.

Linda again, directly quoted Hemitra, "Sue, I love you. Anything you do now, we are both doing. Now, I'm not limited. Stay there for your family. You have work to do. We'll both finish that. We are one. No one questions that. Let it all come back. We'll do it for both of us and be of service. I love you so much and always will."

"She's singing to you." Linda sang, "I'll be loving you, always. With a love so true, always. She's telling you how much she loves you, and that she's with you."

Through Linda, Hemitra said "I want to be here for you. You gave 1000%." She says, "You're going to keep feeling me."

****

Linda continued, "When you dream of her, it's solid and real. You always had intense passion, but true love right away. You have multidimensional soul level sacredness. Now she feels the full expression with her being on the other side. She has her heart wide open and knows the deeper panoramic realization of, and acceptance of, who you are together. She embodies you. How incredible that you had all that in two bodies. You were totally in love multidimensionally connected in intimate space."

My heart felt the expressions of love from my partner in spirit. This reality beyond any boundaries that I'd been taught, opened a gateway of freedom for Hemitra and me. I was enchanted by the messages and grateful.

"Linda, these experiences I'm having push me to the edge of what seems like fantasy or madness. However, even with my vivid imagination, I couldn't make this up. The woman is with me in an amazing and profound way."

Chapter 11

I clung to each of these beautiful experiences. I savored them, went over them many times, and hung on tight because I walked a shaky road. My present reality was like being on a balance board that rested on a barrel. In spite of good intentions and great effort, the slightest wrong thought or wrong step sent me spiraling out of balance into the darkest saddest place I'd ever known. I would forget the amazing messages and then fight hard to get back to center.

I tried to sleep and remember to eat. I didn't want to eat. I didn't want to write a book. I didn't want to do anything but have the pain stop. What am I doing here? Something is wrong. Guilt followed all my weak thoughts. I have responsibilities, a family I love, yet as I inched along, sometimes hour by hour, a nagging underbelly of cloudiness haunted me.

Hemitra repeatedly said, "Stay there. Stay on earth."

I wanted to want to stay, but there was that part of me that longed to follow her, find her, and be free of this. I'm the survival type, not suicidal, but I understand what she saw. She was right, and it scared me. The question became, how could I safely get through this?

Clearly, there was something wrong with me. I tried reason. At one time, I was reasonable. I read about the natural stages of grief; anger, and feelings of abandonment...this is the way it is? We all lose loved ones. The woman had breast cancer. It was her time. But, why didn't you take better care of yourself? Why did you ignore the lump under your arm for months? Damn you! Immediate guilt followed my tirade. This grief stuff is truly like mental illness. It's messy, exhausting and unpredictable. It helped sometimes to simply give in to the insanity. I didn't know when I'd break down into hysteria when I was alone.

Our loved ones don't leave us. I began to get that through my head. Why did I feel abandoned? People sometimes feel abandoned when a loved one passes. I would never have wanted her to stay here in pain and illness, never. However, I now envied Hemitra's freedom. Yes, you do have it easier, and I'm here alone and miserable, while you're free of all this Earthly pain. Hemitra's insistence that everything was great, and I should continue without missing a beat made me angry.

One night, I woke, and my heart pounded violently. I rubbed my chest. How could I go on like this? In a panic, I threw off the covers and sat on the edge of the bed. I struggled like a trapped animal looking for escape from the agony. I saw Hemitra's face, which was one of quiet wisdom and maturity. I felt her hand on mine.

"I know it's dense there. I know it's difficult, but I promise you have more fulfilling things to do than to just get through this time. You're my Goddess, my heroine. Meditate. Stay there. Go back to your routine, be positive."

About what? I answered silently, then conceded, "I will try to make it through this."

"No, you will do it!" came the command.

I lay back down and crossed my arms around my middle. All I remembered in the cloudiness of the night, was that I felt certain those were her arms. She held me so tightly that I wouldn't fall apart, and I slept instantly.

When I woke in the morning and walked downstairs, I heard Hemitra's voice. "Now I will take care of you the way you took care of me."

Ragged and worn, I questioned, "How will you do that?"

The voice snapped right back, "How about last night?"

"Of course, you're right. Thank you so much for that." How could I question? Last night was the second dramatic rescue from her when I felt I could no longer endure the pain, and I felt tremendous gratitude as I processed through this inevitable dark life passage.

****

Linda and I talked a couple of times a week now. I initiated less contact, since I felt how difficult it was for her to witness and handle my intense pain.

Today when she called, I felt the deepest gratitude for my friend who sensed it was important to call at that time. We talked and Linda got right to the point. "She knows how you're feeling and has a message."

Hemitra said, "You're frustrating me. Nurture yourself. Clear yourself. Give to yourself what you gave to me. Keep yourself well. You have a strong body and heart. And yes, you must grieve."

Linda delivered Hemitra's message, "The seasons will change. Have your weather, have your storms. You've got to stay on Earth. I need you there. We have work to do. I'm trying to make you feel better. Don't give up. That's not who you are. I'm proud of you, and I love you."

There was no escaping… she was in my dreams and knew my every thought. I flashed on the first call to Linda and the awareness that I wanted to follow her.

Hemitra continued, "I'll always regret not being there longer, and weird as it seems, nothing could have changed that. You couldn't have done more. You're in a beautiful place. I'm the lucky one. I'm in the most beautiful place."

What if I didn't realize that Hemitra and I could communicate? That concept loomed like another death. The illusion of separation from our loved ones in spirit had gone on too long. She and I with other many others, were tearing down the veils that culture had imposed on human minds. I lived in the borderland somewhere between this world and the next where the natural order of things resided.

63

Chapter 12

At the end of 2013, we met Becky and Teresa at ballroom dancing class where they danced competitively. Hemitra and I had no women couple friends, and we had asked the universe to bring that into our lives. Our friendship grew instantly with the two women, and we found that the four of us had everything in common. Twice when we got together, we were graciously asked to leave restaurants because the staff wanted to close and go home. The four of us couldn't stop talking.

Years before, Teresa discovered that she could see beyond the veils and was a skilled medium. Four weeks after Hemitra's passing, I invited Becky and Teresa to the house for dinner. Teresa had offered to do a channeling with Hemitra.

That night, we lit candles, and Teresa began.

Hemitra said, "I had to go when I did. It was my time."

Teresa spoke for Hemitra, "The soul of Hemitra had many windows to go to the other side. Life is a series of these choice points. She stayed because her soul wanted to connect with yours. She had to meet you and have this piece. She created a difficult early life because her path was about growth. She held out for you, and the two of you are meant to be together always."

Tears wet my face. Would they ever stop?

Teresa continued, "It's not her nature to age. She loved life, and she loves you even more. She has passed to the other side but is so here now with you. She loves you unconditionally. She shows me a waterfall and says, 'the love never stops.' How infinite your love is in all of your lives!"

I wanted clarification and added, "Hemitra was told she would have a long life this lifetime."

Teresa replied, "She lived a long time considering all the chances she had to go and how sick she was as a child. She stayed to connect with you, but her leaving was pre-destiny."

"She's excited about the book. Your plans for that gave her and give her joy. She said the book is the most exciting project we ever had. The book is to happen, but it's your project with her helping. She keeps saying to you that it's not your time, and you must stay here and do the work. She has things she must do on the other side, and she can only get some of the necessary information there."

Hemitra always communicated clearly, and again, she repeated many things that had also been channeled by Linda. The stay on Earth theme came on strong.

Teresa continued, "You are two sparks that make one flame. That flame must happen. You have magic, and she can connect with you. She will look for your invitations. Now it's time for you to do for yourself what you did for her. She needs to know you're safe. She loves how easily you feel her."

Yes, the enticing magic, and the same words that Linda used.

"The connection with Sue is powerful and continues. There's not a weak section in their connection. The next time will be smoother," Teresa continued.

Hemitra spoke, "Turn the page, Sue. You will feel joy again."

I doubted that.

"The euphoria you have felt is her helping you expand your energetic world. She can come to you and feel through you. She eats at the table, and she's in your dreams. You have a merger, and she enjoys that. She's not leaving."

Once more, this was a repeat of what Linda channeled sometimes in the same words. Hemitra was determined to get her points understood.

"Sue provided the grounding for her that she needed. If she hadn't, Hemitra would have been more excessive. Writing the book will help Sue and keep her grounded. It will be a way of staying connected with Hemitra." The session continued through Teresa.

"Sue, you were correct about her body and her lack of care. Her body went off balance at times because of her emotional imbalance from childhood. She had a hard time being in a body and said that was her cross to bear. She sometimes turned away from things that needed to be addressed. The euphoria you feel is her gift to you in her current form. It's helping you expand your energetic world."

Teresa said, "She's very busy, as busy now physically as she was in her mind here on earth.

She thought a lot about beauty. She knows she spent too much time worrying about that this lifetime. She needed adoration and attention."

I listened and thought about getting old and looking old. Without asking the question, Teresa jumped right in, "Don't worry, you will be attractive in your old age as a grandmother and great grandmother. You will be here a long time. She said she got to see you, and your beauty will never leave you. You will grow old gracefully."

Somehow that was no consolation at the moment.

"You are my grieving widow," Hemitra continued through Teresa.

"She shows a kind of pink flowers that meant something to her, and said, 'These pink flowers have so much love in them' and she offers them to you," Teresa continued.

"She said this life you must finish seems like a long time to you, but it will be gone in a flash, and you'll understand when she comes for you."

I felt profound gratitude for another beautiful connection with Hemitra through our friends.

What the four of us hadn't talked about was Teresa's certification as s a non-denominational minister. That night she agreed to do Hemitra's memorial.

Chapter 13

The celebration of Hemitra's life would take place in the backyard on September 15th. Our two good friends, Virginia and Renee, took over the details of the memorial. I was thankful and relieved.

Virginia's number showed on the caller ID. "Good morning. Just checking in. I have something funny to tell you, but first. How are you?"

"Still breathing, but it's minute to minute. I'm searching for the words for my talk at the memorial. Tell me the funny part."

"You and I talked about material to hang as a backdrop in the tent on the end everyone would face."

"Yes."

"Ok, yesterday I was shopping," Virginia continued, "I wanted yellow gauzy material, about 40 yards. I have a use for it after the event. I found what I wanted, but it was $20 a yard. I told Hemitra, if she wanted this to happen she'd better help find it. Displayed at the end of the next aisle was a buttery yellow gauze fabric that was on sale for $3 a yard, and it was perfect. Then I heard a voice say, "And it will drape well too.""

"It's great that you're tuned in and can hear her, Virginia. I don't think I could do this if I didn't know she was here…or here at times, or whatever. You know how much she loves a good party."

Virginia continued, "After that, I went to get beverages and went over the list in my head. There was the voice again—'water, sparkling water, lemonade, wine, champagne.' Anyone who doesn't like that can go home."

Virginia told me that she said laughingly to Hemitra, "You're very opinionated."

Hemitra's retort through Virginia's mind was, "In my opinion, that's the way it should be."

I laughed, feeling the beauty of Hemitra's aliveness, as odd as that seemed. "Things haven't changed. As a matter of fact, the attitude is stronger. She has more conviction in the world beyond," I commented. Virginia and I laughed.

"May I tell you something?" I asked.

"What are you two up to? From what you have already experienced, and what came through Linda, it's hardly over," Virginia assured me.

"I returned her unused shower chair to the pharmacy. As I carried it up the steps, I heard her say, "My legs never felt like that." I do have strong legs, and she complimented me on them often. It wasn't strange but just like us together. She can feel me as if we were one."

"On the way home I heard her say, 'Oh Sweetie you can hear me. I'm so proud of you. You're a channel."

"Amazing. I hope you're writing all this," Virginia emphasized.

"Sometimes," I said.

"How am I going to hold it together to get up and speak?"

"I don't know, but I know you will get the strength and it will be beautiful."

****

Car doors slammed, and low tones of conversation announced the arrival of the first guests. I took a sharp, quick breath. Thankfully, family and friends were the greeters. My hands smoothed the long teal cotton jersey fitted skirt. The mint green top was a good color with the skirt. Getting ready today proved to be an unusual experience. With the quick pass of a brush, my hair looked perfect. How did that happen? It looked

69

as good as it had for the wedding. I put on Hemitra's gold bracelet and earrings.

When I did a final check in the mirror again, the surreal feeling took over. It wasn't me looking at me, but Hemitra seeing me through my eyes. Nothing could be more obvious. The familiar voice in my head said, "You look gorgeous," commented my fashion guru. "Lighten the eyeliner a bit." I grabbed a cotton swab and took off some of the color from my eyelids. She was right there with me. Good, a thumb's up on appearance.

One more time, I read through my tribute. This isn't happening!

Virginia waited downstairs. "Your hair looks beautiful."

"She did it," I answered as absolute fact, and Virginia didn't question. Our friends either accepted these statements as truth or forgave the madness of my grief.

****

In a trance, I walked to the tent. The sky was bright blue, the temperature stayed mild, and a soft breeze rustled through the trees. A sea of sad loving faces filled the seats. They were there to celebrate the life of Jane Cary Crecraft, Hemitra.

Teresa led the ceremony with grace, humor and passion. Just as our recent friendship seemed meant to be, this beautiful gesture was Heaven sent. Our dear friends, Amy and Paul, produced all the music as perfectly as they always had done for our other events.

When my turn came to speak, I watched a part of me, the piece that stood with strength and conviction to honor my loved one. That part knew what she was doing and spoke each well thought out statement clearly and calmly. I witnessed the mourners ride the cascade of words as they rippled from me. The cadence moved up and down, inflections good, my voice strong. A force surged through me, and my body seemed invincible for this moment. I was being helped and held. The audience cried and laughed, as they flowed with the waves of the words, and we traveled together through the precious moments.

"Hemitra inspired and empowered many women. She was a great teacher and teaching partner as well as a powerful leader, who put hard work and passion into all our ventures," my words continued.

"No honoring would be complete without saying this one had great wit and humor. I told her many times, over the years, how grateful I was that she was funny and could laugh easily."

"Hemitra was authentic. She spoke her mind. One of our friends said that she verbalized what the rest of the group was thinking but afraid to say. Authenticity is an admirable quality. However, there were times through the years, that I had to use my anti authenticity tools. They worked something like this…YOU SAID WHAT! Or YOU CAN'T WRITE THAT!" Friends and family laughed and exchanged knowing looks with me.

I ended, "These words are from my heart, yet they are simply words. I would need a new language to describe my cosmic playmate. What a magnificent character! I enjoyed every minute of our 22 years together, whatever the weather. I celebrate Hemitra's life and will every day for the rest of mine."

Hemitra beamed that day as she presided over her glorious celebration. Each family member and friend who spoke did so with deep love and admiration for this beautiful beloved soul.

At one point in the afternoon, our friend Barb pulled me aside, looked me in the eye and said, "There's a radiance about you that's amazing." She didn't explain. I no longer understood my life.

As I hugged the final guest goodbye, there was the sound of a trash can that the kids dragged down the driveway and the click of the long tables being folded marking the end of the day. My kids had worked on every set up detail, and now, they hustled to clean up and restore the place. They lingered as long as they could while the afternoon sun began to fade. The somber looks on their faces showed concern. How had their mom held up on this day of sorrow and celebration?

"It was beautiful, Mom. Everything went perfectly. Are you going to be ok?" Meg asked.

"Yes," I said, not knowing how that was going to happen. "Go home, you did all this work, and I appreciate it. There's nothing more to do." I released them from duty with hugs and deep gratitude, as I stared blankly and watched the last car leave.

It was quiet. A few small yellow leaves from the giant black walnut trees drifted downward, and some landed on the big white tent top. I didn't remember if I'd eaten, since some parts of the day remained a blur. A crew would take the tent and chairs tomorrow, and the back meadow would look like nothing happened here. Empty, like my life. Six weeks since Hemitra transitioned. Six long weeks I managed to drag through. What the hell do I do now?

I made a bad decision, one that my tired body would pay for, but I didn't care. It wouldn't be the first or last mistake I would make. I walked to the refrigerator where the kids had stored the leftover drinks, pulled out a bottle of champagne, grabbed a throw blanket from the family room and a glass from the kitchen, then took it all outside and settled into a lounge chair. We didn't drink often. Hemitra called me a cheap date, because one glass of anything created a party. When we shared a bottle of champagne or wine, we had such fun. Damn it! I popped the cork. We did know how to celebrate!

I raised my glass, "To you, my bright, beautiful spirit guide! With all kinds of seen and unseen help, we pulled off a beautiful celebration in your honor. I don't know what this is all about, or what you expect of me, but I will figure it out. I love you! Hey, thanks for helping with the hair."

Chapter 14

Books began to pile up by the side of my bed. After research on the web and recommendations from friends, I ordered books written by authors who had communicated with those who had passed to the next dimension or persons who reported near death experiences. The books included works from 21st century authors and several from the last 100 years.

Certain that my experiences were natural, I needed to know everything available about the afterlife in order to get through each day and what lay ahead. In the first seven long weeks of shock and grief, what I wanted most was to feel Hemitra's presence and know she was ok. The clear communications, loving messages, and instructions from her were gifts that kept me going. My quest continued to be able to understand the Heaven and Earth connection and balance the two worlds.

The first three books I picked to read were written by Stewart White between 1919 and 1936. They were still considered some of the most important information ever written on the subject of the afterlife. They included *The Betty Book, Across the Unknown,* and *The Unobstructed Universe.* White was a popular author of his time. He often hunted and enjoyed camping trips with his friend, Teddy Roosevelt.

Stewart White's wife, Betty, and her sister Joan, discovered they were both gifted mediums. Through practice and intention, the two women meditated to enter a state of consciousness that allowed them to communicate with spirits in the next dimension. Stewart recorded the information the women brought back from their journeys. The Whites' experiment lasted 15 years and gave them the material for these three ground-breaking books.

The purpose of the experiences with those in spirit or the Invisibles, as Betty called them, was to learn truths that enhanced Earthly life, the lessons that strengthened and inspired us. Betty mentioned that direct communication with spirit had been lost for generations, and she repeated many times that it was important to contact spirit on a daily basis and to develop a balance of material and spiritual energy in order to live a fuller life (White, 2010, pp. 21-24).

I couldn't imagine my life now if I couldn't communicate with Hemitra. My survival depended on that contact. Hemitra told me often that I should have one foot on Earth and the other in Heaven.

This knowledge and daily interaction with the spiritual dimension is our human responsibility, since we are part of both worlds, and we should learn about death before we die. There were many more choices offered on Earth than in the world of spirit, so it was easier to be diverted from the right path for those living on Earth. Help from our guides, angels and loved ones in the next dimension gave us focus and inspiration to be our best selves. We humans must constantly guard against negative thoughts and choose the highest and kindest ones to stay in a positive mental space (Pontiac, 2012).

What I read gave me the same comfort I got from Linda and others who could hear and see Hemitra and consider the communication normal. I needed those with sight beyond third dimensional reality. My hardest job was keeping out of the pain and grief. My thoughts were unruly rockets that were hard to control.

"To develop a direct contact with spirit," Betty wrote, one needed to have an 'open heart' and a sincere desire to develop a personal loving relationship with the next dimension. With practice, anyone could learn to receive and understand these messages and guidance. These messages from spirit were a 'vital force' in our progress on Earth (White, 2010, p. 77).

****

My heart raced. I was getting answers that matched my experiences, and what I read added to my growing new awareness.

The second day after Hemitra's passing, when she told me her blood pressure was fine, I felt totally confused. Also, in one of the channeled sessions, she said she was busy now. She related that she was physically busier than she had been in her mind when she was here on Earth. How could that be?

"The spiritual body is actually material. It is flesh. It is blood. It may not be the same kind, but it is real, as living as your own. It is a pulsing, living body, purified of organic frailty, durable, flexible and capable of more powerful action" (White, 1988, pp. 81-82)

Here was my explanation for the time Hemitra told me her blood pressure was fine, though that information made my mind spin. Many times, I could actually feel Hemitra near me, feel her hand on mine, or know she stood behind me.

Hemitra said through Linda in the first week or two, "I'm so proud of you. You can feel me. You're going to keep feeling me."

Fortunately, I sometimes sensed those things when I was with one of my intuitive friends. They would verify my experience and saw the same thing. These wonderful friends considered the paranormal normal. This was the beginning of my new normal, and it was helping me heal.

The Invisibles told Betty, "The spiritual body has a stronger lighter substance beyond our physical sight. It is the soul, and it has form." They described their bodies as, "like smoke." They said, they have the same body as we do, but they have gotten rid of the "outer shell." They can see our physical world (White, 1988, p. 89).

Years ago, I began to sense when loved ones who had passed were around their loved ones here. It happened spontaneously, and I would see a misty form near the person and know it was a loved one. Sometimes a message would come through from the departed to the person still on Earth. It was difficult to describe what I actually saw, but the best description likened the image to smoke.

****

When Betty was in trance viewing the world of the Invisibles, her husband Stewart asked, "Where are you?" Betty answered, "I'm in a nicer and more comfortable atmosphere, where I can see things. I see what is important and what is not. It's teeming with life. It's a place of unencumbered vitality and desire" (White, 1988, p. 89).

Through Linda, Hemitra said, "Its beautiful here. I can see beyond the edges, beyond lifetimes, planets, universes. There are no boundaries."

Again, I felt envy remembering that comment. I stumbled through each day in a haze, and sometimes, I had to exist minute by minute before crashing.

****

The Invisibles told Betty not to think of the worlds of Heaven and Earth as separate. They counseled, "She could realize the power to overlap the worlds. This expansion of her spirit will give her a wider, freer life." They repeatedly showed Betty how to combine the two worlds. (White, 1988, p. 87)

One of the messages from Hemitra through Linda was, "We're in the same space but different energy fields. I'm in a lighter finer vibration in the same space. I'm always here with you. I'm more alive than ever."

My journey through grief required me to be a citizen of both worlds. I now realized that we were meant to live that way.

Hemitra repeated that I must have one foot on Earth and one in the next dimension. Why had this ancient knowing been lost for centuries? I grew more determined to regain that vital lost wisdom and truth.

Chapter 15

"He died," Mom, told me. I don't remember much at age four, but I remembered that.

I held the limp hamster in my hands. My mom took the still warm body from me, and my four-year old mind tried to grasp 'died.'

In an attempt to ease the traumatic moment, I asked, "Sam died, but we're not going to?"

"Yes, we will." Mom stated the case simply with no further explanation.

My mother was loving and caring, yet on the dead hamster subject, I felt left in cold unknowing. Staring into space, I found no way to figure out dead. Dad and Mom didn't offer any other information on Sam or death, so I put the event aside and continued my four-year old life.

****

Every day after school, for most of second grade, my mom and I would visit my grandmother in the hospital. They gave me money to go to the snack bar, and then I walked the park like grounds of the hospital. They were long days.

At home one night, I sat on the fireplace hearth preoccupied with a small, odd-shaped piece of wood, I found on the flagstone.

My mother talked on the phone, as she told a friend that my grandmother had died. I remembered my stunned silence, and the only thing my mother said after the call was, "You expected her to die, didn't you?"

Expected my grandmother to die? What? I hadn't been prepared by anyone or spoken to about my grandmother's dying. I don't remember any other explanation. I didn't cry and just went to my room. I read my second-grade poem book over and over, but the words had no meaning. I needed to fill the stunned space in my head.

I was not included in the memorial, nor did I witness my parents or family's well concealed grief. My flamboyant grandmother, an acclaimed local artist, was loved by many but now was lost to me. In the years that followed, I hung on to any stories from family and friends about this woman who had been as close to me as a second mother. The example my parents presented to me for handling grief was silent endurance. I learned to fear and avoid thinking about this mandatory transition called death and joined the pervasive emotionally suppressed culture of my time.

Did my mother ever mention the Heaven or afterlife concept? I don't remember. I think she had her own cynicism about the afterlife. Her beloved father passed when she was 17 and her equally beloved mother at age 18. Mother always felt abandoned and couldn't shake her grief and loss. What I learned about this Kingdom of Heaven was that there were many conditions around getting in, and not everyone passed. Certainly, a wonderful option to nothingness, this glorious place remained in a distant and unreachable realm. Grandmother may have changed dramatically. Did she wear a white gown, play a harp, and spend eternity in the clouds?

How would my life and other lives be different if the truth about the process of transition from the physical would have been my gift as a child rather than assuming my grandmother was gone forever? At age seven, this information would have been a start to my spiritual education and understanding of what I now experienced as reality. Losing the knowledge that we could develop a new relationship and communicate with loved ones in spirit left us all open to unbearable grief and disconnection for many generations. My parents weren't to blame for a culture that had gone wrong, as we were ripped from the roots of knowing the true nature of existence.

****

In this life, we raised our girls with lots of animals and nature. They learned to love and respect the Earth. When one of our pets passed, I could still sense or see them from the other side. I shared my many intuitive experiences with my kids, and they developed their own intuition.

Reincarnation became part of the girls' awareness at an early age. They participated in the fun of the 'Come as You Were' parties at our house with my Edgar Cayce study group friends. We would all dress as the person in one of the lifetimes we thought we had lived. Amy described her costume as one of a very rich woman. Meg dressed as gypsy, and Jack followed his Norwegian heritage and became a Viking for those evenings. I always gravitated to my Native American garb, and as life rolled along, we found that our choices all had a foundation in our past lives.

When my mother passed suddenly, and the girls mourned the loss of a loving Grandmother, we were all able to have some connection with her, and that eased the pain of her passing. When Hemitra passed, her communication went beyond my wildest dreams, and I shared many messages from her with my daughters. In my family, I wanted no more denying the beautiful connections humans can have with the Earth and the next dimension.

Chapter 16

Late September, 9:30 am, eight weeks after Hemitra's transition, Linda called unexpectedly. We had agreed that she would check in once a week. For the first three weeks, she contacted me every day and channeled Hemitra, and that gave me the greatest comfort possible. I don't know how she endured my pain and grief, but she saved my life. Her loving friendship will always be one of the most precious gifts I received this lifetime.

My friend sounded terrible as she told me her niece had passed. Her beloved niece was only in her early 40s. They were close, and Linda was now in her own grieving process and packing to go to LA to spend time with her sister. She would call me in a few weeks as soon as she returned.

After the memorial, the phone stopped ringing. It was time. All of our friends needed to get back to their lives and careers and have their own grief experience. Last week, when a friend called to check on me, the scenario played as usual. I reported what I'd heard and seen from Hemitra. I retold what Linda said as verification of my experiences. Could I ever stop talking? Gone was any polite exchange of sharing or asking how anyone else was doing? I tried sometimes. My social graces had gotten lost, and I just blurted out all the Hemitra news. Somewhere in the conversation, I cried. I witnessed myself often sounding like a stuck record and even felt sorry for the listener. However, I just couldn't stop words from falling out of my mouth.

I would say, "Please forgive me, I just keep talking." That didn't stop me or slow down the intensity. When I hung up from a call yesterday, I sank onto the nearest chair. I felt spent, and my heart pounded hard as the PTSD continued to rule my body.

I heard Hemitra's voice in my head. "That was too much for you." She witnessed it. My body and soul were exhausted.

I welcomed the necessary silence that followed, and it was terrifying. Now, I must rest or collapse. I needed to feel the ground under me and to clearly receive Hemitra's messages from a quiet place. I feared the pain that sometimes consumed my every minute would never end. With fewer diversions, I needed to face the dark. As we inched through autumn, and the leaves on the trees turned from brightly colored to dead brown, then bare trees, my grief weighed heavy.

My daughters never wavered in their support and usually checked in every day. They kept me anchored in some reality. Meg stopped over one day. Known for her directness, she looked at me and said, "Mom, you look exhausted and emaciated. Are you eating?"

Was I eating? Sometimes I forgot to eat, and sleeping was in bits and pieces at night.

I tried to do ordinary duties and put out the orders for our small online business, but all the orders were late. I sent emails with tracking numbers and an apology. "So sorry, we had a death in the family." Tiny tasks took forever. I never imagined falling apart like this.

The daily communications from Hemitra continued. I woke one morning at 4 a.m. and stayed conscious long enough to see a glowing orange/gold light in the corner of my bedroom. Half asleep, I knew it was her, and I received the comfort of the visit and slept again.

As in life, Hemitra and I wanted understanding between us. In this new relationship, her communications delivered profound insights to me. One morning as I exercised, I saw her sitting on the couch across the room. The vision was filmy yet vividly her. My body weakened, and I lost energy. Instantly, I knew what she was telling me. She made me feel exactly what it was like sometimes in her body. I felt the struggle and the dissatisfaction as she aged from the lack of self-care over the years. Her experience... so different than mine. I always cared for my health, and she didn't. Encouragement in every way never worked. This beautiful capable woman carried the scars of self-hatred from her abusive childhood, and I couldn't change or heal that. She wanted me to know viscerally what she felt, as if she was saying, "See, this is what it was like for me." The power of the feeling overwhelmed me, and I cried but completely understood the message.

The same scenario happened a few nights later. I woke, and my body felt as though I couldn't move-almost paralyzed. I received another message about Hemitra's childhood that she translated to my body. She wanted me to understand that sometimes she became frozen with fear because of the beatings from her alcoholic father. It almost felt like an apology and reason for her early leaving. Again, she conveyed this with clarity. I witnessed it through the years when she became afraid and couldn't move forward. I was the one to jump into what we must do. After that, she joined me and executed her task and part in our ventures as her brilliant capable self.

Hemitra needed me to have a deeper knowing of her Earthly experience, even though we shared everything about each other when we lived together in the physical. I could feel her pain in this life, but the knowing she conveyed now went beyond what we were capable of sharing when we were both in bodies. I began to understand what Hemitra told me through Linda, "I want to live Earth through you." I never questioned how any of this happened, because now Hemitra's complete perception of my body mind and spirit felt natural. As I read other authors books who were mediums, I gained more verification about those on the other side taking part in the lives of loved ones on Earth.

Events that seemed impossible became my normal. We had two separate phone lines, and I had to replace the phone for the home phone line. When I recorded the message and played it back, the recording was of Hemitra's voice. It was the one she had recorded for the office phone. Meg had stopped by and witnessed the phenomena. I attempted to deduce a rational explanation, but there was no rational explanation. We looked at each other in a daze. The phone message disappeared when I listened again.

My education continued. Somewhere, I read a suggestion that those on Earth could ask loved ones in spirit to communicate in a specific way. Great! That night, I silently asked Hemitra to move the large picture on our kitchen wall. Just make it a little off center, I suggested before I went to bed.

Morning came, and as my first priority of the day, I looked for a picture off center. The picture was still perfectly in place, and I received a vision and message. I saw her with her hands on her hips, scowling. I remembered the stream of past communications from her. I could hear her voice, and I thought about the volts of joyful electric current that surged through me from her, her comforting touch in the middle of the night, and a cosmic, healing trip to the sacred spring in Delphi.

She said, "I gave you all that, and you ask me to move the damn picture! What do you think I am a trained pony?" I laughed out loud and kept laughing.

Her personality hadn't changed. The phrase 'larger than life' felt appropriate, and it made me happy. It was the same. We were together and having fun!

****

Cruising the aisles of Home Depot one sunny October day, a message came. "You were very kind to her." She referred to a phone call I'd had that morning from a woman we both had to tolerate, and sometimes it wasn't easy.

"I learned a lot about kindness from you," Hemitra said lovingly.

My spirits lifted, and I continued walking past the bolts and nuts aisle. I felt grateful for all the love and kindness I had received in my life, and no one had ever shown me more love, devotion, and understanding than Hemitra. Suddenly the familiar sinking feeling began. I started falling. I clawed at the sides of a dark tunnel scrambling to stay upright and falling into the abyss of grief. I heard her voice. "Don't do it. Stay with me!"

It was too late. The familiar pain took over, and she was gone. We couldn't be together where I landed again in the hellish torment far below her high vibration.

The parts of me that still worked witnessed my behavior with curiosity. I handled crisis well, until now. I watched the clean laundry mountain grow on my bed, and the clutter gather. I couldn't seem to feel it's importance. I was just an observer watching someone who had fallen to pieces. In one pile of papers on my desk, sat the death certificates – still many needed to be sent to official places. My bedroom floor lay strewn with notes from multiple books about the next dimension and communications from the other side. Some days I couldn't function.

Who are we? Why do I feel like this? I now experienced the most difficult passage of my life, but I felt I should be handling it better.

For years, Linda had referred to Hemitra and me as Twin Souls, and in all that time, I thought it meant two people who shared a deep, close relationship. I considered the term New Age.

As Hemitra and I first grew close, we didn't need anything but each other. We were a complete package. Opposites in ways, we complimented each other perfectly. She was what was missing in my life, and I was the same for her. Together we lacked nothing. We always wanted to be together, because the connection was overwhelmingly powerful. Adding the fact that we remembered being together literally forever, we created an unbreakable bond again!

Things I hadn't thought of for years, returned to my awareness. Perhaps when a loved one dies, we sift through all the moments we had together, grasping for more, for closure, for anything to comfort us. Again, each event I remembered was as vivid as if it were in present time, and I kept going back to that life changing summer when we fell in love.

Chapter 17

Now, Hemitra and I spent every bit of time together that we could. It felt strange to have become dependent on the sound of her voice and our plans together. I brushed it aside and enjoyed.

From the beginning, there was much to talk about. How could she think I was that interesting? She listened to everything I said, and I remained intrigued with her, not politely, but with full attention. We found the deepest comfort talking, in silence, or in activity. We nurtured and cared for each other with hearts wide open, fearlessly vulnerable. Hemitra knew me better than anyone ever had. I liked that. When we were together nothing else mattered, and many times we would set out to join a gathering with our crowd, only to decide that it would be more fun to just hang out together.

We had surfaced our ancient memories and an intrigue and excitement that no relationship had ever offered. Though I'd never experienced anything like it, this was a natural, comfortable feeling. Plunging into soul depths drew us farther and farther into our story through eons. Moving through time and space together added an irresistible cosmic quality. When we touched, the physical contact stirred even more past life memories. How clever the universe was in its method of bringing us together again!

Just a couple weeks before, we met Linda and had a reading that revealed snap shots of our life together in ancient Greece. We were women lovers living a lifetime of service. The life in Delphi always felt like a healing balm, and Linda's information added to the picture of two souls bonded in love through millenniums.

Being in the same space, ordinary physical touch or closeness was now filled with passion and longing that couldn't be acted on. This perfect joyful friendship setup, as our forever together movie played in the background, made it impossible not to fall in love again. All innocence had disappeared.

We struggled everyday against the temptation to fill in the missing piece and become lovers. It became intensely hard to avoid. One day sitting side by side, Hemitra spoke with a hopeless edge to her voice, "What are we going to do?"

By August of the summer that changed everything, there was only one course of action. My hands trembled, and my heart raced as I drove to meet Hemitra at her house. Gulp! What am I doing, and how do we do this? She's a woman.

As long-lost lovers, we tumbled into the endless depth of each other's eyes and the dizzying sweetness of our first tender kiss. We had found each other again with the same passion and pull between us that we always experienced. We remembered the mysteries of our past and surrendered to an unknown future. Heart and soul, body and mind merged in sweaty ecstasy, as we fulfilled long awaited desire. The both women part we figured out, and we delighted in the irresistible magnetism with wild abandon. The decision that day, closed the door on Act I of my life and dramatically heralded in Act II. Those hours were a phenomenon that we talked about in the years to come, and we repeated the scene as often as our busy life allowed.

Looking back, the odds were a million to one that we could stay apart. Presented with someone compatible and irresistible on all levels, and as we witnessed our history of love in many lives, the temptation proved too much. Our time had come.

Yes, Hemitra, your secret love, the one who reflects you better had appeared. I'm glad it remained a secret this long. This secret love was dangerous at that moment and needed to be closely guarded to keep it secret. There would be many years ahead when we remained masked from a public that existed in closely drawn boundaries of should and must. This was not ancient Delphi.

****

I woke up the next morning, and in those first moments out of the dream time, I faced the realization that I was a married woman having a love affair with a woman. The most difficult passage in my life thus far, had begun. It was a long slide into dark waters and way over my head. I couldn't fully grasp its meaning. Of course, this was impossible. What should we do?

There was nothing to do but carry on. We began working on more women's circles, full moon gatherings, sweat lodges and classes for women. The first time we advertised a full moon circle, one woman joined us. Her name was Jacqui, a lovely woman about our age. Jacqui would become the Reiki Master for our future center and a mainstay and pillar, who stood with us and worked with us through all kinds of weather, as we experienced great fun and fulfillment as well as hard work.

Word spread and women filled our available space. They arrived as all ages, backgrounds and circumstances. Hemitra and I loved this work and our common bond with the women. Just as we filled our back yard, other women gathered all over the globe in circles and groups because it simply was time. The mandatory great "Shift of the Ages" was in process, and we were here for more than the right to vote. The rise of a fierce feminine force united us, and somewhere in us all was the mark of the Renegade.

****

We thought sometimes that our surprise love affair could be a passing thing, a beautiful storm, though my doubts for that resolution mounted. We made some attempts to end the steamy affair, but that only lasted a short depressing day or two. Hemitra continued to look for the right man, as she dated every so often and was disappointed in the results. Of course, we knew I could never leave my marriage. I was committed, bonded and in place.

I hated the lies I told. I loathed the deception. The marriage I had always worked on, treasured, and fought for now turned to a life of betrayal. I became a good actress, as this journey now necessitated immediate and convincing stories to cover my tracks.

Breaking all of my own rules was a humbling experience. It seemed I had become the unforgivable villain. I reflected on my life with Jack and the girls. Our protected family was not without its challenges but ran on caring and joy. Our home had been a love circus filled with kids, friends, animals, and a whirl of activity. Growing up, the girls had horses that they showed, our chickens clucked contentedly in the yard, and we had a few litters of puppies and kittens among a long list of critters that the girls adored. I fed my family organic and was a wholesome Earth mother and loyal wife-until I wasn't.

I questioned, what happened to my normal life? Searching my memories on how I viewed gay relationships, I wondered if I would have experimented with women if social values had been more liberal? I'd always had boyfriends and loved my girlfriends for similar thinking, sounding boards, and wonderful fun relationships. Was it just conditioning?

In college, the Dean discovered a girl in my sorority with her female lover. Word spread quickly, and the sorority members took sides. Should this woman be tossed from the sorority? You're kidding right? My reaction and my friends' reactions were, so what?

In that moment years ago, I searched for help, and I remembered a friend of mine used an intuitive who lived out of our area. I didn't want to talk to Nick about Hemitra and me at that time. I thought about Linda but decided to flee to a place where no one knew me. I needed answers.

Chapter 18

My nerves were on edge as the 50-minute drive ended, and I parked at the curb of a neatly manicured lawn on Dogwood Drive, which was a quiet suburban street. Brightly colored mums lined the mulched flower beds, and the colorful dried flower wreath on the front door welcomed visitors.

Elizabeth, a woman wearing grey slacks and a peach colored top, answered the door. She looked about my age, and I relaxed as soon as we met. She worked as a channel and had been highly recommended by my friend, who had consulted with her for years.

Elizabeth led me through her house which was decorated with tasteful furniture and modern artwork. A small room at the end of the hall was an office with two chairs, a desk, a recorder, a phone, and a lovely grouping of seashells. The woman made small talk for a minute, and then she told me to get comfortable, so we could begin. Did I have any questions before we started?

"No."

Elizabeth closed her eyes and began to breathe deeply. In a moment, her voice altered slightly, and she began. She asked for my full name and date of birth.

"Yes, I have your vibration. I see nature spirits around you, and you are attuned to the nature kingdom. They appreciate that. You're living in a time of change."

"Yes," I offered in response.

Next, Elizabeth asked me to begin my questions. Here goes, I thought. "I've become close to a woman named Hemitra," and I told Elizabeth her date of birth.

The woman paused and then said, "Yes, I have her energy."

A statement came through from beyond, "She's a lot to handle, but there's much to be offered."

"That's true." I smiled.

"The two of you are very well matched and compatible. Is there a problem?"

"I've become very dependent on her and this relationship. I'm used to being more emotionally independent." The words tumbled out.

"Why is this wrong?" the channel's other voice continued.

"Were you not dependent on your mother and aren't we all dependent on each other?"

"I guess," I answered, not convinced.

"And what of the sex?" Elizabeth asked. I hadn't bridged that one and inwardly winced. "Is loving someone ever wrong?"

"No," I said. *Yes, in this case*, I thought.

I continued, "When we're together we spontaneously travel to other times and places, past lives."

"Yes," the response calmly delivered. "What's coming up strongly now is a lifetime in ancient Greece."

"Yes."

"In that lifetime you were together a long time and very dependent on one another as a lifestyle. You were everything to each other."

I swallowed. "How many lifetimes have we been together?"

From the distant realms of wherever Elizabeth traveled, came a laugh that caught me off guard. What was funny?

Following the laughter, "Oh so many, and most of them highly sexual."
What was I to say? I was in big trouble.

The reading ended, after some details I don't remember.

****

Hemitra and I always traveled between the worlds where time and space blurred. This connection spanned millennium, and we witnessed civilizations on Earth originate and fall to dust. She and I had met again at what seemed a most inconvenient time and circumstance. Turning away would close the door to this mysterious encounter. I wanted someone to share these things with. I wanted a cosmic playmate.

I knew that the ones we love and the players in our world were not a first go around. Souls join together over and over again, as they unconsciously found one another in many lives to learn lessons together. However, our story was reinforced with seeing and feeling the other lives we'd lived and the verification by those who could pierce the veil of ordinary reality.

Hemitra and I enjoyed the glimpses of many shared lives. Some were simple and plain, and others were filled with high adventure. In Hemitra's and my first summer together, the life I was to be shown next would make a stunning appearance as it played, and then it would lay dormant. It would reemerge decades later to offer bizarre and challenging information.

Chapter 19

On a warm, late, August evening those many years ago, as I cooked dinner for the family, I heard the sharp, rhythmic clip clop of horse hooves on stone, and in my mind's eye, I saw a horse carriage and driver. I was startled by the sound, as well as the vision, and even more so as an elegant looking young man with a top hat and a long black waistcoat opened the door of the carriage cab and stepped down onto a cobblestone street. Suddenly, I was no longer barefoot and relaxed in shorts and a t-shirt. Instead, I was wearing a tight corset under a long Victorian-style dress that was made with lots of material. It felt uncomfortable! Even though all of this was happening in my mind, it was as real as the lettuce I was washing in my kitchen.

Several times, over the next weeks, the sound of the horse drawn carriage on a cobblestone street repeated, and I saw what looked like a scene out of one of my favorite childhood books, *Black Beauty*. Some memory wanted to be recognized, yet I remembered feeling some annoyance as it insistently broke into my normal thoughts.

Hemitra was back to work, but we got together as much as possible. She called one day to say that an old love from college days was flying from the Midwest for a visit. She was happy with the news. I was not. Maybe this marked a turning point. I had no right to want to stay in this crazy, painful, and hopeless situation.

Ted, the boyfriend, arrived two weeks later. Two days into his arrival Hemitra called, her voice discouraged, if not downright disgusted. The man arrived with too much luggage, including 40 ties, and he was obviously looking for a place to land after a failed marriage. It took three weeks to extricate him.

During the Ted weeks, Hemitra decided we should all go to the annual formal ball in Philadelphia. The plan was for Hemitra and Ted, and Jack and me to attend. The men reluctantly agreed but quickly backed out. Hemitra and I decided to invite a girlfriend, since this wasn't a couple's event.

The night of the party, I was at Hemitra's place waiting for her friend, Victoria. We decided to meditate.

The man from the carriage, complete with top hat and long waistcoat, appeared in my head a few minutes into meditation. He walked arm in arm with me, a woman in an elaborate Victorian dress. The man opened the door of a brick building, and we walked in. The address on the outside of the building was #10 Downing Street. The gathering of people inside acknowledged us as a couple with a polite bow or curtsy, and we waltzed together, as if we were one.

The meditation and the vision ended, but I remained half in another time and place as I shared the experience with Hemitra. She was the man I waltzed with 200 or so years ago. At that moment, she sat aside me as the attractive woman I loved again. Victoria never showed up for the party, and Hemitra and I went alone. From the 11th floor of the large building where the party was held, we mingled with 500 people that night. When we glanced out the window at the Schuylkill River running under a bridge, I only saw the Thames River passing under London Bridge, as I remained lost in time. That memory took me to emotions not yet explored in this life.

I needed Nick to find out what this latest lifetime was about and called him the next day. Nick said that in Victorian England, Hemitra held a seat in British parliament, and I was the wife. Nick called me the "power behind the throne," or what I later decided was the sharing of our usual partnership.

The movie flowed forth from there. I saw images of a manor house on a large piece of land. It had windows with many diamond shaped panes, a library full of leather bound books, and a large well used dining room. In one scene, I saw us riding horseback together on the beautiful land. There was a rabbit hutch, and I thought we may have kept the rabbits as a food source.

The images continued, especially when we were together, and also when I was alone. We were a couple in love and living what looked like a good life. The story played in sequence, as another deep bond between us was revealed.

There was no Internet at that time, so Hemitra and I visited the library a mile away, where we found a picture of 10 Downing Street, the home of British Prime Ministers since 1721. I didn't remember ever having seen any picture of this historic British building before, but the image on the page and the image from my meditation looked exactly alike, and a cold chill ran down my spine.

More history revealed that the waltz was introduced to English society in 1812. Hemitra pointed out a paragraph that said the Prime Minister sometimes entertained the Queen at Downing St. I hadn't seen Queen Victoria in any of the past life scenes I remembered.

One day, I saw myself as the Victorian wife watching the poor, ragged, dirty street children. My long fancy dress almost touched the filthy London sidewalk. The scene brought tears to my eyes and reminded me of *A Christmas Carole* by Charles Dickens, one of my favorite writers. Dickens' writings were a social commentary of his time in Victorian England, and he depicted the poor middle class of that era. Though the British Empire stood as the world's most powerful nation in 19th century England, the rich and poor were miles apart. Industrialization brought depressed living conditions, child labor, sickness and poverty to the English work force.

Another time, I saw a vision of me in a beautiful church wearing an elaborate off-white gown with a long train. My eyes and heart were focused on a handsome man, and there was a large stained-glass window behind him. The event was our wedding. He wore a dark blue suit with brass buttons and decoration. I thought it was a military uniform, and it seemed to make him feel like a wooden soldier, stiff and at rigid attention. I also felt my dress as heavy, perhaps a clue to the way we endured the restrictions of the repressed Victorian era.

The underlying foundation of these memories came from the depth of love we shared in that lifetime. Again, I thought of Charles Dickens and his social commentaries of that period. In *A Christmas Carole*, the main character, Ebenezer Scrooge when he addressed the spirits and asked, "Spirits why do you show me this?" I could relate.

As I shared every detail with Hemitra, she jumped right in and provided details from her own deep memory bank. Together we processed this past love and felt the pain of being here at the end of the 20th century unable to be together, as we continued to live a mysterious secret.

One day, as we worked on another part of a course curriculum, Hemitra pressed her hand into the left side of her spine, saying her back hurt. When I massaged the spot, another trigger fired. I saw a clear image of us riding horseback together. I think she, he at the time, rode a dapple-grey horse and was thrown. It seemed to be a painful and lingering accident. I related the vision, and after the massage and the surfaced memory, the pain disappeared. She didn't mention her back again.

The next 200-year-old event replay started with deep sadness and tears flowing down my face. Again, I heard the sound of horse hooves. This time, I was riding inside the carriage. My husband sat opposite me in the carriage cab. He was wearing a grey "boiled wool" suit, and I knew he was dying. I heard the word consumption, which is the old-fashioned word for tuberculosis, and that dreaded lung disease was prevalent at the time.

When I saw Hemitra that afternoon, I wrapped my arms around her afraid to let go and hung onto the moment of being together, whatever the circumstances. What were we to do?

After the vision of the man I loved about to die, I felt finished with that life in England, but a phone call from Nick a week later prompted the story's ending scene. When I spoke to him that day, he asked me if I remembered how I had died in the English life?

No, I hadn't.

"How do you feel about fire?" he asked.

I didn't have an answer until after we'd ended our conversation. Nick left me on my own to figure it out.

I wanted to deliver Nick's information in person, so I jumped in my car to drive the 10 minutes to Hemitra's house, as the next installment of Victorian England unfolded in my mind as unstoppable and disturbing images. In the bedroom of our manor house, my bed had a canopy and curtains, and I saw a lit candle that had fallen over. There was with a glass of wine tipped over next to the candle. Flames engulfed the bed and revealed my death scene.

I watched the woman get up from the bed and walk toward her husband, the English Lord, who was now in spirit. He wore the black waistcoat and waited just a few yards away to greet his wife as she left the Earth realm. The last thing impression I had, on that day long ago, was a strange feeling of disappointment or incompleteness, as I viewed that life end, but I couldn't understand the feelings.

I explained what I'd just remembered about our dramatic English life as Hemitra and I sat on her sofa.

She asked, "What happens when you die in a fire?"

I shrugged my shoulders. "I guess before the fire gets to you, you die of smoke inhalation."

I changed the subject, and minutes later we had our arms around each other. In a few seconds, Hemitra began to cough and pushed me away.

"I can't breathe," her face was pale.

I realized what happened and took her hand. "You're doing what you always do. I have one of these images, and you join in. We were reliving our two-hundred year-old marriage, and the memory made you feel like you were choking on the smoke from that fire."

Hemitra's visceral reactions to the past continued. We walked a favorite trail that wound through a part of Valley Forge Park. The same thing happened each time we walked. Her voice would deepen. She'd say, "I feel like a man." I will always remember those walks with the man in a dark waistcoat and top hat. We began to consider those experiences our unusual normal.

****

Denial was the only path I knew to stay sane, as Hemitra and I lived day to day growing closer and more inseparable. Jack, Hemitra and I spent time together since she was at the house a lot. We had fun together. Not facing the truth of our situation gave relief, at times. With Jack's travel schedule and my dodging, fencing ability, this state of limbo lasted another 18 months. However, I grew noticeably distant from Jack. Our daughters and their dad had discussions about Hemitra and me. Suspicion increased, and one day, Jack confronted me. What was going on? Our passion was not a containable secret.

My defense was denial, and then I charged back with an offense about his emotional and physical absence. It was a pale, lame reaction, and from that day, the nightmare began.

Hemitra's passing sparked all the memories of life 22 years before in every vivid detail. Stop, enough, I screamed in my mind. I focused on the next day and my present painful life. I had an appointment with a medium who lived an hour away. My friend, Pat, had recommended Danielle, and I was grateful, since I missed the amazing conversations with Linda.

When my friend Pat told me about Danielle, I emailed her to make a date for a reading, and she wrote back and said, "I can tell how close you and your partner are."

Chapter 20

Danielle opened her front door, and I felt a comfortable connection with this attractive blond in her mid-forties. Danielle's eyes reflected compassionate knowing. Her home radiated serenity. After our initial greeting, she led me downstairs into a room with a soft lavender light shining on a water feature, crystals arranged on a table, and a cozy couch and chair. We sat, and she told me to close my eyes and bring my awareness to center. She began....

"Who has the pain in the abdomen?" Danielle asked.

"She did," I answered.

"Who's having the shortness of breath?"

"She did at the end."

"Who's getting the headaches and fuzziness in the head?"

I paused, confused. "Oh, it must be me. She never had headaches."

Danielle responded, "She says, it's you. She's worried about you. She says you're not sleeping and not eating, and you're dizzy because of it. Do you have anxiety?"

"Yes," I answered

"You know how she took care of you? She's cradling you. She's wrapping her arms around you. She's worried about you." Danielle continued.

I asked that nagging question one more time, "What more could we have done? I would have done anything."

Danielle confidently replied, "She says, you did everything you could have done. Everything. I'm sorry. It couldn't be helped. It wasn't your fault. There was so much pain, heartache pain. I couldn't be here."

"You mean for a longer time?" I questioned.

"Yes," Danielle spoke, "She's thanking you so much for taking such good care of her.

She says she's still here. She's making me feel nauseous. She talks about the blockage. She said it spread everywhere. She's showing me with her hands."

Danielle motioned with her hands moving over her torso.

"By the time it was diagnosed, it was too late. It was metastasized breast cancer." I filled in the details.

"There was nothing you could do."

"Could we have done something earlier?" Could I ever let this go?

Danielle affirmed, "No."

Danielle raised her voice, "She loved her life! She loved her life! She loved her life, and you're the reason she loved it! You need to know how much she loved her life! She loved every moment. She loved every single second, and she is so grateful!"

I cried.

Danielle began to cry. "I don't get emotional at readings, and I feel such emotion. She's emotional and you're emotional."

Danielle said with emphasis, "This love that she has for you, she has such love, such love for you!"

I tried to stop crying and reached for the tissues behind me.

Danielle continued, "Something with the infinity symbol. It's infinite. It will never end. It's just the beginning."

I grasped for more, "Other lifetimes like this one?"

Danielle continued, "Yes. She will wait for you. She'll be the one to come for you. It will be infinite. The two of you spread joy and love."

I smiled, "It wasn't always perfect. I had to put her in her place."

Danielle laughed. "She's a pistol! You were the only one who could handle her, the only one!"

I laughed, and it felt good.

"She needed to be put in her place," answered Danielle.

"We understood each other completely," I commented. It was wonderful to hear these words.

Danielle began again, "You both needed your space, and you respected those boundaries with each other, and that's why you lasted. Even though there was no separation, you had your own individuality, but you grew together."

"We learned from each other," I added.

I thought about the pain in my left side. "There has been a pain in my left side for a long time."

Danielle frowned, "Yes, she keeps giving me a twinge there. Something needs to get checked out. There's something there that needs to be investigated. She knows how stubborn you are. Something that you would manifest. You want to be with her deeply."

"I'm trying to stay. I want to want to be here," I expressed my current struggle and nagging desire to abandon ship.

"Can I avoid surgery."

Danielle paused for a time, "You will be able to. You need to get it checked out, but you will not need surgery. That's one of the reasons you haven't gotten it checked. She's showing me with the people you have around you that you will get this under control. You have the right team in place, and with your strong mind and those others, you will get back on track. You have a lot of support around you, but it's not her. You're a powerful creator.

Danielle quoted Hemitra, "Stop it!! Don't make yourself ill, because you're working on it. You know how to reverse it, and you can do it quickly. You're very good at that. You know how easy it is to go the other way. Your work is not finished here."

"I wanted it with her," I tried not to cry again.

Danielle assured me, "She will help you write and do it all. I feel Hemitra is going to channel with you."

"I see lights flickering," Danielle changed direction.

"The lights over the vanity flickered this morning. I thought the power was going on and off."

Danielle began a stream of observations, "She gave you the sign that she was there with you. Something with a bird. She'll come to you in the sign of the bird. I see a blue bird."

"She loved birds. She said I could feel her in dreams," I said.

"With dreams it will be a visit. This is a visit, but dreams are more of a visit since you are out there beyond the body. She's with you all the time." Danielle's words comforted me.

"You are so fabulous, you are so fabulous!!" Danielle quoted Hemitra, and she and I both cried.

"I feel that way about her," was my answer.

Danielle continued, "You made her better."

"We made each other better," I commented.

Danielle translated my partner, "But you're fabulous on your own. She wants you to really know because she knows how lost you feel without her. You will be back. When you were together you had a purpose. You built each other up and you fed each other. Your soul must have a purpose. You were fulfilling that and assisting many. You did a lot, and you were growing, and she is doing more than she could do on Earth."

"Do we grow together?" I had infinite questions.

Danielle said, "Yes you grow together. You'll do the book together. When you're happy it frees her, and your grief ties her. She won't leave you. She'll never leave you; it's not like that. As your spirit elevates, so will hers. You're supposed to learn more and take what you're doing to another level. Whatever you were teaching, do it. After the book, I see you speaking in front of people. Just because you're grieving... this is an Earth experience... part of being human. Humans chose to have emotions. It's part of your life lesson. You will feel the loss. Not making yourself sick is a very different statement than feeling the loss of your partner, your other half, someone you shared everything with. You elevated each other's vibration, and now, that has been shifted. How do you maintain that vibration when you can't do it together? You can do that. You absolutely can feel the closeness, because she is absolutely here. It's not just the memories. She's absolutely physically, spiritually here. She's definitely with you. She picks out your outfits. She compliments your hair, she fixes your hair, she tweaks your hair."

"Yes! I have conversations with her all the time. I hear her answers, and it's just like before. Is it my imagination?"

Danielle answered emphatically, "No, she's with you. Know that! It's not over. She keeps showing me the moon and the stars. It's something about, I love you to the moon and stars and back again. Over the rainbow, and there's something with a butterfly. These are signs for you."

"She's dancing," Danielle reported.

"We danced the waltz at our wedding. I've never felt anything like that."

Danielle said, "That gave her memories of your history. She talks about the waltz. She said you were floating."

"Waltzing together was a memory from a lifetime when we were a couple in Victorian England," I added.

Danielle continued, "She said you have a question."

"Will we be together in the next life?

Danielle quickly said, "Always. There isn't a life that you won't be together."

"Why do I keep asking that?" My lost feeling surfaced.

Danielle revealed, "You had a tragedy and you were separated, and that's the heartache. You were pulled apart. Twin souls search for each other, and they may be ripped apart, and they search and search to be together."

Twin souls? Just like Linda said, I thought.

"I always think about being with her in ancient Greece."

Danielle, "Greece was a similar life to this, and you were lovers and best friends and served together. I see you both in white robes. It was a beautiful life where you were very happy. However, in your many lives together, there's something I would like to look at to be healed for the next life. There's something that needs to be healed in the soul. What work needs to be done? Why is the soul leaving the Earth? I'm hearing, whoever is leaving, the soul is not able to accomplish the lesson that needs to be done, and choses to leave. It manifests as illness. In every lifetime, you always take on lives of service. If you have chosen to be twin souls, you must agree to have this experience. You must agree to make the most of the Earth experience. You were about to fulfill what you came to do, and her body wasn't able to do that anymore. It was a whole bunch of things such as the abuse from her father. That wasn't up to you to heal. Next time in spirit, agree to choose an easier path. She chose a path of resistance to learn life lessons. You must agree that in order to assist beings you are here to help, that you choose a path of least resistance."

"That's the heart of my grief. It's that feeling of being left again." Danielle had just identified my pain and confusion.

Danielle, continued, "You can still learn and be together; you don't need abuse. That's why she had to go first. There was nothing else. You were doing everything you could do. You're still together in this life. You will always miss her. You're supposed to. You had each other's heartbeat."

The session ended, and I thought about the deep ties between Hemitra and me and all humans. We grow together? I had many questions, but now, I was looking forward to a break in the routine. Next weekend, our friends would gather in Cape May, New Jersey to have a private memorial for our Hemitra.

Chapter 21

"Tell them. Tell them." Hemitra referred to the memory that filled my mind.

"They've heard it," I answered silently.

"Tell them." She wouldn't give up, but I held back as I listened to the others who shared loving, sometimes funny stories, as we sat around the wooden table in Renee's secluded back yard. Renee and Johnnie's beautiful Victorian house in Cape May offered the perfect oasis to join together for this more intimate memorial to honor our Loved One in spirit. We all arrived Friday and filled the house with laughter and tears, as we attempted to allow Hemitra's passing to sink in. The early October morning sun warmed us, as we basked in the comfort of each other and the rightness of our communal grieving and celebration.

Together we cooked a gigantic Sunday breakfast laid out in colorful bowls and platters. We passed steaming scrambled eggs and bacon, warm muffins, fresh from the bakery, and luscious fruit, while Joan poured us each hot tea from a red ceramic pot.

In a few minutes I spoke, "Ok, I give up. I know you've all heard this, but she insists that I tell you."

The women's faces lit up. They smiled and welcomed the story. What a blessing to be together. Everyone completely accepted Hemitra's presence from her place in the next dimension and my daily communication with Her. They shared their own stories of feeling her with them and remembering her visits in recent dreams.

I told our tale. It was two years after Hemitra and I had fallen in love. Jack and I still lived together, but the marriage was a nightmare, and my children hated me from their safe space in college. I suffered from a dark, hopeless place because I felt everyone's pain; Jack, the girls, my parents, his parents. Life as I knew it died, and a new magical life had begun. The grief of a broken marriage tearing at my insides, and the other part of my life with Hemitra was a state of bliss. Hemitra and I had tried to be sensible and turn back to friendship, but our relationship was like nothing either of us had ever imagined possible.

One day in September 1989, I was driving home from running errands and was stopped for a red light. The light turned green, and I looked both ways as my foot reached for the accelerator. A large grey truck sped through the intersection running the red light. I had a split-second impulse to hesitate, and that saved me from a violent crash with the reckless truck.

I moved through the green light and thought on the way home about what an easy way out it would have been to be run over by that truck. The quick death illusion gave my mind a brief moment of relief. No, I can't do that. I have Jack's car came the next thought. The irrational feelings scared me.

****

On a cloudy grey day, two months later in November, I was driving home from Hemitra's house, where we were creating lesson plans for our classes. Some trees hung onto a few dead, brown leaves, and others were bare and stark. I dreaded going home. On the last mile stretch before my house, I pulled to a stop because of an eight car backup. A large deer lay on the road in the opposite lane. No cars were damaged.

That's my deer I thought, as some primitive force surfaced. I pulled the car to the side of the road and walked to the wounded animal. A man in a grey suit paced and talked on his cell phone, as he apparently tried to reach the police or someone for help.

The beautiful doe struggled with labored breath, and blood oozed from the corner of her mouth. It appeared her injuries were fatal, and I leaned down to stroke her neck.

"Don't touch that," the man barked an order.

I didn't pay any attention to the guy who assumed to be in charge. I spoke softly to the doe. "You're so beautiful, and you're badly hurt. It's ok to go now."

It felt good to touch the wild animal. I ran my hands down the doe's neck and head, as I repeated to her, "Just let go."

In a minute, the animal's breathing stopped, and I felt relief for her. I grabbed the doe by the front legs and dragged her off the road. The cars had been stopped because the deer took up a whole lane and created potential danger. Cars coming from the west faced a slightly blind corner, and then they were confronted with a blocked lane because of the animal.

The stalled traffic moved on, which left me and the grey suit alone. He lingered, paced and called another number. My heart raced. The deer was going home with me. I walked over to the man.

"One time during the day, we had a sick raccoon staggering around in our yard. It must have had distemper or rabies. I called the game warden, but no one came. I had to shoot it myself."

The man stared at me dressed in jeans and a hoodie. Without a word, he turned, and made one more call then drove away.

Growing up in the country, my dad taught my brother and me to safely shoot guns. I didn't like to kill anything, but when one of our animals was sick or dying, we lovingly put them down ourselves. That was country life.

I jumped in my car and drove the mile and a half home. Jack's car was parked in the driveway, and I ran in the house. "Come quick, there's a deer just killed on the road. Could you please help?"

I was grateful to see Jack smile as my unusual request broke the now intense tension between us.

We took my car and drove to the doe. Jack grabbed the back legs, and I took the front, so we could hoist the beautiful creature into the back of my station wagon. She completely filled the back of the car. Jack said she must weigh 125 pounds.

When we arrived at the house, I took a deep breath, since the prize was in hand. Together, we pulled the animal from the car and put her on the lawn next to the garage.

"Now what?" Jack asked.

I stared back at him, "I don't know exactly, one step at a time, I guess."

The deer must be gutted quickly to keep it from spoiling. This part made me nervous, and it would be best to do it before thinking too much. I grabbed a pack of single edge razor blades and rubber gloves from the utility room cabinet. Armed with the not too perfect tools, I walked to the deer where she lay on her side in the grass. I gulped and then took the sharp razor and cut through the flesh starting at the pubic area. The skin opened like it was being unzipped. As I cut through the abdomen area, the insides spilled onto the grass. Steam rose from her body cavity, and a deep reverence sweep through my heart, as I felt the perfection of this animal.

My wildlife training from Dad paid off. As I finished cutting through the doe's skin, I noticed the liver was dark and clean, which showed a healthy animal. Feeling triumphant at accomplishing this part, I hurried to the kitchen, rinsed the blood covered rubber gloves, and placed them in the sink. I excitedly called Hemitra to ask if she would help me skin the deer in the morning? She responded with big enthusiasm. I was proud of her.

I asked Jack to help me hang the deer, as he walked out to check on my progress. We both lifted the doe and carried her into the garage. I got a plastic bucket, and he took a sturdy nylon rope, then he adeptly tied it to the deer's back legs and slung the rope over the center beam above. We both pulled on the loose end of the rope to hoist the animal into the air. I put a tarp on the floor and a plastic bucket under the doe to catch the blood as she hung upside down her head inches above the rim of the bucket.

Jack wished me luck then turned to leave. The sadness that invaded the house returned. His kindness brought tears to my eyes. We were engaged in a silent, bitter battle, and the temporary truce between adversaries felt wonderful. I never could have imagined these circumstances.

"Thanks so much." I offered, as he briefly caught my eye.

"Yeah." Jack walked away, the moment of distraction over.

For months now, the love between Hemitra and me had been revealed, and the truth sent my family into shock and rage. How could they stop this madness and get me to return to my senses? My heart ached, as I felt the pain of my loved ones. Jack's mother, who I always considered my second mother, was devastated, yet after she had time, she supported me and never stopped the love between us. I didn't tell my own mom and dad, as long as I could possibly avoid it, as I processed the impossible situation. Neighbors and some friends revised their opinion of me and expressed bewilderment and outrage at my insanity. My reputation quickly went from well liked to She Devil. How could anyone do that to Jack? The atmosphere in my world was hostile.

Chapter 22

According to Native American wisdom, the medicine of the white tail deer is peace and gentleness. These qualities enveloped us that day. Many times, we expressed our gratitude for the sacred gift of this animal.

In the morning, Jack went to work and Hemitra arrived to help me. I got the single edge razor blades, and we both wore rubber gloves. To start, I held the skin where the deer was cut open. We learned how to pull the skin tight and cut the layers of fascia, the white web that held the pelt of hair to the doe's body and holds all the muscles in place. We worked slowly making sure we didn't cut holes in the precious coat.

Sunshine spilled in the garage windows, the November day remained calm and warm. Usually we talked endlessly, as we found subject after subject to explore together. Now we focused on the task at hand surrounded by the presence of the deer, exchanging a word here and there, sometimes commenting on the details of our work.

I paused the story and looked up at the women who were engaged in the long-ago tale of deer harvesting. It felt real, as if it were happening in that moment. Hemitra's presence was strong and vibrant. I knew she loved feeling the joy of our gathering and the story that she wanted told.

I continued…….

It took a couple hours to finish freeing the deer pelt from the body. We held the beautiful hide, and we each took a side of it, as we admired the tawny hair with the white tail.

Next, we grabbed a round plastic table and laid the pelt upside down on the surface. I took four cups of sea salt and sprinkled it generously on the inside. The salt would keep the skin from spoiling until we could take it to be tanned. We agreed from the beginning on preserving this treasure.

After a lunch break, the next task was to cut the head from the body. Hemitra never flinched as I took a hacksaw and easily severed the doe's tawny head. I was proud of this woman beside me and relished our sharing that day. The whole activity seemed normal, even though we'd never done it before...this lifetime. Sometime, some place before on this planet, we remembered preparing and thriving on game like the beautiful doe.

Hemitra suggested we do a ceremony to honor the doe. I dug a hole in the back of the vegetable garden, and we placed the head gently in the space, as we stroked the soft ears and face before covering her with the earth and marking the space with a rock.

We raised our arms, and each in turn thanked this beautiful animal for her life and for the peace she offered. We both felt deep reverence. Without words, we put our arms around each other and walked back into the house.

In the garage again, we looked at the large body now ready to be cut into pieces, another first. Grateful for my dad's advice on butchering a deer, I found the two sharpest knives in the kitchen and showed Hemitra how to begin. First, we cut the tender backstrap muscle that ran along either side of the spine and sliced it into portions. The rest of the day proved to be hard work, as we sawed the rest of the meat into cuts that were recognizable. We did a pretty good job, and our arms were tired as we wrapped and put the last pieces of venison in the freezer.

****

"We'll never forget that day and what was to follow." I paused and caught Connie's eye. She had been there from the beginning and knew the meaning of the rest of the story. She and eight other women joined us for the first Woman Wisdom training, a nine-month experience for women. That autumn long ago, Hemitra and I spent hours refining the curriculum, as we put our creative spin on the most valuable teachings that we received over the years. All the women around the table were part of the training at different times, and all but one had become teachers of the program.

****

Two weeks after the day with the deer, I was at Hemitra's house. The phone rang. Hemitra picked it up and handed it to me. It was Anderson, a friend of Hemitra's and mine, the woman who had sponsored a hula workshop at my house, two years before. I didn't know her well enough to expect a call and was puzzled that she wanted to talk to me. She lived in a nearby town and had just published a book on shamanism.

After a brief greeting, Anderson delivered a message I clearly remember. "I'm worried about you. I'm afraid for your life." She stated it in a matter-of-fact way, and I didn't know how to react.

When I asked why, she said she didn't know. It was a feeling, and I had popped into her mind. She cautioned me to take care of myself. I didn't pursue the questioning. My world was torn and shattered at the moment, so denial was helping me cope, and for some reason, I wasn't afraid. I told Anderson about the deer and the sacred day Hemitra and I shared.

In response, she lowered her voice and said, "That was supposed to be your deer. She gave her life for you." The words dug deep into my soul. This woman spoke with certainty, and her words caressed the deer with honor and reverence, as it should be.

Because of my bewildered state, I don't remember how the conversation ended. I do remember that her words were true, because the doe and I had become one heart that November day long ago.

Chapter 23

The story went on, and our friends continued to give it their attention. Post deer adventure that year, the holiday season filled our family with sadness. Disbelief stayed with me, as I moved through each hour without the ability to comprehend the whole or what to do about it. I matched each family members pain and felt it with them and for them. Was it guilt? Yes, yet how does one not fall in love? The sharp winds and snow of January settled in the northeast region.

****

It was the third weekend of our training, and the group energy bubbled as the women reunited after a seven week-stretch. We exchanged warm hugs, and the room glowed with exuberance. What great women we were blessed to have join us!

That day, I couldn't match the enthusiasm. My side hurt. It was probably a bug of sorts, I thought. I didn't eat lunch, which was very odd for me and my healthy appetite.

By end of day, the abdominal pain increased, and I asked Hemitra to take over one of my teaching pieces. In our closing circle, I remember Fran, one of our group, looking at me with tears in her eyes. I didn't know why, but she sensed something.

All the women showed concern, but I'd become such a health freak that I had a natural cure for almost everything. Part of our training time was devoted to homeopathy, herbs and vibrational medicine. I thought I'd figure it out and be ok.

****

Three days later, neither nature nor magic made the pain go away. Hemitra and the girls checked on me often, and they all acted scared. Even with the pain and anger, the kids felt toward me, they sensed something was very wrong with their mom. I hung onto the idea that this virus was a passing thing, but to ease their fears, I promised that if I wasn't better in a day, I would call an MD. Jack was on a sales trip, and I enjoyed the peace and quiet, although I became worried when nothing brought relief from the increasing pain.

On the third night, Hemitra and my two daughters hovered around my bed. I agreed to go to the ER but moving wasn't possible since my abdomen had become so rigid I couldn't get out of bed. Someone called the ambulance.

As I was hauled down the steps by two men in big black boots and yellow outfits and plunked into an ambulance that cold January night, I saw terror in the eyes of Hemitra, and my daughters. "I'll be ok. Don't worry," was all I could muster.

****

I spent eight days in the hospital after surgery for a ruptured appendix. The first days, I lingered in a morphine coma. My surgeon commented that I was fortunate to have come through the ordeal, because there wasn't much time left to decide to make the trip to the ER. The toxicity had progressed to the critical point. The grief and depression had caused me to lose my survival instincts.

Tearfully, Hemitra told me when she visited the hospital that she'd never been so scared, and she didn't sleep all night because she just couldn't face losing me. Terrified the night I was taken to the hospital by ambulance, she called our friend Nick. Nick said I would be back, and her fear was based on times when we were together and I left and didn't return or the reverse was true for her. Again, he referenced the countless times we'd shared love on Earth.

When I left the hospital, I was wild to begin again and incredibly grateful to be alive. It was obvious Jack and the girls loved me and I them, but now I must make a decision.

I called Nick, and early in the conversation asked, "Didn't I have a purpose with this family?"

"Of course, a very strong purpose," he replied. "You can go back to your family and continue your life. However, I'll tell you this, your soul level purpose and her soul level purpose at this point, is each other and your work. You agreed to come together for this life when you were between lifetimes. You don't have to do this. It's your choice."

Inch by inch, my life force had slipped away that fall. The agony and hopelessness became overwhelming, because my heart and soul knew, if I were to be honest and whole, that living life without Hemitra wouldn't be possible.

A new vitality filled me. I was aware that I'd passed through something of big significance and faced near death. What else could happen? With a clear mind and a heavy heart, I filed for divorce.

A month later, I spoke to Anderson and caught her up. She said often deer allow themselves to be killed by cars. It's some kind of a sacrifice and is a voluntary act. They represent the soft, nurturing, receptive qualities of the heart that humans need to develop or remember. The doe touched my life with love and healing. The mystical event of this gift was arranged on the subtle invisible plane. I won't fully understand how the threads of that day were woven together until I'm on the other side.

Hemitra, from her broad perspective, now saw this deeper meaning, and how it all played out. She knew the reason for something that could never be explained by my human mind, and she brought new life to the details that she wanted told. The white-tailed deer offered her medicine to me at a time when I needed it most, and I will be forever grateful.

I stopped talking and the story danced all around and through us. I'd relived it all, and could feel Hemitra with me, but now I came back fighting tears. It was all too new, and she would argue that she was with me, but the absence of the sight and touch of her overwhelmed me. There were tears in other eyes. These women friends had shared with us and played with us, and we'd known good and hard times together over many years.

****

It was the perfect story, and Hemitra wanted me to tell it, because my near-death experience and the incidents around it, was the shamanic beginning of our next 15 years teaching together and opening our center, Heart of the Goddess. My partner in spirit showed how much she was participating and loving this time with our friends.

For the rest of the weekend, we took long walks on the beach together, as we felt the deep sand under our feet and the cool ocean waters splash around our legs. We hugged and cried, as we shared grief and laughter. These women knew the depth of the love Hemitra and I shared, and that awareness helped in my healing.

Each woman at our private memorial had joined us for our Woman Wisdom training that stretched over a nine month period, and four of the women became amazing teachers of the program with their own groups.

For 15 years, we worked hard and loved the women and each weekend. We created experiences that allowed those wonderful women to remember their connection to Earth wisdom and the ancient culture that revered the feminine, each other, their inner knowing, and their hearts.

The time with friends in Cape May was a relief from my daily path through a maze of grief and learning the rules of play with my partner on the other side. It was only the beginning of my testing time in this soul workshop.

Chapter 24

Where are you when I really need you?! The insane voice echoed through the empty house. It was mine. Who do you think you are? You won't talk to me? You said, "I can help you so much more. I'm always with you and always will be." Your words to me and now this!

****

Almost three months after Hemitra's transition, I discovered my computer upgrade had deleted precious emails and e cards she'd sent me, and that pushed me over the close edge I walked. I cried and called my friend Michelle. It was after 10 p.m., and my reasonable self would never have bothered her. Michelle listened, comforted, and listened more. That evening, and the many times after that, as I trudged through the next months, she was always there for me. She was also a gifted intuitive, and she could hear and see Hemitra. At times, I must have taxed her inner strength, patience and the spiritual depth of her many years of Buddhist practice. Our times communicating like this gifted me with the true knowing of compassion.

My solution that night, besides the flood of tears, was to frantically spend the night making copies of all the sentimental messages that Hemitra had sent me from her computer. By 2 a.m., I was deep in anguish, with a lot of printed paper cluttering the office. Clearly, I'd lost my reason.

Morning didn't improve my hopeless mood, as self- pity plunged me to a place deep in emotional sludge. Linda was back, and I called her as early as possible and described the crisis. I asked her to contact Hemitra. Linda grew quiet and then reported, "I can't access her."

"What do you mean? I don't understand. Is this how she is always with me to help me through?" Linda's pattern consistently began with my enthusiastic departed one filling the airwaves with advice and loving praise.

"I don't know," Linda's voice sounded different.

"Where is she?"

"She won't come through right now." Linda saw or felt something that she held back.

My heart sank, yet that was the final word. I thanked Linda, and we ended the call with her suggestion to 'talk tomorrow.'

In the past weeks, Hemitra had been there for me instantly when the grief got too much to endure. What was going on?

After one session and a follow up email with Danielle, I'd felt an instant friendship with this caring woman, but I knew she had a demanding schedule. Now beyond polite rules, I emailed her and spilled the story.

A return email arrived in an hour but brought no relief. Danielle said, "This has never happened in any reading that I've done. She doesn't want to communicate and told me, she wants you to raise your vibration."

Never happened to Danielle before? Hemitra's only been in spirit a short time, and she started making up her own damn rules. It figures! Everything I've read about those who'd had Near Death Experiences wrote about the place called Heaven as indescribably loving and beautiful. Don't you have a team of angelic teachers or a standard book for rules of engagement with loved ones left on Earth? What about keeping promises?

The barrage continued in my head. You can't treat me like this. You said you're my guide now. Your guiding techniques, after only a few weeks in the next dimension are unacceptable!! Remember who you're talking to! This isn't our relationship. Are you even there?

My thoughts sank further. When we were on Earth together, we stood by one another, and we brought each other back to center if one of us was in trauma or afraid. Now we were arguing between dimensions, or I was arguing by myself alone and miserable. Actually, we rarely argued on this playing field. It was easy to figure out disagreements and be completely vulnerable with each other. Beneath my raging lay the ever-present fear of abandonment.

Worn from sleeplessness and reeling from my perception of unfair treatment from Hemitra, I staggered through the next hours on autopilot doing the necessary mundane. The October sun began its descent. Sunshine spilled through the kitchen skylight and glass door facing west. I glanced at the counter top across the room. A small notebook and pen was tucked in the corner to the left with some of its pages crumpled and opened in the middle. I picked it up and read the place where it opened. These were some notes I'd transcribed from the web, and I reread a piece from a well-known channel whose beloved husband and business partner had recently passed.

A few weeks ago, I'd copied her words and felt comfort from her experiences with her partner on the other side. She talked about the closeness she knew with him now, that wasn't even possible on Earth. Even devoted to one another in Earthly life, there could be no closer relationship than the one from his new vantage point in spirit, while she was on Earth. He knew every thought she had and every move she made, and he still participated in their work together. She mentioned this phase as a new relationship, just as Hemitra repeatedly spoke of our new relationship.

The channel said that this beautiful exchange with her soul mate in spirit could only happen when she went beyond the pain and raised her vibration. I stared at the words and smiled, as I lifted from my dark space. Instantly, I felt the familiar euphoria, as the powerful electricity coursed through me from her. I got it. The image in my mind was Hemitra smiling her charming smile, as she shrugged her shoulders and giggled putting her hand over her mouth. I knew the gesture, and this time it said, "See, I made my point."

I sank into the cushioned seat in the oak kitchen chair next to me and laughed. We were together. Of course, you're right! Sorry to be such a mess. I just miss you like crazy! This is the hardest thing I've ever done. I was even too tired to cry.

Suddenly, the tight spring in me unwound, as I folded my arms on the round table and rested my head for a few minutes, exhausted.

I remembered what Hemitra said through Linda. "Nothing is more important than you. You are what I'm doing. You are my project. You're the work I'm doing here."

"Ok, you're my guide, I understand. You made your point. You're not in the vibration I sank to as my Earthly self. You're taking your guide job seriously but ease up. I'm hurting." I directed my request to the invisible one. I thought it would be good not to tell too many about this event.

Will she always be my guide? Is this just to get me through the grief? Why did I ask the same questions and carry this anxiety?

How embarrassing! I felt relief that I had made it through another emotional breakdown, as I attempted to understand my partner in the next dimension. We always expected a lot from each other, and we each consistently delivered, but having a temper tantrum with someone no longer embodied showed a scary loss of control. The me I knew wasn't there. I'd become unrecognizable to myself. Grief and mental illness seemed to be the same thing. How can I navigate this obstacle course? I must get some sleep.

I expressed gratitude for our friends who interacted with Hemitra, the ones who saw and heard their friend on the other side and knew it was normal. I was much more comfortable now with the paranormal, the bigger normal.

I would speak with Linda tomorrow, but I emailed Danielle my report. The next morning, I received an answer.

Danielle said, "I knew you could do it." She related Hemitra's words, "She loves you very much. She's so proud of you, and this is only the beginning."

Chapter 25

The plan for Halloween was to meet at Joan's house near New Hope. Our friend, Connie, picked one of her favorite spots where we would eat lunch. After eating and catch up, we planned a drive around town to look for the witches, goblins and ghosts on the lawns of the houses that went all out with decorations. At days' end, our friends, Joan, Connie, Barb and I would light a candle for our loved one in spirit, Hemitra.

In preparation, I pulled a ¾ length black silky skirt from the closet, attempting to find the makings for a roaring 20's costume. The problem to solve was what top to wear. At Chico's in a nearby shopping center, I poured through the racks and asked my guide and fashion guru extraordinaire, for help. Having gathered all the longer black tops, the saleswoman put them in a dressing room, and the search began. When I slipped on one item that fell at my hips and was cut on a diagonal, I heard, "That's perfect Sweetheart." With the words came the familiar loving rush of energy. She was right. As if custom designed, the top could have been on the rack for the last 90 years from the Great Gatsby era just waiting for this occasion. The message was surely from Her. I wasn't in the habit of calling myself Sweetheart.

In front of the mirror outside the dressing room, I explained the costume idea to the sales person, and she gave me an enthusiastic review. She said the top looked great and was the 'perfect' 1920's addition. I didn't explain that my wife on the other side also gave her ok. It was always fun shopping together! Thanks Love!

I returned home and went online to search for roaring twenties costumes and ordered a glittery black headband with rhinestone jewels and a feather. From my jewelry box and Hemitra's, I found all the rhinestone jewelry from beloved family females, my mom, Hemitra's mom, and Jack's. A wide rhinestone bracelet and a perfect rhinestone necklace completed the outfit.

On the hour drive to Joan's house the next week, one of my downward spirals began. The grief came from nowhere, the unpredictable slide to the bottom, as I felt the pain, loss and sadness. Three months had passed, July 31, 2014 to October 31, 2014, since my world collapsed. It was the longest, hardest time of my life. I tried to reason that the beautiful experiences we've had on our two planes were beyond this world, and how blessed I was to be able to perceive this, but nothing helped.

Disoriented, I missed the turn to Joan's house in the last ten minutes of the trip. I said out loud to myself, "What I need is a horse!" Good grief, where did that come from? I had no idea, but the irrational thought served as a pattern interrupt to my mind and allowed me to just let go of the loss of reason and flow with it all. I returned to a more positive place, though I couldn't explain why, that horse lightened my spirit. I forgot my phone, but I'd find someone and get redirected. There was plenty of time, and I looked forward to seeing everyone.

The road ran along a sunlit meadow, and a lovely grove of trees arched over the road. A black SUV was parked there, and a man and little boy seemed to be looking at something in the wooded area. I pulled over to the side of the road, and the man walked to my car. I asked him for directions. He said I'd missed the turn two miles back, and he told me how to backtrack.

I thanked him and felt appreciation for his kindness and for finding someone in the middle of a deserted country road. He looked at me for a fleeting second, and I saw something in his eyes I didn't understand. "By the way," he said sweetly and with enthusiasm, "You look really great!"

"Thanks. Happy Halloween, and thanks again for the directions." I drove off on the right path again.

It felt like the man wasn't looking at me as much as witnessing what was happening to me. Sometimes recently, my heart felt like it spilled over, and the loving energy went everywhere. It flowed into everything, and that was happening now. I felt love for every tree and the moments in this countryside, the man and his son, the air and all things around me. It was a touch of the divine in my Earthly self. It seemed the way it was supposed to be. I would suddenly appreciate people I didn't think much about before but now felt a deep empathy and caring toward.

I pulled into Joan's driveway, opened the car door, and was greeted by the sound of galloping hooves and a whiney, as a horse stopped on the other side of the fence by my car. I'd seen this horse before in the meadow below Joan and Bob's country home. He always stayed in the lower meadow eating grass or standing under a tree. Hummm, there's the horse I needed. My life now unfolded as a series of never before happenings.

Joan walked over to my car, I got out, and we hugged. "That was some greeting you got from Harry horse! He doesn't normally do that."

I told her about my spontaneous need for a horse and went over to pet Harry and thank him.

Good friends live in many dimensions with you. We both simply knew Harry delivered a message from our Hemitra, as she helped to guide me. From then on, Harry would repeat this performance when Hemitra had a message for Joan, or when Joan asked her a question.

The others arrived, and we gathered in Joan's yard for pictures on that cloudless blue-sky day. For one picture, Joan told me to stand at the edge of her little grove of trees. To my left was the large, sunlit meadow, which was Harry's place.

Next, we piled in Connie's car for our day together. We all felt Hemitra's vibrant joyful energy, as it filled the car, and we knew she celebrated with us loving that her friends were together. It was to honor her. Why wouldn't she be pleased?

After a glorious day of friendship, good food and honoring our friend with our laughter and tears, we looked at all the pictures taken that day. In the picture of the 1920's me, I was at the left in the picture, and the meadow took the other half of the frame. The camera didn't capture the brilliant sunlit grass but was covered in a white mist. We briefly questioned the camera and found that the mist was only in that one picture. We laughed and knew it was another message from Hemitra saying, "I'm here with you." I was going to see Danielle for a second reading next week, and I would show her the picture.

Chapter 26

I loved Danielle. This was only our second meeting, but I felt a deep soul connection with her.

When she greeted me, she said Hemitra came to her in the morning and was really excited about the reading to come.

I showed Danielle the picture from Halloween.

"That's her. The mist is her without a doubt, absolutely 100%."

Hemitra added, "I did that! Isn't it cool? Isn't it amazing?"

I laughed. Hemitra's glorious self was shining in Spirit, just as it had on Earth.

I told Danielle that the blue bird she talked about in the last reading had announced itself.

Three mornings ago, at 5 am, I woke up to a noise that was loud enough to sound as though someone was trying to get in the house. Are the kids here? I got up and looked out the window to see a blue jay on the roof over part of the kitchen that was outside Hemitra's bedroom window. It was pecking the window sill, as if it was attempting a break in. I'd never known a bird to make such a commotion. I watched as the bird soon flew around the yard and then made two circles in the air, before it sped off. The show was amazing and so her! How perfect to announce her presence as a saucy blue jay.

Danielle had also mentioned a butterfly in our last reading. Days after the reading, I walked outside and stepped over the kitchen threshold where a huge blue and black butterfly sat motionless. I knelt down, and the beautiful butterfly didn't leave, but moved its wings. "Are you ok, I asked?"

It looked perfectly fine and still lingered. I sat next to it to admire its beauty. At point, I realized it was another sign from my girlfriend. I never experienced that species of butterfly as big or wanting to sit and chat. I related the story to Danielle who immediately said, "That was her!"

"Did she like her memorial?" I knew the answer.

"She loved it!" Danielle said enthusiastically.

"She did my hair."

"Yes, she did. She's hysterical with the hair. She says it looks great now! She likes the sweater also. She's stroking your sweater." Hemitra's presence beamed.

I looked at the rings I still wore, mine and hers. "When we first sat down, I saw her sit down with me and take my hand."

"She took your hand and turned all the rings upright; I mean she made the gesture. She went like this and touched each one." Danielle moved her hand to show turning the rings.

Danielle and I laughed. She led us in a centering meditation and began the reading.

As before, Hemitra started by addressing my health. "You're not taking care of yourself. You're not sleeping."

"I am sleeping. I'm unconscious anyway. I think I'm sleeping." I thought I was sleeping.

"Your sleep schedule is off. You're not sleeping long enough." Hemitra wouldn't give up.

"Can I get credit for staying alive or something?" I felt she was taking her guide role too seriously.

"She's tough on you. She expects a lot. She expects perfection from you," was Danielle's explanation.

Hemitra replied, "Where we're going you've got to get in line. We have a lot of work to do."

"She is demanding from her new position," I responded.

"Just a little bit," Danielle smiled. "The way she's making my body feel is interesting. I've never felt this before in a reading. Your situation is so unique. I literally feel her physical presence in my body. She's making me feel foggy. That's exhausting because you're carrying her vibration day and night with your own. Because of her high vibration, you constantly have to raise yours. When you're not in sync, that's when you feel foggy and scattered," Danielle explained. "You need to recharge and rest. Although your vibrating is powerful, you're still grieving. Until you're in alignment, you have healing to do. You will be healing together as well, but you must work on your own heart. You are grieving the physical body relationship, but you understand the relationship isn't over. There is an interchange. She is very helpful, and you're not abandoning her assistance in your grief. She can be with you 24/7, and you're always channeling her, but it doesn't give you time. Where is the opportunity for your own soul? You must have your own space to recharge and strengthen," Danielle's advised.

Hemitra said through Danielle, "It's ok for you to set boundaries. Where I am I don't get tired, and I don't know time, so I get excited."

"Excited enough to arrive as a noisy blue jay at 5 a.m.!" I commented. We laughed.

Danielle continued, "When you go to sleep, you must set boundaries. Have a conversation with her. This is what we're going to do. You told me I need more sleep, and I need to take care of my body. I'll be with you tomorrow. When you don't' feel her, it's not that she's left you, and it's not that she will ever not be in your vibration. She's not going anywhere. There are times when her vibration won't be as strong, but know this clearly, if you need her, she will be there, and she will be there instantly, and you will feel her immediately!"

That brought up the abandonment I felt from the beginning, and it kept nagging me. I heard the words but even after all the promises, I still questioned if she would always be there.

What was wrong with me? Maybe it was just that my body and mind were exhausted from the last year when we treated her cancer, and now I had to adjust to communicating with a high voltage, enthusiastic partner on the other side.

"She's assisting you and writing with you. You feel when it switches. There's a physical feeling that you feel when she comes through. She wants to affirm that she is coming through. She gives me this lightheadedness and tingling in my body, and that's her coming through. She's showing me that she's seeing through you. Do you understand? My eyesight feels different," Danielle continued.

"Yes, it's amazing."

"I want to make you understand that you are not losing your mind. This is truly happening to you. This is truly spiritually happening, and I don't want to discourage this because it's a beautiful thing, and it's part of your spiritual path. There have been encounters since her passing when she has come to you and embraced you, and she wants you to know that it's her."

"There's no mistaking her," I answered.

"She wants you to know that it's because your spirit is so free that you are able to allow yourself the freedom to go to where she is. The journey you took in your Earth life has enabled you to go where you are going now. Most people when they lose a loved one, it's over. It's not over for you. There will be people who will say you're not dealing with your loss," Danielle continued. "What you're doing is using a certain part of your brain, and you're expanding your consciousness. That is what humans did thousands of years ago. You're not dealing with the shell, and you know this is not the only realm."

Danielle saw Hemitra literally jumping up and down and saying, "You're expanding your consciousness so that just because I'm in this body doesn't mean I can't meet you."

"She's so proud of you!" Danielle commented.

"I just can't stop the grief." I sunk back to that.

"You must remember that when you lose the love of your life, or when you lose a child, or when you lose a husband or wife, it's important to shift your mind not to focus on death. You're grieving the loss of the physical relationship, and that's going to take time. Loved ones left on Earth must focus beyond the body. You're grieving the loss of the body, but the spirit is still here. The grieving will be easier, and you can open yourself up to a new relationship. That softens the grief and opens a new doorway, and that's needed. It opens a new empowerment so you don't have to accept that the relationship is over."

"I couldn't have handled that," I responded. "We can continue this relationship until I go to be with her?"

"Yes, this is not the end. She's always with you, Sweetie. She just gave you a really big kiss, and now she's talking about your visions."

"When I see her and hear her. Is it always real?"

"Yes. Absolutely. There's a stream running through you. Did you lose your keys?" Hemitra jumped from subject to subject.

"Yes."

"She found them. She helps you find things." Danielle confirmed.

"Yes. The one who sees through walls and around corners somehow directed me right to them."

"There's more that she wants to tell you. She says you're doing a good job. She's really proud of you. She's so proud of you! What's she's excited about is that you will both help a lot of people. She wants you to know that what's coming next is going to be the most beautiful chapter in your life because of your spiritual vibration together, and how amazing you are, and how free and open you are, and that you are willing to let go of this physical realm. You're willing to accept other dimensions, and because of this willingness, your relationship will only grow and evolve."

"We had an awesome life!"

"You did, you really did!"

"She's telling you again. It's only going to get better." Danielle's assurance and information always comforted to me.

"What was the purpose of this lifetime?" I asked.

"The first word I hear is magic. She said it's just the beginning, it's just the beginning."

"We always had magic."

"You still have that, and it's been elevated to a different realm. The magic is so strong. The magic keeps coming up over and over. Even when you both had bodies you were able to transcend realms then. On Earth, you always moved into different dimensions of consciousness. She also said healing. You must tell your story."

I wasn't totally sure.

"Your love is beyond the shell, and that is a unique thing. When the energy of one on the other side can be seen, that has to be shared. I know that you understand that beings have come to this world and have been sent for specific reasons. We all have a purpose. You're here to be an example to others that there is so much more in the unseen realms."

We easily played in different dimensions, I thought.

"She talking about the magic you have with nature. You have a unique way of seeing nature spirits. You see the energy in the Earth, and you must expand on that. I see little fairy lights all over. Incorporate that back into your life. You must find that joy and magnificence without her. When the two of you were together that beauty was wrapped up in the two of you.

You must find that beauty within you. Then you'll understand how she sees you. That Light is in everyone and everywhere. Most of us search outside ourselves, and you must find the Light within. The more you expand, the more you will grow to understand there's nothing you can't do now."

At that moment, her words of advice felt like a big job.

"Now when I have a memory it's like it's happening again. It's so vivid," I said.

Danielle explained, "Hemitra said you go there. You go to the energy of that place and time."

"Does anything need to be forgiven? How could we have made things better for us?" I asked.

"Better?" She says, "Oh Honey," Hemitra's response.

I added, "We always had each other."

Hemitra stepped in, "There was no one better. Were we perfect? No. We were perfect together, and we still are. There's nothing to forgive."

"Is there anything you need to forgive from her?" Danielle added.

"No, nothing." I meant the no, yet in a short time, I would discover something that I labeled unforgivable.

Hemitra continued, "Are there things we could have done differently? Yes. Would that have changed anything? No. There's nothing to forgive. We had what others dream of, and we still have it. If we would have changed what I had for breakfast, or we would have changed one thing here or there, it wouldn't have made me live longer."

"The infinity symbol is very strong between the two of you. She showed me the infinity symbol three times." Danielle moved on.

Linda repeatedly said she saw the infinity symbol.

"She has to tell you again. It's only going to get better," Danielle repeated. I still didn't feel it, but it sounded good.

"You have this very interesting energy between the two of you. You tried to control her energy, because she had no sensor," Danielle continued to channel.

"I was her sensor at times."

"It frustrated her when you tried to rein her in. She understands why you did that, but she wants you to release yourself. She wants you to free yourself. Don't be afraid to fly."

Walking steadily was my only goal at the moment.

I added, "I'm trying to get the balance of being me and us. Sometimes, I see differently. You said she sees through me. Many times, when I look in the mirror, I see myself differently like she would see me."

"Yes, absolutely."

"What about dreams together?"

"Your dreaming is work."

I told Danielle, "Her nephew called and told me about a dream that he had. He said I was there in the dream with her. I came in the room first. So that means I'm traveling with her at night." I had to clear up a million unknown details.

"Yes, you are. You're working. You're writing," was Danielle's explanation.

Danielle repeated, "You need to rest and recover."

"Is that just being codependent?" I smiled.

"I feel that you are you, and she's her, and you're the two of you. You're connected, as always. She's excited. She never sleeps, and she's doing her own work. She wants to share that with you," Danielle explained. We both laughed.

We called that living the dream, because we felt happiest being together in life and now in life and afterlife. Together as much as possible was as natural as geese mating for life or being a pair of wolves. From what I learned so far, that was always us.

"We were each other's joy."

Danielle added, "And you still are."

"Do you have exercise equipment?" Danielle continued, "She showed me you exercising. That's really good for you."

"It would have been good for her."

Hemitra didn't miss a comeback to me. "Don't get picky." We laughed.

"She showed me this journal. Are you writing in a journal?

"It's all the notes that Linda channeled and my experiences." I knew Hemitra referred to the yellow lined tablet, some of it barely legible.

"She's looking over your shoulder, and she's pacing back and forth," said Danielle. Hemitra's interest in my Earth life gave me hope and consolation.

"Here's what she's telling me. You have to have faith that your connection will only grow, and when your strength and your vibration increases, her vibration increases, and when they both increase then your connection grows. It only increases in beauty. It's such a beautiful thing. I'm learning so much from the two of you. This is an amazing thing, and it gives me such hope! You must tell your story. What's amazing is that this isn't the end of your relationship. She knows that with certainty."

The vital information continued through Danielle. "She said that you hear her. So how it's all going to play out. She's giving you the courage to follow through and sometimes the words. It's almost like you don't know where it's coming from. Whether they are yours or hers. It's how you blend together. Again, I keep seeing the infinity symbol. You will know what to do. It's just going to come. It's just going to come naturally. She said you're very hard on yourself."

"We expected a lot. I feel as if she's in this place of perfection, and I should be more. She does inspire me to be more. Now I understand why when someone passes, the loved ones left are motivated to elevate themselves and grow," I explained.

"She has a very relaxed feeling about her, and she's excited." Danielle shifted the subject.

"I feel her euphoria, and the communication is amazing. There's an expansion I never experienced. We had a great love here together, and now it feels more extensive." I tried to put into words what sometimes was hard to express adequately.

"It's amazing!" Danielle commented. Again, I was comforted at how deeply Danielle could sense us.

"Isn't it a long time not to reincarnate if I'm here to grow old?" I had many questions.

"She says there is no time, and also that time here is moving slowly for you."

"So slowly," I confirmed.

"She said it won't always be like that. Things will change for you very quickly. Things are already changing for you. Different people are coming into your life to uplift you. She said everything will happen for you with ease." I listened.

The beautiful reading ended. I made an appointment for the following month. There was much that stirred under the surface, and it needed to be revealed. I went home and transcribed the recording and read it again and again. Danielle and Linda served as my life raft to navigate the stormy dark waters of grief.

Chapter 27

My instability continued with some more irrational breakdowns. However, I slowly began to accept my state of mind as part of the essential human process after loss. There was no concluding this journey in six months. It felt best to stay isolated and work though the emotional holocaust.

I'd done some of the unpleasant job of sorting Hemitra's clothes and personal things, as I donated or passed on items. My ever-present guide didn't seem to miss anything—no thought or action of mine went unnoticed or without comment. I received more instructions.

"Give that to Joan." Good idea I answered the voice in my head, when I picked up a goddess necklace that was perfect for our artist friend Joan.

As usual, Hemitra took her duties seriously, and at times when I wasn't even focused on the dissembling of our physical life together, I would get a message that a piece of clothing or a book or something should be given or thrown away. Everyone had these guides, but perhaps Hemitra just persisted more intently. Those thoughts we sometimes get, an inspiration or idea must come from somewhere, and I began to realize that, many times, it came from the invisible realm. Danielle and Linda had commented that Hemitra was a very strong spirit, and my lovely new spirit guide wanted to show me a reality that defied science and expanded natural phenomenon. Our continuing magic elevated to a higher plane, and I remembered her devoted antics through the last months that kept me getting out of bed in the morning.

Electricity always seemed easy for her to manipulate. As it got dark one day, I turned on the ceiling lights in the family room. The next minute, they all went off. I turned them on again, and they stayed on. This happened throughout the house, at times since her passing, and there could be no other explanation than Hemitra's exuberant other worldly interference.

How did I know it was her? When she seized my attention, every fiber of my being focused on what she was showing me. It was as if I suddenly went into a trance and a space of suspended time, where nothing else existed. Of course, she got my attention when she caused the house to suddenly darken.

The familiar gloom surrounded me another day that fall. As I walked, the clouds lifted, and the sun shone and continued to shine. Hummm, I thought rain had been predicted, but I really appreciated the bright warmth. After two miles, I headed inside. As I did, I heard her voice singing in my head, "You are my sunshine." Once in the house again, the clouds covered the sky, and a light rain began to fall.

Another day, I walked in the back field fighting depression. The maple leaves had turned a warm yellow, and I watched as a few of them tumbled from the top of the giant tree at the edge of the field. One of the floating leaves caught my attention, and I followed its drift as it turned and turned in the current and headed toward me. This large perfect yellow leaf landed on my left side right over my heart and stayed there as I moved another 20 feet.

Sometimes, these things left me dazed and questioning, but I wasn't clever enough to fabricate her cosmic feats. She had said through Linda, "See it believe it." Hemitra constantly reminded me that she was always with me. I loved the amazing ways she showed her presence, and I was beginning to understand how to have one foot on Earth and one foot in Spirit. That was the way it was meant to be. Now, I couldn't do anything else. However, I would travel through many places of questioning, before I completely digested our new status.

Rushes of love always came from Hemitra as we transcended worlds together. Music became a great way for her to deliver messages. Though I rarely turned on the car radio, sometimes when I was driving, I automatically reached for the on button, and the absolutely perfect song played. No matter what mood I was in, my spirit wife would send words that lite my heart and made me shake my head in wonder. I began to ask her questions and knew when to turn on the radio in order to receive her answers by song.

Loved ones in spirit could help us in many ways. I did question that at first, but she went beyond my wildest expectations in the help and advice department. Our guides are only a thought away.

I believe one of Hemitra's interventions potentially saved me from an accident. We had a great conversation in my head that morning, and I rode on the high as I packed my car to the brim and headed for Hemtira's mom's house. Some of the boxes, filled with Hemitra's things, were for her sister. The pervasive words in my head echoed, "Slow down."

A short way into the trip, the car in front of me traveled at half the speed limit, and I couldn't pass. Annoyed, I remembered the slow down message. After shaking that car and a few more miles, a large white-tailed deer darted in front of my car, and I missed hitting her by only inches. Again, I shook off the extra adrenaline and smiled about the slow down message. However, still on my morning high, I didn't slow down. Close to the destination, I'd crossed a main highway and now traveled on a side road. Next, I heard the siren from a police car behind me. I pulled over but didn't understand.

A young officer came to my window and said, "Ma'am, do you know how fast you were going?"

"No," I answered the obvious.

"You're in a 25-mile speed zone, and I clocked you at 49. Besides that, your car is packed so full you have no visibility in the back." All this was news to me.

I played the card, "I'm sorry. I just lost the love of my life, and I'm not doing well."

The young man's eyes softened, and he spoke kindly. As he wrote my ticket, he said something about my being a danger to myself and to please slow down. In those few minutes, my senses returned, and I actually felt gratitude to the officer for doing his duty. My ticket of $187, plus four points, came as a sobering realization to slow down. My long past driving record had no accidents, only a few speeding tickets and a few parking tickets. I used to be a safe and adept driver. From then on, I did slow down, at least behind the wheel.

I told Linda about the incident, and she channeled my guide, Hemitra. "You were completely out of your body," Hemitra sounded alarmed. "You were here talking to me and not paying any attention to what you were doing." Guilty as charged. I was giving Hemitra practice handling the difficult assignment of being my guide. It was fitting.

A cold snap came, and I went to Hemitra's bureau to claim her share of our warm, wool/silk socks. We both had several pairs, and I put on a burgundy pair that were hers. They were worn and thread bare on the bottom.

"Throw those away!" Hemitra delivered an instruction in my head.

They're fine, I thought my response. I put the socks on and walked into the bathroom on the porcelain tile floor, and an icy cold came through the socks.

Oh, I see what you mean, I smiled. I threw the socks in the trash and had a vision of Hemitra laughing and shaking her head. It surprised me that my spirit guide had time to micromanage a thing such as holes in socks, but how sweet. If you love someone, you want them to have warm feet. At the same time, she could also be somewhere else in a distant galaxy totally understanding quantum physics and the nature of creation.

Though Hemitra went beyond trying to show me that she was with me, the hardest part in getting assistance was simply remembering to ask. When I finally gave up and said, "Help please," she directed me right to the lost glasses or keys and more. Hemitra had said through Linda, "I can help you so much more. I can give you so much more."

Messages arrived in different ways. I clearly heard her voice in my head. Even when I wasn't thinking of her, she would interject a comment or give advice, and then it would be her voice that I heard in my mind. At other times, we had conversations in a series of what seemed to be my thoughts. The talks were just like we always had, yet were they between me and me? I questioned both Linda and Danielle, only to be assured over and over, that those conversations were authentic, and how much it pleased Hemitra that I could sense her in so many ways.

In this modern mystery school training, I continued reading. "In order to establish communication with those who have died, we must adapt ourselves to hear from them what we ourselves say and receive from our own soul what they answer. Those still on Earth must adapt to that method of contact" (Steiner, 1918).

****

I was in process.

A few times, when I was talking on the phone to close friends, I would make a statement, and it felt like my spirit guide had spoken her opinion. I would get this kind of response from the friend, "That was Hemitra." We would both laugh and agree that the statement came from her.

My daughter, Amy, applied for a new job. She was perfectly qualified, and I felt the new position could be an easy success. I asked Hemitra if the job would be Amy's? My personal oracle showed me an instant visual with a comment. Hemitra wore a brilliant indigo robe and dramatically opened the robe. She was wearing a colorful cake under the robe. The words I heard were, "piece of cake." Amy called a few days later, and happily told me she'd gotten the job. Though I missed Hemitra's physical presence more than words could express, we still shared our usual comedy and side-splitting laughter together.

My moods changed like an up and down elevator. Sometimes without warning, I became a somber grey battleship in Arctic waters navigating through dense fog with sonar disabled and hidden icebergs everywhere. I dealt with life one minute and kept thinking positively, then suddenly I'd hit the submerged wall of icy pain and tumbled into darkness.

I had one of those sinking sadness from no-where moments, as I allowed every awful illusion to come to mind. I thought about being told that I would be here and grow really old. What if I forgot her? Hemitra's instant response was, "Try it!" I laughed out loud.

Hemitra loved birds, and they were great tools to deliver spirit messages. She used them often ever since the early morning visit I received from a blue jay. Another day, I had trekked through the trails in the woods and returned homeward at dusk. A broken record, I asked inside, "Where are you?" I should have gotten it by now. I wasn't expecting anything, but in under a minute, I noticed a moving speck a distance away. Quickly, it projected itself right toward me. In seconds, I recognized a barn swallow in flight. It was flying the same height as my head. About 15 feet before a possible collision, it turned straight up and flew away. It must have taken effort on Hemitra's part to bring such experiences into the physical, and I loved it. She was saying, "I'm here. I'm right here with you." What a wonderful partner!

As I walked around the flower garden one day, out of nowhere, a catbird suddenly appeared and did a quick dance, which included making a circle in the air three feet in front of me. It fluttered wildly, before it sped off. "How do you do that," I asked?

Another day, as I walked to my car, a little green hummingbird flew close over my head. The day after, I found a tiny hummingbird feather on the driveway and recognized it right away. It was so little and perfect. Linda said that the beautiful feather was a gift from Hemitra, and she was very proud of the coup. I can imagine snatching a hummingbird feather might take an advanced skill set.

The feather collection grew. I found blue jay, cardinal, crow, a red-tailed hawk feather, an owl, and some I couldn't identify. They were in strategic locations, on the steps up from the terrace, and all around the property. The feathers were in perfect shape, and I always felt that charge as I happened upon them.

Was she ever present? It seemed so. On a warm bright October day, I ate lunch, absent mindedly, at the island in the kitchen.

"Go outside and sit down." Her voice seemed to be a reminder of the obvious. My happy life had changed to one of no pleasure and lots of stress. Good idea I thought, since it was a beautiful day.

I relaxed in the warm sunshine. In a minute, a red-tailed hawk flew into the yard and circled the tree lined property. It flew closer and lower and passed right over me. A second hawk appeared and did the same thing. They glided the air currents gracefully, circling me and staying close together. In a minute, the show was over and they left. I said thank you for the beautiful message!

The classes Hemitra and I taught included a weekend on the shamanic interpretations of animals and identifying our individual power animals. The red-tailed hawk often showed itself to both of us as a totem animal. The meaning we knew of the hawk was that the bird was a Guardian of the Earth Mother, and those it appeared to wanted to educate others to value the Earth. The hawk reminded us to use our intuition in daily life and see things from a higher perspective to increase our spiritual awareness. The message Hemitra delivered was perfectly appropriate.

One of her best bird feats happened on a sunny beautiful autumn day when I was outside and noticed a shadow pass over me. A large vulture flew over the property, then another and another. Those birds, with four-foot wing spans, circled low and close, and I stood directly under the flock. The sun reflected off the underside of the vulture in the middle of the group, and its feathers shone a beautiful golden brown. Next, they all landed on the house roof, and there were eleven. I stared at them, spellbound. I'd grown tired and depleted by this time. Were they coming for me? I hoped that I wasn't that close to my departure.

The vulture I noticed with the golden underbelly was a sign from Hemitra. I felt that the message of the vultures was poignant, and it said that I should accept the natural cycle of death and rebirth. These large birds purified the Earth of death and decay and should be honored for their work.

I smiled thinking of my glamorous Hemitra delivering her message as a vulture. We did the glamorous thing when necessary, when we taught together or worked at our center wearing the clothing and jewelry we sold. Fond memories came forth, because we could be happy on our haggy days working together outside in the yard sweaty and dirt covered.

I guess I won't understand all the experiences until I'm on the other side. However, as I poured through my research, I found a passage. "The dead start their lives two kingdoms higher than we do on Earth. On Earth, we know the animal kingdom only from the outside. Between death and a new birth, the first most outer activity of life consists of acquiring more intimate and exact knowledge of the animal world" (Steiner, 1918, p. 145). Hemitra now joyfully learned inside secrets from her beloved birds, and my education about the next dimension continued.

A month had passed, and tomorrow I had my scheduled appointment with Danielle. We would delve into the murky area that had haunted me since Hemitra's passing.

Chapter 28

"She said you have questions," was Danielle's first statement, as our next reading began.

"I know feelings of abandonment are normal when someone you love makes their transition. That emotion haunts me. I can't get over the tragic leaving we talked about. For example, losing her in Victorian England. Why did she leave? We had everything; love, abundance, and apparently, status."

"She passed young in that life too. There was trauma in Victorian England. It was a very traumatic life. Who was hurt," Danielle asked?

"Years ago, when we were just getting in touch with the English past life, she complained of a pain in her back. As I massaged the place on her back, and I saw us riding together on beautiful land. There was an accident. She, he at that time, was thrown from a horse."

"Yes, I see that. I feel pain in my body. And she left first." Danielle confirmed.

"Yes, I saw a vision in meditation at that time. Riding in a carriage, I sat opposite a man in a grey wool suit, and I knew he was dying. I felt such sadness and heard the word consumption."

"Is that something with the lungs?" Danielle asked.

"Yes. It's the old term for tuberculosis."

"I can't breathe," Danielle's held her hand on her chest.

"Why the unhappiness? The love between us was over-powering."

"You always had deep love. That was never the problem."

"I don't think I stayed long after he died."

"The grief was more than you could bear."

"I remember dying in a fire. What do you see?" We plunged deep into that life.

Danielle paused. "It wasn't that you set the fire. It was a tragic accident, but it happened because you were so devastated."

"You mean I created it unconsciously?"

"Yes."

"I know you're right. Did we have children? Lately, I felt like there might have been children."

Danielle paused, and her face grew serious, as if she didn't want to continue. "Three children were also taken by the fire. They were ages seven, four and younger than two."

My heart hurt, as it began a rapid dance of anguish.

"Don't take that on as guilt. Your pattern was to follow along into the next dimension when Hemitra left." Danielle's answer would haunt me.

"I saw three children also. We had to be so young, and we suffered all that tragedy in a short life. Why? I can't get beyond this. You said it's up to both of us to correct these recurring calamities."

"I keep hearing that your souls were separated again and again. It feels like in the lifetimes you've had, there was a hesitation in staying together and following through. When you have the happiness, fear comes up, and it has been repeated time and time again, and it's usually her."

"It's too bizarre, and I feel angry. You said in our first reading that whoever is leaving, that soul doesn't accomplish the lesson."

"This is what I'm getting. I said why can't you be together? I heard that neither of you felt worthy of the love. She didn't feel worthy of your love and you didn't feel worthy or her or his love at that time."

"What? We just give up and move on to spirit, where it's easy?" I was quickly sinking into a dark hopelessness.

Danielle continued, "It happened differently in different lives, and there were different scenarios, because the self-worth has been compromised with both of you. You bring different life lessons into your lives to compromise the life. Mundane life was hard for her. She understands your sense of balance, and why you had to rein her in, and she understands that you're more grounded than she was."

"I'm angry and confused." I didn't even know what to say.

"Be patient with yourself. It's ok to have those moments. Be kind to yourself, and she will help you through it. She said that you're going to be mad, and you're going to be mad at her sometimes, and that's ok. She can take it."

Danielle's last words before the reading ended were, "Be good to yourself. You know that's what she wants for you."

****

Driving home grey clouds consumed the sky, and dark leafless tree skeletons lined the roads. I began to process what Danielle had channeled. The muscles in my forearms tightened, and my shoulders ached. I reached over and turned up the car heater shivering against the December chill.

Today, Danielle put words to the torment in my unconscious, as we unearthed the details of Hemitra's and my 200 plus year old story. The details sucked the air from my lungs. I flashed on Danielle's face and the shock in her voice, "You were tragically separated. It happened over and over again."

Those words were the only ones from the last hour that I could remember. Why? It didn't make sense. Hemitra, in whatever human form, almost always left first. Many times, from illness at a young age. No, that wasn't possible, not lifetime after lifetime. We would have learned. The feeling of abandonment had nagged me ever since she transitioned. This terrible anguish felt familiar. It was crazy, impossible, and it repeated again and again. That couldn't have been the plan. My head pounded in violent protest to the thoughts, and I wiped the tears from my face. I took a deep breath, then another, trying to ground myself.

Danielle saw three young children, and they were all lost in the fire. "Don't take that on as guilt," Danielle had emphasized.

Danielle confirmed that the lives of our three children had ended tragically, as I left soon after Hemitra in that life. I struggled with a horrible vision of a young mother exiting Earth with her children screaming in terror as the manor house burned! Intense self-hatred filled me. All the bliss of this life with Hemitra, and the loving communication were forgotten. The life we romanticized as a life of love had turned to a nightmare. How did it happen? We returned lifetime after lifetime to be together. Tragedy followed. How unevolved! We never learned. My mind attempted some comforting thoughts; we all agreed to situations as we returned together in lives, there are no victims, stay in the present, these are just lessons, but I only felt hopelessness.

In the first reading Danielle had said, "She loved her life, she loved every minute, every second of her life and she loved it because you were in it." We have that kind of love, but why the past tragedies? Why do you always leave first or leave early? That isn't love. No answer was delivered from beyond.

When Hemitra passed from breast cancer, I felt my life was over, but I could see her, feel her and embraced the incredible love that she poured from the next dimension. Before this new information, I vowed I would share my experiences that taught me about the eternal nature of relationships and love never ending. I would make the best of the loss somehow. Now the awareness of recurring tragedy and lives cut short loomed as senseless and unsolvable.

"You were tragically separated, and it happened over and over again." I kept hearing Danielle's words.

I won't write about the never-ending tragic pattern of our lives! No strategy can soothe this! Plans and promises were made and never completed. The thought of repeating this pattern again, being left again, and then somehow creating my own early death was hideous. We caused pain for each other and those around us. I couldn't stop the hot tears. My knuckles whitened as I gripped the steering wheel and struggled to focus on driving.

****

I declared out loud, "I can't do this. You can't always break my heart like this. There's no purpose. I can't do this again. No more lives together!"

Chapter 29

"It's over." I called a longtime wonderful friend of ours, Anna Marie. She had been there from day two after Hemitra's passing, and she did her best to help hold me together.

"Are you ok?" Anna Marie heard my distressed voice.

I told her, "Danielle saw that Hemitra and I were tragically separated over and over in many lifetimes. She leaves first. She must like it better in the next dimension. She gets sick and dies young leaving me to pick up the pieces. I won't do that again, so I broke up with her."

Anna Marie was in the middle of gathering groceries at a local farmer's market. She seemed to fall away, and her voice sounded muffled. "I'm sorry," she said trying not to laugh. "I wasn't prepared for that." She told me later, that she had to lean against a pole at the edge of the market and hang on because she was laughing so hard.

"I understand it's bizarre, and laughable. Grief is like insanity, and this may be the last thread severing me from reason. I would laugh too, if I wasn't totally crazy. To realize that so many of our lifetimes ended tragically, is more than I'm capable of handling. Strange as it seems, we're just not good for each other. Remember one of the first channelings and what came up? It's not her nature to age. She felt embarrassed because that wasn't what we were about. We taught women's empowerment. Let's not make this public, but I broke up with her."

Anna Marie replied, "It doesn't seem fair. Tell her to stop that, because I don't know if you can actually break up with her."

"Over the last many lifetimes, I may have mentioned that. Now I'm taking a break from us. Damn! Are we really having this conversation?" My life kept getting stranger. "It's done. No more communication. The book isn't necessary. There's nothing to teach. From now on, no more agreements, and no more lives together!"

Holding back tears, I revealed the rest. "There's more...in those lifetimes when she left first, I followed shortly after. That fatal fire I told you about in England, 200 years ago; I must have been young, because we had three small children who also died in the fire. They were ages seven, four and two. I feel such self-loathing! Everyone's Earth lives have had tragedy, but there's something wrong with this partnership and me."

Anna Marie paused for a second trying to take in the information. "Look, you can't know the whole story, and you won't until you're on the other side. There are reasons why humans do things."

"We incarnate on Earth to learn lessons, right? Why aren't we learning to complete our promises? I know it's dense and sometimes hard here, but nothing changes. It's always heartbreak and usually mine." I raved on without giving my friend time to respond.

"Our entire Earth experience together has been a joke. There's no endurance or integrity. I'll put that on my cosmic resume. Entire Earth existence with soulmate incomplete, no progress. How's that?"

"You sound really angry," Anna Marie finally got a word in.

"Angry is better than living with tragedy and disappointment through eternity. When she talks about eternity from the other side, what she means is that we will repeatedly create unbearable pain. Listen, I know how insane this sounds. How could anyone understand? Hemitra and I shared a magical life with love and joy beyond words. Our relationship was the best two people could imagine on Earth. Not always, of course, since we were just human. She had breast cancer, and she lost that fight. She said from the other side that she stayed longer this time. How can I be angry like this? But I am. We persist in a pattern I must break or be broken by it. Are people aware when they have an emotional breakdown?"

"I know you two had a new life planned after the wedding. I've never seen either of you happier. You must feel such disappointment." My friend tried to make sense for me.

My tirade continued, "Now she tells me to do it without her. I don't want to."

"Anything you must go through is ok. Grief has many stages, and this is probably the hardest thing you'll ever face." Anna Marie comforted me as best she could.

I didn't stop talking, "Even after she passed, we were still one. I felt her, heard her and saw her in visions. We even had a few good laughs. I thought with that closeness, one day I would recover. Now, knowing our pattern through time, the grief and pain is like a nightmare. I won't do that again. There will be no more lives and no more communication."

"Do you want me to come over?" Anna Marie asked.

"Thank you but no. I must let you go. You're a good friend to listen to this crazy talk. I'm really sorry."

****

Each day, the sunlight lessened with stretches of cold rain. I was a dark void without feeling, and I was free falling through this last shadowy part of the year. It felt like the night I left the hospital at 4 a.m. July 31, and life changed forever.

I robotically drove here and there checking off errands. Avoiding the trip upstairs at night sometimes pushed bedtime to after midnight or 1 a.m. Once asleep, I awakened often, as I tried to shake off bad dreams. Getting out of bed was an act of courage. Sometimes, the clothes I wore were the ones thrown on the floor beside the bed the night before. I made no effort to do yoga, meditate or to connect with human or spirit. The bitter cold wind drove temperatures below December norms.

The woman I sometimes caught glimpses of, as I walked by the mirror, had dark circles under her lusterless eyes. I didn't attempt to hear Hemitra or think of her. The nightmares while I slept were replaced by the visitation of frightening images by day. I saw myself in a military plane at 30,000 feet. Suddenly the door opened. "You, get out!"

"Where? I need instructions," I fantasized.

"You'll figure it out," someone shouted, as arms pushed me from the plane. I fell through space and landed in deep sand on a lifeless island covered with strange vegetation. I watched the grim scene with curiosity. There were no animals, no birds, no sound, just dull grey scrub bushes with paths leading to somewhere.

As part of the waking dream, I saw a cliff by the sea. I hovered on the bank of that craggy cliff. It was an inlet where the waves crashed over rocks. The other side of the cliff lay 20 yards away. Between the two grey steep cliffs, hung a tightrope. I often pictured myself walking this rope to the other side, as I looked down at the cold dark water that dashed over jagged rocks. Letting go would be easy and quick. Sometimes I slipped and hung from the rope. Other times, I clung to the side of the cliff then pulled and clawed my way up. The image recurred daily.

At times, I stepped aside and witnessed my own unraveling. This was not healthy, I would self-counsel. Stop! You can't do this to the children. You know something nasty could manifest. Look what you're doing! I didn't listen to the wisdom of my observer, and the painful hours passed. The record low temperatures and wind continued. I turned down a few holiday invitations. Days ended as an undefined blur.

Anna Marie called and asked, "Are you drinking enough water? Are you eating?"

I shared the haunting images of being on the lifeless island.

"Write it down. Write it all down and how you feel."

"Why?"

"You must write it all," she insisted. "You sound like you're far away."

I said I was fine. Don't worry. Hovering in a surreal limbo state, the numbness was better than the pain of what I called reality and lives with no meaning. The children knew their mom's life had disintegrated, and they didn't know what to do or how to help, but they called.

"Mom, come over for dinner," the girls would ask.

"Thanks, not tonight."

Amy repeated more than once, after Hemitra had passed, "Mom, if you dare give in we will haunt you into eternity. I mean it!"

My daughter's perceptive comments chilled my spine. Somehow, Amy had an awareness of how deeply I was wounded. Had she witnessed or been part of my family when one of those tragedies or early escapes from a lifetime had happened? Did I abandon her at some point? We came back with our loved ones over and over again. A lot of love existed in our family, and I knew we had been together many times.

The weather remained dark and frigid. I was always cold. I didn't want to think of my life with Hemitra or past lives, but one day, seven days after my reading with Danielle, the grieving widow from the 19th century hijacked my thoughts. The woman I scorned, loathed and judged for leaving her life and her children, surfaced. She looked sick, worn out and devastated. The slender, waxy pale woman wore the black garb of a mourning widow. Her lifeless eyes reminded me of my own face right now. I wanted to stretch the material away from the arms of the dress that imprisoned the ghost. A flicker of compassion passed through me for the young Victorian widow who lost her beloved English Lord. She was left alone in a cold, massive home in a harsh historic time that didn't honor women. This woman had felt like a stranger in an alien setting.

I noticed the sunlight streaming through the bay window in the kitchen. I loaded the dishwasher and pressed start, then I sat at the granite countertop breakfast bar to write out bills. The water swished and gurgled. I took a deep breath and ran my hand over the smooth counter splotched with brown, grey and cream-colored stone. Leaning over and putting my head in my arms, I thought about how much Hemitra and I loved our home and appreciated being together. A vague sensation of relief crept into my body. How odd to be this disconnected! We lived 22 years as the Goddesses of pleasure and sensuality. Presently, my days were only about staying in my body and dealing with the visions of a strange island and the fragile rope that stretched across the sea cliffs below.

Suddenly, a whole new awareness flooded my head. I was recreating the same repetitive pattern of wanting to abandon this life too soon. I unwittingly had slipped into the same destructive scenario by creating a delusion that only lead to another path of self-destruction. This was just a way to remain in a hideous cycle, and the horror of that knowing came like an electric shock. I was allowing myself to be deceived by my grief and heartache. Thinking I was making a correct choice, I fell into a mire and blamed Hemitra. No! This was mine to unravel! No matter what choices she made, I had free will. I vowed that this time, in spite of what I felt, I would change this now!

Once more, I thought about the English lifetime and the children lost in the fire. Family tragedy leaves its mark for generations, and our choices can cause intense pain for our loved ones? We carry emotions from the traumas of our ancestors. I imagined my kids and grandkids if I left this agreement early and felt revulsion at what I now saw as selfishness. My anger and pain was not just about Hemitra. It was my own self-loathing because of my decision, even if unconscious, to leave the life in England and the other lives. My choices now would dramatically affect my loved ones in this life and many lives to follow. My own soul evolution invited me to break a long pattern and free myself.

I didn't communicate with Hemitra at the moment, but since our thoughts broadcast to the universe, I'm sure my mom brought this teaching memory to me. Several years ago, Hemitra and I, and some of our students joined a friend of ours on a sacred site tour to Sedona, an incredibly high vibration place on the Earth.

At the end of our trip, Sarah, an intuitive who co-lead the trip, planned to do a spirit circle for us, and she would contact a loved one in spirit for each woman. When it was my turn for a reading, my mother appeared. Sarah seemed slightly startled at her vision. She said, "Your mother's really beautiful, and she's only wearing fox furs."

I laughed because our group had just returned from shopping. At one place, there were gorgeous furs for sale. I spent time appreciating a beautiful red fox pelt and bought a rattle and a turquoise bracelet. My mom loved furs and all animals. She was a woman who loved and cared for the Earth. Mother spoke her message to me, through Sarah, "By freeing yourself, you have freed me."

Instantly, I knew the meaning of the message. This lifetime, I followed my deep heart and soul longing and joined Hemitra on another wild adventure. At the time, my mom and dad were devastated by Jack's and my divorce. My parents loved Jack. However, I did free myself and accept the agreement with Hemitra made between lifetimes, though it was difficult and uncertain. Outside of convention again, we created our lives from our own imaginations. Though Mother only met Hemitra once, now from her Heavenly front row seat, she understood how perfect we were together and appreciated the beautiful qualities and joy Hemitra offered me in our relationship. My mom told me how much my actions had freed her, which showed how deeply we influence one another by all of our decisions, thoughts and actions. I declared freedom from my destructive patterns now!

Navigating Earth was tricky! From the Betty Book, it was said that on Earth there were many more choices that humans could make to fall into negative patterns than in the next realm. Our loved ones on the other side could only watch as we stumbled and learned the hard way. They couldn't offer help if we didn't raise our vibration and connect with them for guidance. If humans just stayed out of negative thinking that would be progress (White, 2010, p. 77).

Hemitra said the same thing when she counseled, that if we only make a little bit of progress on Earth, we were succeeding. The kids were grown, and I didn't set fire to our home this time. Considering my recent thoughts and my history in other lives, I claimed that as progress.

I got up, and put on my down coat, grabbed a pruning shears from the garage, and marched outside to cut fresh greens. Winter Solstice was approaching. The pieces of spruce I cut smelled fresh and enlivening. I looked up at the giant Norway Spruce and said, "Thank you!" I was alive.

Inside again, I caught a glimpse of myself in the living room mirror. "You are so adorable!" said Her voice in my head. The accompanying vision was Hemitra, as she beamed at me, and her eyes sparkled. The hat I wore was a gift from her. It was lavender with purple and was called the 'Jester' hat with a squared top and a tassel on the top right and left. It looked like a hat from image of the Fool in some tarot deck, and it made me look like a 12-year-old. Adorable? Hardly, but in those moments, I had rejoined the living. How good to hear a loving message from Hemitra again! I smiled.

I set up the rest of the lights and all of the glittery things Hemitra and I loved. The youngest grandchildren helped me with the tree a week before Winter Solstice.

On my list today was to cancel the appointment with Danielle which was five days away. Since I severed my multi millennial relationship with Hemitra, there was no need to have another reading. The readings were for the book and to verify my experiences I had with my partner in the next dimension. I hesitated. No, I'm going to talk to Danielle. It was scheduled be a phone appointment.

Chapter 30

Danielle's call came at 1:00 p.m. Danielle reported, "I must tell you, I was meditating and at 12:59, Hemitra said, "Come on let's go," and she clapped her hands together." The reading began.

"She said you're not taking care of yourself, and she is not happy about that."

"I just haven't been in communication with her because I've been in such a dark place that I didn't want to talk to her." I said. "I didn't think she was around."

"She is around. What she's saying to me is that you're mad at her," Danielle answered.

"I was mad at her, because after our last reading, it seemed as though our Earth experiences together were co-created tragedies."

"You're mad at me for leaving first," Hemitra spoke.

"Not just this time. You're always leaving first and early. I understand that people die. I was at a place that I felt I could live with it, as long as I knew you were still with me, and we could communicate, and we would be together again. We had such ecstatic moments, but now the tragedy and abandonment came up, and I had to recently fight off that same pattern of jumping ship too soon. I wanted to figure it out."

I addressed Danielle. "You agreed that every lifetime we loved each other deeply?"

"Yes, but in that life, it was very traumatic for both of you. It had a lot of low level vibes attached to it. It was as though the spirituality had been sucked out of that time and place," Danielle said.

"Why?" I didn't understand.

"It was part of your transition," was Danielle's only comment.

"What did people think of us?" I pressed on.

"You were not well loved. It feels like it was hostile," Danielle explained. "Did it come up before that you were working with something that was regarded as strange?"

"I thought we were probably esoteric, but I read that there was a spiritual revolution going on in Victorian England. Even Queen Victoria had séances to contact Prince Albert on the other side," I replied.

"Where you were location wise, it was not like that. You were not well liked or trusted. It almost had the essence of.."

I interrupted, "It was like the witch burnings."

"Yes," Danielle confirmed. "You were very ethereal, and it wasn't accepted. You both were intuitive, and you read tarot cards. Most of your clients were women, and many times, you would tell them their husbands were having affairs. When the women found out, they cut their husbands off from sex."

"That wasn't politically correct or wise on our parts." Of course, we did, I thought.

"Yes," Danielle continued, "Lack of understanding and acceptance came from those around you who were part of those times. Again, you were and always will be teachers, so pushing the boundaries and being outside the norm has been something you always chose to do. You do that so others will accept themselves. You helped others grow. It hasn't always been easy, and this was one of those times. You attempted to stay there, but it didn't work."

"We picked a difficult and repressed time." I felt sure of that.

"What she's showing me again is that you both defied the times. You didn't wear the corsets, and you let the kids run around without shoes. You had romance and lots of sex."

"Good. We loved each other, but you mean that wasn't accepted?" I asked.

"It was not accepted. It was disapproved of by many. What's she's telling me is that relationships were of convenience and not for love."

"And ours was for love?"

"Yes, Hemitra said there were lots of affairs. Couples were in chains in their marriages."

"We didn't' do that."

"No, you didn't need to, said Danielle.

Hemitra said, "When would there be time to be with someone else?" Danielle and I laughed.

"You had something that everyone wanted to have in their relationships. You had something unique. You were equal partners, and partners didn't exist in marriages at that time."

"We came in this time as two women, and that wasn't approved of either."

"Look how far you have come. She said that you have come so far since then, and she says she's so proud of both of you. This current life, although you were separated physically, was meant to heal those lives. This is an important life, because in those other lives, you didn't have an understanding that it wasn't the end, and that was the anguish. Now you have the understanding. That's why you've been given this opportunity and insight. You have the body, mind, spirit, and the vibration in your being this lifetime to make the connection. It's such an instrumental life for you. It's a pinnacle lifetime."

Again, Linda used the exact words, 'pinnacle lifetime.'

"It's instrumental that you're here. I understand why you want this for yourself, but you're doing it for more. I believe you're doing this for a Light purpose. You are meant to be teachers, and you're both healers. You have the opportunity to raise that vibration to the highest level and remember who you are. You're a part of the Light here in this world. I believe it was a spirit agreement, and there is an ultimate purpose in you being here and her being there with the joining of your spirits on Earth."

Danielle continued, "Hemitra says she understands this break from each other, and she will be patient with you. She says she has big shoulders, and she can take it."

"I just want to know why? Why she's always leaving and not just in England? You said neither of us felt worthy of the love." I had to keep questioning.

"There are a couple reasons, and it's on both your ends. Why for you? You need to understand how important you are. You need to do this part by yourself. You're very close in this lifetime to understanding how important you are on your own. You lose yourself. Sometimes that's a good thing. You must understand what you are to the two of you. You're so close to a breakthrough."

"I don't feel a breakthrough as much as a breakdown," I confessed.

"The pain in your heart and the pain in her heart were similar. You sought healing in different ways. She said you're so close to a breakout. You're going to discover that this time around. This life is critical."

She says, "Even if just one of you discovers enough self-love, it's everything, and it will work."

"Self-love?" I didn't understand. My life had been filled with love and kindness from family friends, lovers and the universe. What was wrong?

Danielle said, "There was this always this immense fear with the two of you. She had this fear that you would leave her, and you had the fear that she would leave you. It's connected to your own inability to recognize your own worth. She didn't feel worthy of you and you didn't feel worthy of her. You never had any problem loving one another. You had problems loving yourself. What she's trying to tell you is that you must search for and find the answers in this quietness and reflection that you've been going through. She's so proud of you! It's a really good thing. You've never given yourself time to do that. Within the dark is light. How do you find the Light if you don't go within? She knows everything you've been contemplating, and she won't allow it!"

"What am I contemplating?"

"She says you're contemplating leaving. She says she won't allow it. She will not allow it."

And how was she going to stop such a thing, if I should decide to leave, I thought? "It's an unconscious thing because I know I have to stay. I'd like to make it feel like I'm finishing a term, and this had begun to feel like a jail sentence," I complained.

"She's showing me that right now it's as if you've been in this dimension. She can't even say that you were numb. It's so painful, that it's difficult to feel. She knows she can't help you through the rest of this right now. It's something you must do on your own. It's not even something you can put into words. It's a heaviness. It's actually a dimension of time. This grief that you have, it's as if you died, but you're on Earth."

"It feels like I was in the underworld," was my description. Linda said that I died along with Hemitra.

"What she's showing me is that you will be reborn. Here's how you are the Phoenix. It's the two of you in a new way. There will be a resurgence of you both and reconnecting in a new way. What you will find is that this connection you've done in the beginning is nothing compared to what you will experience in the future. It's only the beginning. She's showing me that you will rise out of these ashes. You will find yourself, but not only yourself, you will rediscover all the lifetimes. With her somehow, you're going to connect everything and all the lifetimes. It's as if everything will be healed. She shows me every lifetime. She zips up all the lives. She lifts them up."

"Is this the last one?" A new thought now presented to me.

"She said you're both finished. You can both decide to come back, or you can stay in spirit, and you will make that decision together. What you forget is that you will have eternity with her. What you're focused on is the physical. You're still grieving the physical loss of this life. You've forgotten, and that's completely understandable," Danielle continued.

Hemitra said, "This is not the end for us! This is only the beginning of eternity for us."

Danielle said, "She keeps showing me the infinity symbol. She is simply waiting for you to finish out your life's work, which means your life's work together. There are still things you need to share, and you will channel together. Once you have completed this, then you will decide whether you become spirit guides together or come back. There is so much you two can do without a body. The relationship that you are referring to is the physical. The relationship you have shared is eternal."

"We've been together from the beginning?"

"Yes. That's her."

"When I was angry, I said I was going to achieve that with someone in some lifetime who completes an agreement," I added.

"You're out of the high vibration." Danielle reminded me.

Danielle spoke for Hemitra. "She said that's ok. You're allowed. You'll get a kick out of this. She said, "She'll allow it." We laugh.

"You mean thinking this whole Earth thing has been a waste?" I tried to interpret.

"No, now she says that's really not ok." Hemitra didn't like me referring to our lives on Earth as a waste.

"Here's the thing. The two of you have shared so much. Give yourself a break. You're so hard on yourself, and you expect it all right now," Danielle said.

"Where I am, there is no right now and there is no then," Hemitra chimed in.

Danielle relayed Hemitra's messages. "What she's showing me is something quite beautiful. She's everywhere and everything and every time, and she's enveloping you. I mean not just body and spirit and mind and soul. She is you. She's lifting you up. And I feel this is working at the cellular level. She's trying to give you healing. She wants you to understand. This is very important. She said let me go. She doesn't mean her. She's showing me her body. She said that's not me. We had this plan to grow old. If you have a plan, it doesn't always go. What if we had our wish? What if...picture me, and I'm still here on Earth, I'm 110. I'm wrinkled, and I know you would still love me the same way, and you would look at me with those eyes, and you would still see me with that spirit. Where am I, what am I, am I my body?"

"What about me? I still have this body and I must stay in it!" I responded.

"What she's saying is that it still goes on. Your relationship goes on. She said you're stamping your feet, and that's ok. She said we want it all. We want everything." Danielle said.

"I didn't sign up to come back with her forever and ever for all this pain." I had difficulty giving up and continued stamping my feet.

"Don't you and I have forever and ever?" Hemitra countered.

"I guess." I made that concession.

"But it's not good enough. You closed the door on me." Hemitra continued.

"I did." This incredulous dialogue went on, as we argued between dimensions.

"You want forever and ever on your terms. Your terms, your way!" Hemitra hit back.

"Between lifetimes you prepare for your next life." I answered.

"Yes, and now I'm preparing, and you're not letting me in." Hemitra was not giving up.

"This call was meant to change all of that." I said.

"I know you're mad, and I know it's not according to your plan, but things are not always on your terms." Hemitra kept up the good fight.

"Or is it always according to hers? What about her terms? She always wants things on her terms since she's left this mortal plane." Back at you spirit woman!

"She's hesitating, she's actually hesitating." Danielle laughed. "She seemed to get things her way a lot."

"She didn't this lifetime." I referred to her early life.

"I know. She said she fought to be with you," Danielle said.

"I know, and I fought to be with her." We had gone through a lot to be together.

"What's she's learned is that it isn't in our control," continued Danielle. "You have to let go." Hemitra said, "I really trust in the whole way that it's all working. I know that we will always be together, and we are always together. There's no way we can be apart. It's just not possible." I felt myself softening.

"I love what we had. Not being able to be together in two dimensions was like death again. That was keeping me here," I added.

"I completely understand that. I really do." Danielle said. "She said you're very upset with her."

"It's the never-ending tragedy." I was still on that subject.

"Here is what she wants to talk about. She said she couldn't do it because she wasn't strong enough," Hemitra spoke from beyond.

"I know," I answered.

"Do you understand how insecure she was? She was insecure with everyone. She said she's not anymore. The outside was an act. Even though she was free with you, she was always afraid. She constantly struggled." Danielle brought up Hemitra's deep pain, and my heart hurt, wishing that she could have always seen herself. She excelled at whatever she did and was an extraordinary brilliant, talented, luminous being.

Danielle continued, "What she's trying to tell you... she wants to say this because you are so close to a breakthrough, and she was so far away from a breakthrough. She's showing me all these pictures like her ups and downs. Her chakras weren't balanced. She would have these extreme highs, and then she would crash. Mundane life was hard for her. She understands your sense of balance, and why you had to rein her in, and she understands that you're more grounded than she was." I understood.

"She says, she's sorry to put this all on you. She says it's ok if you don't. No, she says she doesn't understand. She says you have to, you must!! She will wait. She will be patient for you to be mad at her, but she won't stop bugging you. She says you have to do this for both of you. You just have to!! She doesn't want to say it's all up to you, but it's all up to you! This is the one that's going to decide everything! This is it. This is our chance to change everything!"

I'd never heard such emphasis from Hemitra! Our chance to change everything? She wanted me to stop our painful patterns and carry on. I had already decided.

"I intend to do that." I voiced my signed agreement.

"She wants to say something else, she says, trust your own instincts," Danielle channeled Hemitra.

"They haven't taken me to good places lately," I responded.

Hemitra said, "That's not true. First of all, you are still here. You're questioning things. Questioning is always good. Where it becomes a problem is when you stop listening to yourself. You must trust you. She said you have really good instincts."

"Sometimes." I wasn't too confident after the last few months.

"She says all the time. When you're quiet, and when you listen, your instincts are always right on. It's really important to trust your own inner wisdom. We have doubted ourselves for too many lifetimes. No more!"

"I wish there was a handbook for this." I swam in deep water here.

"There is no expectation on where you should be or on how you are supposed to feel." The counseling continued from my guide.

"I must stay alive." At least I'd gotten clear on that one.

"And you are. Just because you don't' feel a certain way, because you aren't doing what you think you're supposed to do doesn't mean it's not working. It is within your normal. You've never been within the normal. Take a breath and trust it. She could never be within the normal. That's why you worked so well, because neither of you were what others considered normal," Danielle stated.

"That's in all our lifetimes?" I asked.

"Yes. You both defied expectations with each other, and you defied others' rules. You never expected each other to be normal or put chains on one another. Why would you put chains on yourself now?" Danielle continued.

"I don't know. This is pretty new territory," I said.

"Don't allow anyone to tell you what your normal is. You must decide for yourself what feels normal." Danielle responded.

"Right now, doesn't feel normal at all. What felt normal, before I went into this slump, was to talk to her and know we were together and to know that there is no death, and that we go on loving and being. I could live with that."

"What she suggested," Danielle began.

Hemitra interrupted and said, "I'm not ok with this break from each other. Do what made you happy, and what made the two of us happy. It's been so long that you've felt your own joy."

Danielle added, "Joy without her physical presence is difficult."

"I was feeling it with our communications. I was feeling the other worldliness, the magic, and the humor. You said it went beyond anything you knew." I addressed Danielle.

"Yes. You defied what those rules are," Danielle agreed.

Hemitra continued, "Where have we ever fit in? We always had joy. It just ended too quickly because we were stupid. You need to stop it for us. Look what path you're already going down. What are you doubting? Yourself. Us? I guess more than anything, yourself. You're saying where do I fit in?"

"Sometimes my human self wants to fit in somewhere." Is that really too much to ask, I thought?

"Where have we ever fit in?" Hemitra repeated and came on strong again. "We haven't. Do what makes you feel good."

"She's smacking you by the way." Danielle reported.

"I'll smack her back." The madness continued.

Hemitra said, "Seriously, we don't fit in. They fit in with us or they don't."

"That means dead or alive or whatever?"

"Yes. Don't try to fit in. Just be you, be us, do what makes you happy, and don't worry about the rest," came Hemitra's conclusion.

"Good advice, and I still miss you."

"She knows that," answered Danielle.

Hemitra replied, "What you lost is the physical sense of me. The me that you know is still here. Honey, I'm right here."

"I just needed to know that this wasn't a big cosmic joke." I persisted.

Hemitra continued through Danielle, "Everything we shared since the physical part of me has been gone is, I know that you know better than to think that we're a joke."

"I know. I meant the tragic leaving," I responded.

"From now on, us being one and moving forward, this is it! This is our time! We can do it!" My guide led the cheer for our evolution. "I know you can do it. No, not that you can, you're doing it and will do it. Think of the freedom this will give our souls."

In that moment, a deeper awareness surfaced in me, and I truly understood how those on Earth and in the next realm co-created and evolved together. We always said we could do anything as long as we were together, and once again, we joined as a powerful team.

Danielle continued. "Hemitra's asking you to do this with trust. Really follow your heart and your joy. There is a sense behind your spirits to follow the path of the higher self. Just follow your joy. You're releasing your soul. You're free to soar, and then you're free to connect with not only her spirit, but your higher self, and that connection is truly free. That's what she's trying to teach you. That's what you're here to teach and to learn."

"Freedom?" I asked.

"Yes." Danielle confirmed.

"It was a good lifetime," I said.

"It is a good lifetime, and it's a lifetime of remembering and sharing, and it's just the beginning," Danielle continued.

"It's a painful new beginning." I was still getting my balance.

"In that pain, you'll find healing, if you're able to come through it, and I know you will. You have so much Light and so many lessons within it."

"Ok, Hemitra, we're on again."

"She's happy, and she's excited because you needed to go through this. You needed to push her away and connect with yourself and be with your own energy. I feel you will be so much stronger when you come through this. This was a breakthrough for you. Anger is power."

"It wasn't fun." I understated.

"Honey, she didn't ever leave you. You needed to leave and walk away. She will always be there. You're allowed to have some space and shut the door. She is so proud of you!" Danielle affirmed.

****

"I'm putting up the Christmas decorations."

"She loves what you've done. She loves it! Did you get a new angel, a new decoration? Was there a nutcracker? She's talking about the nutcrackers. She loved, loved, loved the holidays and the decorations."

"Nutcracker? I don't know." I didn't know of a nutcracker, but Hemitra did, and she would actively participate in the decorating with a surprise intervention.

Saying good-bye, I hugged Danielle and didn't want to let go.

"Thank you, Danielle!" I said out loud on my way home. Danielle and Linda brought me through a long dark night of the soul with love and endless patience. What great women to take on these two souls who pushed boundaries and never played by the rules. Never normal! How normal is it to fight between two dimensions? We rarely fought when we walked here together. None of the books I was reading by mediums talked about cases of couples arguing between Heaven and Earth.

"She's smacking you, by the way." I smiled as I remembered the dialogue. "I'll smack her back." She's right. We don't fit in.

Chapter 31

"I'm on my way home, and I'm right around the corner. May I stop? I have a present for you both," Anna Marie announced in a cheery voice.

"Sure, please do. I have a present for you too."

The day after Hemitra's passing, Anna Marie had shown up with a day's worth of her efforts contained in a large bag of organized material for legal and logical details needed when a loved one passed. It included labels, folders, notebook, dividers, and all manner of stuff. She carefully laid it out, yet somehow knew most of me wasn't there to take it all in. My friend was one who stood by me and checked in through the darkest passage of this lifetime. Her car pulled into the drive.

With a mischievous smile, twinkling eyes, and a brightly colored holiday bag, Anna Marie appeared, and we hugged when I opened the front door.

It was wonderful to see my friend! We talked excitedly as I heated water for tea and found cheese, crackers and nuts to eat. With a tray of snacks and steaming mugs, we sat on the sofa by the fire.

Anna Marie handed me a present tightly nestled in a lovely holiday bag. "Merry Christmas to you and Hemitra!" With a few tugs, a nutcracker emerged.

"I never, I mean I never buy nutcrackers. I don't even like them," Anna Marie began. "A friend's daughter was in the Nutcracker at Forge Crossing this season, and I went to the daytime performance with her. There was a table outside the auditorium filled with nutcrackers for sale. Of course, I ignored them. After the performance, we walked by the table. Halfway to the exit door, I turned around and marched back to the nutcracker table and bought her. You know she made me do it."

I held the nutcracker in my hands, and we burst out laughing. "Isn't this a look alike?" The nutcracker, a woman in a red glittery dress, saucy expression, and big, curly, brunette hair stared at us. She had ample cleavage and held a black glittery night bag. My eyes widened in disbelief. "It's her, it's the best caricature of Hemitra I could imagine!"

"I couldn't get out of there without it," Anna Marie laughed.

The spunky little nutcracker stood on the coffee table facing us. I told Anna Marie I had a reading with Danielle a week before she had gone to the nutcracker. Danielle said Hemitra loved the holidays and the decorations I put up. She kept talking about a nutcracker and that she loved nutcrackers, but we don't have any nutcrackers. This is the piece she was raving about.

"She already knew she'd get me to buy the nutcracker? You are living in a space between the worlds, and I'm playing there too." Anna Marie kept grinning.

"There is no time. Wrap your head around that." I passed along some Hemitra wisdom teaching from the next dimension.

"Well, she loved you, and you two obviously are in the same pipeline, or you and I are easily manipulated from her new place." Anna Marie smiled.

"She's feeling her spirit power and is having fun," I added. As we sat laughing, we both felt Hemitra right there with us enjoying.

Anna Marie looked at me, "I've talked to you a few times, but tell me honestly, are you ok?"

"I'm back from the darkest place I've ever known, besides the loss of her physical presence, and yes, I'm ok and figuring it out."

"You've been trying to figure out the whole way the universe works. Could you give that up, at least for today?" Anna Marie smiled.

"Being here in body, if we're lucky, we can understand about a drop of the water as compared to being in spirit and perfectly perceiving the whole ocean." I gave my explanation.

"I'm glad you're back," Anna Marie offered.

"Every close relationship I'd ever had, I loved being together and then loved time apart. Those relationships ran in parallel tracks. In my relationship with her, those parallel lines merged, blended and became one. We were opposites and gave each other space, but now I realize there was no me or her, only us. We loved it, but what now?"

Anna Marie raised her mug, "All I can say is congratulations on the reemergence. We were worried."

"I was able to forgive that young woman in England. I understood how much she suffered. I forgave all the incarnations of me who followed Hemitra into the next world. It's also unnerving to know how patterns persist lifetime after lifetime, and how we easily slip right into them. This pattern must be broken."

"Are you writing?"

"Sometimes."

"Keep writing."

That holiday Anna Marie gave Hemitra and me a great gift by happily diving into our expanded other worldly madness.

****

Winter solstice, the longest night and the coming of the Light, was a new beginning. I lit a large white candle. Every holiday light ablaze, I set two places at the kitchen table, and made tea and heated muffins, as I talked to my invisible partner, the presence of loved ones in spirit, the angels, fairies and the spirits of the land. Hemitra and I were together. We felt euphoric and triumphant.

Hemitra loved the moonlight, and Danielle had channeled her instructions that I should spend more time in that feminine Goddess energy. The memories of our moon ritual groups and sweet evenings outside were felt with gratitude and not pain.

I bundled up in layers and a long down coat and went out into the bright light of the full moon. I'd never felt such intensity from the moonlight. My senses heightened, as if I'd stepped into a different reality. It was the expanded world that was our togetherness. Danielle said Hemitra requested that more of her ashes be scattered on our property, and she wanted them in the gardens she loved. I carried the box, which felt like a strange token of her mortal remains. I took off my gloves and walked around, holding the ashes in my hands, as I gently tossed handfuls in our flower gardens. Then I sat in a chair on the deck under our favorite Dogwood tree. Thanking the spirits of the land and honoring the coming of the Light, I offered her muffin to the fairies or maybe a lucky raccoon or skunk who happened along.

For some reason before bed, I went into Hemitra's room and looked through her jewelry. A large silver and gold dragonfly pin landed in my hand. It was a piece of jewelry we bought for our center's gift shop. "Give that to Danielle," I heard clearly in my head.

"Yes, great idea," I agreed, answering out loud. Smiling, I went downstairs and reopened the computer to write.

Dear Danielle,

Yesterday, our friend Virginia had to cancel her Winter Solstice party in town because she was sick. Hemitra and I created our own celebration here. What I felt and did say on the reading was that, after the 7- day period of feeling like it was my own death and mourning all the tragedy in our past lives, I gave it up and started to live again. Not having contact with Hemitra was very unnatural, and I now accept us as a new type of dynamic team. Hopefully, I finally truly know that our loved ones in spirit are not only in the spirit world, but they have a vested interest in their loved ones lives who remain behind. It took some kicking and screaming on my part.

As Hemitra said, the beauty and wonder of our encounters since she passed are things that dreams are made of. The humor and guidance, and the joy that I felt in moments when I am aware of her, is to be celebrated.

I called this a new start, as we honored the coming of the Light. I celebrate her Light, yours and mine and the Light of all beings. I scattered more ashes as she requested. I put them in the flower gardens we loved to work in, around the pool and hot tub where we fell in love, and 22 years ago, we remembered being in ancient Greece. Time traveling from the beginning.

What I found is that, whatever form we are in, it still feels best to be together doing our work and sharing our life. Just as in ancient times, the knowing and conscious working with the ones on the other side of the veil, must return.

Would you ask her to make a comment on last night? It feels that we're back and moving on.

Look for a small package from us. I will explain in the note. Last night, you were part of our Winter Solstice time.

Much love,
Sue and Hemitra

A week later I received an email.

Dear Sue,

I'm sorry it's taken me so long to get back to you. I was away visiting my mother for her 70th. I just got back yesterday and was overwhelmed with emotion when I opened your card, and I was immediately drawn to the energy of the dragonfly pin.

175

Thank you from the bottom of my heart. I will cherish it always. The dragonfly has been a great teacher of mine and has come to me in beautiful times during my life. It has been a powerful symbol. Hemitra was so right! Thank you for listening and sharing that gift.

On that note, I've been meaning to tell you she wanted you to know that during your party, she felt magic, a unity of your energy, and a surge and reconnection of your souls. She said it was beyond anything that beings here get to experience, and she is so grateful to be sharing it with you. It was timeless, and it was beyond this world. She also wants to thank you for meeting her there. She understands that you needed to leave her in order to find her. She loved being with you in the moonlight and garden. She said it's a meeting place.

I'm sending you much love, light and strength,

Danielle

Chapter 32

I was incredibly fortunate because Hemitra and I were together. It wasn't the way I wanted it, and it wasn't as good as having her here with me, but my dynamic powerful partner went beyond the rules of engagement even from the next dimension, and she enhanced our new life. Loss is always going to be part of the human experience in some form. Life didn't end here. Our relationship was different, but the relationship continued. Being able to connect on a personal level changed everything, and the veil was lifted.

After unraveling the haunting feelings of abandonment and knowing the facts from the English lifetime and others, I began to move on. Somehow remembering and understanding allowed the healing to start.

Danielle had said that most humans don't remember their lives in such detail. We kept drawing the same pattern to learn those unresolved lessons, as everyone does. Because we identified our repeated patterns and the lessons we had to learn, the feelings were more traumatic. However, the remembering and breaking the pattern would bring a final healing to us both.

Above all, I vowed that no matter what transpired in our future lives, I would have no part in creating more Shakespearean tragedies, like *Romeo and Juliet* or Juliet and Juliet. We played the star-crossed lovers and followed the theme of all those, 'I can't live without you' songs one too many times.

Impatient though I was, grief takes its own time. Each time, I fell into pain then inched my way back to center, I felt Her rush of support. It came as a powerful loving adrenaline surge. My coach witnessed it all and knew that we would win. I had crawled through the darkest night of my soul, and I would keep my promise to stay here.

I became aware of many people in a different way. One of my good pals happened to see an acquaintance of ours, and the acquaintance asked my friend if I was still trying to talk to Hemitra. She scoffed at the thought with pity for my insane notions? It made me wonder if the scoffer had lost the love of her life, and her departed sent signs to her, would she be able to receive them? Are we that trapped in dogma and what we are being told?

Another friend avoided contact with me at all costs. At first, I felt hurt, but later understood that her response was an example of our life's training to exist in an emotionally shut down culture.

A woman I happened to meet along my journey had lost her teenage son four months before. After a two-week absence from work, her coworkers didn't mention her son at all. Grief is messy and complicated. With some, it creates distance instead of intimacy.

With my cherished friends, magic happened. Linda, Hemitra and I shared an eternal multi millennial relationship that gave me profound comfort and healing. We three worked through many situations, as I trudged forward and backward in my soul transformation. I treasured the brilliance and accuracy of her messages and the depth of meaning from Hemitra, complete with a play list of songs that Hemitra pulled up to sing to me. They were always perfectly aligned to her messages.

I reread the beautiful transcriptions from Danielle that documented the history of Hemitra's and my soul, as we plunged in and out of our Earth experiences. Many lessons lay in those words. The time Danielle, Hemitra and I spent in Danielle's celestial oasis were priceless, and Danielle did her best to help me stay on Earth.

The heartfelt kindness from my friends carried an added bonus. Everyone who surrounded me could somehow receive messages from Hemitra or travel back with me to my obsession of endless past life memories.

In our conversations, Michele, my long-time friend, tuned into intriguing details about many things related to Hemitra and me. Once, we focused on Victorian England, and she brought forth the fact that our home in that century was known all over. Hemitra and I, the man and woman version, had books that we hid. They were esoteric literature that we kept private because of the climate of the times. Michele vividly described our library of leatherbound books that stretched from floor to ceiling. She saw leaded glass windows. I had also envisioned large diamond shapes in leaden glass windows. Michele added to the details of a stained- glass window, big wooden tables, and Hemitra and me in those other bodies, sitting by the fire reading to each other. She said we had mediums, or spiritualists come to the house for gatherings. We had a reputation with mixed reviews. Michele also repeated Danielle's comment that we had lots of sex. That sounded like a perfect pastime in a repressed culture. Those details reinforced the channeling with Danielle from Hemitra about our never fitting in.

Therapeutic conversations with Ellen soothed my heart and added to Hemitra's and my endless story line. Ellen met Hemitra and me at our center, Heart of the Goddess. She brought two lovely daughters, Sarah, age nine and Rebecca age seven. For the next many years, Ellen and the girls participated in our classes and seasonal celebrations. Hemitra put her heart and soul into creating elaborate meaningful celebrations for all the Earth holidays. Ellen and I reminisced often, remembering Hemitra in all her theatrical glory as High Priestess of Spring Equinox, Summer Solstice, Autumn Equinox, and Winter Solstice with 50 or 60 women in our circles. We made it all came alive again; the dancing, the music and drumming, as everyone did their part for the rituals. Hemitra's eloquent voice and dramatic presence brought richness and passion to the events.

This lifetime, Hemitra had no children, but loved Ellen's girls as if they were her daughters. Hemitra created May Day dances for mothers and daughters and beautiful Coming of Age ceremonies in which both Ellen's girls participated. A grown up, lovely Rebecca, flew in from China to grace us with her sweet presence at our wedding.

When we spoke after Hemitra's passing, Ellen also saw pieces of the English life. She told me she didn't do this peering into other lives except with Hemitra and me. Ellen would be silent then say, "You were children together. I see you, Sue, in a tree, and Hemitra as a young boy. He liked you right away." Then, as adults, she said, "The way he looked at you. He was enchanted with you, and you were with him." I had also remembered Hemitra and me being children together, and Danielle also confirmed it.

One winter day on the phone, Ellen related a story to me. My gregarious friend had been shopping and met an interesting woman. They struck up a conversation, and Ellen mentioned me and Hemitra's recent passing. The gist of the story was Hemitra's and my ongoing communication. The woman said that her passing was tragic but was meant as part of the story, because I had work to do and must stay here to do it. I would live a long time.

Hemitra's passing devastated me. It was wrong! However, she repeatedly told me from her spirit home that this was the plan all along. I fought her on that, as I kicked and screamed. Of course, she spoke the truth. Even a complete stranger told my friend Ellen we had selected the course.

Ellen had never met that woman and perhaps would never see her again. The incident reminded me that all events, thoughts and actions were present and permanent in the vast collective unconscious, and they were accessible to all who could contact that realm. There were no such things as secret thoughts or hidden information.

"We are broadcasting even our most secret thoughts and desires. We are accountable for what we send out." It's our responsibility, "as far as human frailty will permit," to think and send out wholesome thoughts (White, 2010, p. 107). Hemitra constantly reminded me to raise my vibration and to stay in alignment with my life's responsibility. I could relate to the 'human frailty part.'

****

In the last reading, Danielle had asked whose birthday was coming up? Hemitra's birthday was at the end of January, and she requested that I celebrate and not be upset. I guess we were having a party, and she wanted it to be festive. What friends could I ask to a party for someone in the next dimension? I would invite Anna Marie and Damini. They were a special part of the angelic team that put up with Hemitra and me.

Damini was a woman I'd known of for 20 years, yet our paths rarely crossed. She owned a wellness center where she did acupuncture, and Anna Marie did her PT sessions. Three weeks after Hemitra's passing, Damini invited me for some acupuncture treatments. I was receiving acupuncture from our beloved acupuncture MD who treated Hemitra the year of her cancer, yet Damini's offer felt kind and right, so I gratefully accepted.

On the massage table at Damini's center, I looked in her eyes and heart and instantly knew the comfort of being with an old friend. At the same time, I felt the presence of her mother close by, though her mother had passed years ago. Damini clearly saw Hemitra with me and could channel messages from her. From there, a wonderful kinship began.

Damini was matter of fact. She told me, "Your pulses are going backward," and asked, "Do you want to be here?" She insisted I see her every week until she felt I wasn't a critical wreck. She wasn't ruffled by anything, as I shared the many channelings and my experiences at that time with Hemitra.

The evening of the party, Anna Marie and Damini arrived with one too many bottles of champagne and beautiful flowers adding to the roses I bought. I decorated the dining room table and made a special effort to clean and refresh the house. I bought a cake from Hemitra's favorite bakery. It was encased in a ton of butter cream icing, with Happy Birthday Hemitra in letters of bold purple sweetness.

The event became a forever memorable party. Both women had perception, and they either heard or saw Hemitra, as we laughed and shared. I set a place at the table for our birthday guest. Hemitra super charged the night with her electric, other worldly presence, as she enjoyed her celebration to the max. We all knew how much Hemitra appreciated still being acknowledged as part of the gang.

After dinner, the girls told me to stand at the dining room table next to Hemitra's place setting and her picture. Both women agreed, "She's standing right there," and pointed to my left side. The picture Damini took showed a haze around my shoulders and down by my side. It looked like Hemitra had her arm around me. I guess I should say, she had her arm around me.

What a gift to be with those who considered it matter of fact to include and celebrate with one who was no longer embodied! At that moment, a birthday party, complete with a dinner place setting for my pal on the other side seemed perfectly normal, but in the future, Hemitra would have to celebrate with me on the subtle, since I might quickly run out of priceless friends like those two.

Chapter 33

Three days after the birthday celebrations, I had a phone reading with Danielle. Danielle began, "She's very excited about the party you had for her. She says you did so many little details. She loved the flowers. She says thank you for the flowers. She had so much fun and she really enjoyed Anna Marie and Damini's energy. It was fun because they felt her and saw her. What did you do with pictures?"

"The second year of our relationship, I created a birthday ritual and dinner party with two friends. I wanted to surprise Hemitra with something meaningful. The pictures were of that evening, 21 years ago. Connie and Judith were our two friends. They joined our first year six weekend Woman Wisdom Training classes and were the only ones who knew our story of past life memories and secret love. It was wonderful to be able to openly share with them."

"She loved the pictures. She says, thank you for the pictures."

"I dreamt about the birthday a week before the post life party with Anna Marie and Damini and knew those pictures were special to her. I put them out on the coffee table. Hemitra was good at implanting vivid details of our life in my mind. As I planned the party, I found the pictures and saw a clear image of Hemitra holding them to her heart and smiling."

I would never have thought to put the party together the way I did, and I knew from my dream and the thoughts in my head that Hemitra gave me the ideas for her celebration. I also realized it was my choice to listen or not. We can reject the influence of our loved ones in spirit and guides. However, it means more than can be fully understood to co-create with our teachers on the other side.

My original idea for that long-ago birthday was conceived because sometimes Hemitra could be unnecessarily sharp and reactive in her dealings with others, and that didn't serve her well. At times, she threw uncensored remarks at the unsuspecting, and I made it my task to set her straight, especially when it involved our business. We got the boundaries between us established in the beginning of our relationship, and she never spoke to me like that.

There had been a target bow and arrow set in the attic that belonged to the kids. It was a nicely made, oak colored, wooden bow, a little over four and a half feet high with a red grip in the middle of the bow. I covered the wood on the bow with strips of white rabbit fur. My self-sufficient parents raised sheep, chickens, and rabbits, and I now had many sheep skins and rabbit pelts in a box in the attic. Next, I found several dark brown rabbit furs and sewed them together to use as a top for my costume.

Before that year's past evening, I told our friends about the secret ritual, and when I went to Hemitra's house the night of the party, they helped me hide the bow and costume. Soon, I excused myself and brought out the bow. I wore my Artemis the huntress costume with rabbit skins over one shoulder, secured at the waist with rawhide twine; the other half bare breasted.

Going through Hemitra's things, I found the birthday card I'd written to her for that celebration. "Happy Birthday to the woman who changed my life forever, my best friend, my partner, my cosmic playmate. I honor you and all the facets of you. You are intelligent, quick witted, a dynamic leader and a powerful force. That powerful force is a great asset, however your messages are sometimes delivered with a hammer. This gift is a reminder that power can be gentle like a soft breeze, a breeze that has hurricane force quietly underneath. Conviction and knowing is a feeling inside, and it comes through better with kindness."

"She loved the gift, the message and the evening. She hung the bow on the wall of her bedroom where it remained. I decorated the coffee table the night of her post life party with the bow and two pictures. There was one of the Artemis me kneeling in front of Hemitra, half clothed, handing her the bow and a picture of all of us laughing and happy," I explained to Danielle.

"She loved that! When you did that, she said it taught her a very valuable lesson. It changed your relationship." Danielle got Hemitra's message. "It helped her to see people differently, and she thanks you so much for doing that for her. You toned her down. She appreciated that. She truly did. You balanced each other beautifully," Danielle continued.

"Did you create a grid for your party? The table? Are there crystals around? Did you rearrange them? She likes what you did. She said you rearranged the crystals."

"I cleaned them. There are crystals all over our house. They had such sad energy."

"What is the symbol? Native American. Is it a medicine wheel? I see the Earth, Air, Fire and Water."

"I set the table and honored the four directions. I did that because I wanted to be who we are."

"Just know that she saw that. You did that in her honor, and she really loves that you did that. She is truly celebrating it."

"There's a heart shaped box. There's something in that for her?" Hemitra wanted to go over all her party details.

"Yes, I gave her a gardenia scented candle in a bag with a heart on it."

"Thank you for the candle," Hemitra responded.

"That party years ago, turned into a memorable evening."

Danielle began, "She's been talking to me about magic the last couple of days. She says, with us it's beyond this world."

"It always was."

"She said it still is." Hemitra never stood for any past tense references.

She said, "We're living beyond this world, and we're living beyond this dimension. We're in a dimension together. We are existing together. It's as if we've created another dimension together. You understand? It's the coolest thing ever."

I'd continued to read about experiences with those on the other side. A young couple who fell deeply in love were separated by the man's untimely death. The woman expressed her grief and her desire to leave her life on Earth and go with him. The man from the his Heavenly dimension told his love that he would go on living through her, and she was to move ahead in her life and live it to the fullest. We can create a new dimension of existence with our beloved in spirit, and live life on Earth. It was the coolest thing!

Danielle continued, "Hemitra is enriching her spirit, as are you with this Earth experience. You're doing both. It's just important that you honor both of your spirit works. She was with you every moment you felt and heard her. She wants you to know how strong you are. She wants to make sure you know that about yourself." Hemitra regularly repeated comments she felt I needed to hear.

"You feel her hands."

"I see the images in my mind, and I know she's touching me. I can feel it subtly."

"She gives you give you such incredible hugs. Do you feel her hugs, because she hugs you?" Danielle asked.

She enjoyed a total sense of me, but my sense of her was definitely subtle.

Danielle continued, "By allowing this experience the way you are and being open to it, you are both continuing to grow as individuals. And there's no stopping you. You are doing it. What she wants you to know is that now you need to work on your own inner being. You must be the highest you can be. You can connect with her with ease because of your soul connection, but your connection with her can be so much deeper when you raise your vibration. You're also supposed to connect with other souls."

My new guide never stopped with the instructions.

"Now three times she brought up yoga. She shows me that you must do yoga. It opens you up, and it grounds you."

"We took classes together, but she always dropped out." We laugh.

"She has a very good sense of humor now about herself. She's always with you, but she has crossed over. She's where she is, and she's where she is. It's very interesting. There are some spirits that refuse to leave. She's not one of them. She has left this dimension. She's still doing spirit work, and she's doing work with you." Danielle kept instructing me on the rules of the universe.

Hemitra said, this is why you stayed, and I didn't. You stayed because you were always more disciplined."

I was more disciplined with the physical, and Hemitra was incredibly disciplined with her spiritual practice, meditating twice a day for most of her life. She now reminded me when I didn't meditate.

Danielle continued, "This is what she wants when you're healed more. She said I'll be patient, a little bit. She wants you to treat your mind and body like a temple. You really must. She wants you to be more aware of what you eat. There are certain foods that will elevate your senses."

"I was the one who took good care of myself and tried to take care of her."

"She's changed. She says, she's learned, and she wants you to be vibrating up here. That's why she will be a little patient."

Give me a break, woman. It's only been six months, I thought.

"Did you get a new outfit," Danielle asked?

"A new top," I answered.

"She loves it. She says it's really pretty. It's a good color for you."

"Have you been dizzy?"

"Yes, I feel lightheaded."

"She says your holding too much energy. It's the vibration. You know the natural flow of things, but you're holding on instead of letting go."

"Holding onto her?"

"Everything. The intense emotion of it. She said, "Even though the grief hurts so much, it's still her, and because of that, you won't release it. You must let the pain go. There's the fear that you will let her go. You must come to a point where you're willing to shift that.""

"I understand. It's a reaction grieving people have."

"That's it. You feel left. It's the abandonment feeling. Again, she encourages you to raise your vibration. This grief is too draining for you. What you are beginning to understand is that she hasn't left you. It's just that you don't feel her that intensely. It's her stepping back so you don't get hurt. Two things will happen. You'll raise your vibration. It will be so elevated that you will be able to go in and out whenever you want, but you won't need to. You will have moments of intense connection with her, and you will also have moments in your Earth experience when you have time for yourself. You'll be balanced. That's what she wants for you. She's with you every minute, and she can be."

Danielle continued, "She's released so much. She wants you to know that she's in such a good place. She wants you to know that she is in such a good place because of you. You didn't have a choice about her leaving, but you could have chosen not to let her back in."

"I couldn't do that."

"She loves you so much. She's doing something really really sweet! She's bowing at your feet. She truly honors the essence that is you. She just honors you so. She says don't forget you. Promise me." I cried again.

"You two have an amazing connection. Your energies have merged, but you are still individuals, and that's beautiful."

"We felt that right away."

"You toned her down. She appreciated that. You balanced each other beautifully. You are twin souls without a doubt. You are the equivalent of each other's souls. There are no boundaries that define her. She's with you on walks, in the car, everywhere."

The reading ended when Danielle said, "If you could make a love potion of what the two of you have and give it to everyone then we would have peace."

"It will come. It will all be exactly as it should be."

Chapter 34

When Hemitra first passed, the comfort of her communications kept me going. When she said I became her assignment, that sounded like job or duty. Didn't loved ones in spirit contact loved ones still on Earth to console their grief and help them? Would feeling compassion or just plain sorry for my limited Earth self, wear thin? After all, Hemitra lived in the company of angels now, had unlimited knowledge and vista of the multiverse, and the beauty of Heaven couldn't even be understood by us mortals.

That was a misconception, and from the beginning, Hemitra enthusiastically involved herself in everything I did and all things she once loved. She did so with a force that couldn't be ignored, as she told me that she was much more alive and active now. By this time, I fully realized what our loved ones in spirit loved here, they passionately involved themselves with from the next dimension. Now, she truly had clear vision, and I accepted what she said, "I can help you so much more, I can do so much more for you," and she did.

Danielle said Hemitra heard my thoughts and said, "Remember, no one's Light is brighter. Just because someone is more evolved or vibrating at a higher frequency their Light is the same. She couldn't possibly tire of you because she's seen your Light and knows how beautiful it is."

This was my Eternity 101 course.

"Gradually we come to realize that the so-called dead and indeed the whole spiritual world are involved in and care deeply about every aspect of Earthly life. We can actually enable those on the other side to share our physical life. Their powers focus on us, they look at us, act in us and add to our strength. They flow into our souls" (Steiner, 1918, pp. 21-22).

In a conversation with Linda, I commented that I counted on Hemitra's insights. Linda related Hemitra's response. "I count on you too. We count on each other. You're my mission, and the mission is love."

"Our task on Earth can't be done alone, but only through those we love. For the work of the Earth is love and working with the dead is an important part of our task" (Steiner, 1918, p. 23).

****

Hemitra said once through Linda, "When you take care of yourself, you take care of me." We effect one another's evolution more than we imagine.

I realized that I chose to continue our relationship, and if I had decided not to allow Hemitra or any loved one in spirit to share my life, my free will determined that. In the books I read, I found agreement from several authors who said that if any conscious interchange is to take place with loved ones who had passed, it must come from a feeling of the heart. If the person who passed had been abusive or cruel, those left on Earth could choose not to communicate or forgive the departed, and the person passed would see and feel the pain they had caused.

I continued my sessions with Danielle as that first winter wore on, and this one started with another discussion about our English life.

Danielle said, "You've done a lot of healing regarding the lifetime in Victorian England. That proved difficult for you because you aligned with centuries of genetic pain and all the tragedy of your many lives. You have clearly identified those patterns and moved on from those lives, and what you need to do now is chose a path filled with ease." I was determined to do that.

Danielle said, "She stated that she is with you and you will always remain on the journey together. She is here and growing with you. The only difference is she doesn't have a physical body. She's aware of the challenges that continue to cross your path, but she is completely confident that you are both on your way to a life filled with Light."

"I tried to break up with her," I reminded Danielle.

Hemitra was quick to respond, "Fat chance that's ever going to happen." We laughed.

"I had to relive those memories to get to a place of forgiveness for myself. I took responsibility for my part, but isn't there another side like Hemitra's part in all of this?"

Danielle paused, then Hemitra said, "I was careless with the lifetimes I'd been given and selfish."

Danielle added, "That was hard for her to say. She said she didn't take care of her body. She was defying her physical being."

Hemitra spoke, "It was hard for me to be in a body. I resisted it. Many times, I didn't pay attention to my body signals, didn't sleep right and neglected my body. More than that, I felt I didn't deserve you. I had lots of self-hatred from my childhood."

"You didn't take care of yourself. I forgive you," I responded. I remembered twice that Hemitra asked me through Linda if I forgave her for leaving?"

"No, you don't," Hemitra answered.

"I love you, and it hurt watching you," I admitted.

Danielle began, "She is sorry for that. There are many layers here, and this is the tip of the iceberg. There's lots to do with the body, and there's something she's working out with that."

I remembered Hemitra telling me that a long time ago, one of her spiritual teachers told her she must remember she had a body.

Hemitra spoke, "Disrespecting our physical bodies is also disrespecting our spirit, and I separated the two, but they are not separate. The more we care for the body, the more we are able to access different aspects of ourselves. I didn't do that. I disregarded that. I've done a lot of learning in spirit and from your growth. I've also learned because we're together."

I brought up that from the beginning of Hemitra's transition and communication, she always talked about my body and had an awareness of every physical cell and every thought in my mind.

"She wants you to treat your body and mind like a temple. Watch what you are putting in your mouth. She wants you to be aware of everything. Eat more greens."

For months, I hadn't taken perfect care of myself, as I usually did. I answered, "I'm the one who always took care of myself."

Danielle said, "She's changed. She says she's learned, and she wants you to be vibrating up here." Danielle raised her hand to demonstrate Hemitra's message.

Hemitra said, "By you taking care of your body: it's more up to you to raise your vibration to come to me. Yes, I know that was convenient on my part. I understand…She has trouble saying this… I know this is harder on you. I know that. So what? Stop crying about it, get over it and let's get this done."

"I am doing it." She was much more intense out of body, and we were on a painful subject.

"But, we can do it more. Let's get this done. We can do this." The tirade continued.

I asked Danielle about the discrepancy of who Hemitra and I were in this life, and what Hemitra kept saying from the other side about not being our bodies, as if she was ignoring the sacredness of the body. Our classes for women included the Sacred Feminine, self-care and treating the body like a temple. Hemitra kept saying we're not our bodies, and I bantered with her about it, as I argued that we taught that the physical body was a vehicle for expression of the divine.

Hemitra spoke, "You know how we are, and we always tell each other like it is. I never meant the body was insignificant. You missed the point. I'm in all dimensions. That's why we can still have this exchange. You are in an Earth dimension. The body is the temple, and that's where we started, and that's part of our connection but don't limit us. That thought process limits by defining dimensions. We go beyond all defining. You are in an Earth dimension, and I don't have a physical body."

Danielle began, "What she's saying is that our bodies don't limit us, even on Earth. The soul is never ending. That's why you had this awareness of the other lives. What she's saying is the body ends. She says you're being very good and listening, and this feels so important for your work. This body is a vehicle for the soul. It's part of our soul but not all of it. Our soul is a visitor in this body and uses it."

So far, I stayed in alignment with the remarks.

Danielle said, "What about when we come back and do this over and over, and we don't master those lessons? Her pattern hasn't changed, because the lessons were in an Earth dimension. When we bring in Earth experiences, it changes the dynamic. When we are in source we are able to evolve, and we see more clearly. There are so many other influences in a body. When we add Earth obstacles or lessons such as grief, financial, or family trauma, our souls must rise above those challenges or not. In your case, you are rising above those. What happens is that your actual vibration elevates, but not without those realizations. Let's face it- you repeated many of your lessons too."

"Of course, I did. I went right with her over and over. This time I understood how much pain I caused my loved ones, and I don't want to repeat that lesson again."

Hemitra said, "Did I ever really leave? If we can really get to the point: what if all those times, what if it's always to realize that the body isn't to define the relationship in this shape? What if we are supposed to keep coming back only to realize that we are always connected? The only thing that changes is the dynamic of our connection. Our purpose isn't to define a relationship in this body box. From where I am, I know it's part of our journey but not all of it. The difficulties…it's as if we were aligning to different energies, and the illness and tragedy just fell into place. We didn't make those choices, but the energy we lined up took us down that path. It's a vibration. We are lined up to a frequency. We have to once and for all, and you know there isn't a once and for all; we must change our frequency through awareness and understanding."

"I'm intending to do that," I said.

Danielle continued translating the intense conversation. "She said you're doing an amazing job. She could not do what you're doing. She said you're doing everything she couldn't achieve. You have made a really strong choice, and she is so grateful, not only for you, but for her as well, because it's bringing much healing to both of you."

"Absolutely. She said you're still grieving my body, and she gets that, but you are looking for my body, and you're still angry. She says you still don't like it and if she were you, she wouldn't like it either."

"Yes, I was angry, but I don't feel angry now. I knew this lifetime was different, and she stayed longer, and I don't want to be difficult."

Danielle spoke, "No, you're not. This is really important. This needs to be uncovered. I would be angry too. You're getting to big layers here."

Hemitra continued, "You're mad at me because you had a realization when you looked at your family. I can't inflict this pain. Why wouldn't I have had the realization that by not taking care of myself, that I would cause this pain in you? How could I have done that? That is holding us back."

Hemitra's comment that my judgment of her process was holding us back made me stop and think. I couldn't hold us back. The price was too great.

Hemitra said, "It's really important that you understand. We have different experiences in our upbringing and our marriages. Shifts create or close doors. My experiences in all lifetimes were different than yours, and even though we lived in parallel existences, even though we had similar traumas, I internalized pain differently. Being like a bull is part of me. It wasn't my intention ever to leave."

"It was so much a source of her body not being honored. Not by you. It was no wonder that she couldn't stay," said Danielle.

"I would always help you in any way I can," I said.

"That's the key," Hemitra began, "It's not up to you. You don't have to like it but having that understanding that we all learn differently is what I did. I did come to learn unconditional love for myself, and that's what I wanted to do. We're all here to do that, everyone. We all have a unique fingerprint. That's not an accident. I loved my time here on Earth. I don't see it as failure."

I spoke up. "Failure, are you kidding? You had an amazing life, and your being here has been a gift to many, especially to me. Failure was not possible."

Danielle said, "You must evolve in a body and she avoided that. She says the lessons she needed to learn were different than yours, and she had such pain she couldn't embrace hers. It was up to her to feel that. You are farther along in understanding that feeling unworthy about you is only going to hurt your time here on Earth. In a way, you are judging her process and how she got to where she was. She needed more time in spirit. She wants you to look at where you are and look how you have changed from her passing. You are embracing your time here. You are doing it for you, and she's part of that, and you are claiming your life for you, and she is happy about that."

Danielle continued, "One of the hardest things for you and me, is when people we love are struggling. When our family members and loved ones have hardship in their lives, you and I feel that pain, and we are judging their process. We are fixers. Why does it have to be a struggle? They chose that."

Danielle added, "You and Hemitra have connected so deeply, and you're are getting these issues out of the way."

Hemitra said through Danielle, "There isn't a predestined path. We promised to be together. That's not a path; that's different. That's just who we are. We are together, but how we interact isn't defined. We are choosing an Earth existence. We have free will, and it changes the path. We do come to learn unconditional love."

Danielle said, "This lifetime for both of you feels like you have the opportunity to make that choice. It's as if you've been given a review option. This lifetime has given you the chance to bring your relationship to a new level. It's really quite remarkable. You've been through so many lifetimes with all this pain over and over again, and it's taken a lot of evolving to get to this point. That pain and what you've learned has trained your spirit. It was in that pain that you found yourself and your strength. You didn't have to learn through pain, but it was a valuable tool because neither of you were getting it until now."

I didn't like the sound of the pain, but I had learned profound lessons from that pain. I also knew that Hemitra and I co-created our lives together, and both our choices did lead us into whatever difficulty we experienced. I could have stopped following her into the next dimension many lifetimes ago, but the pattern continued. I'd lost my boundaries. I judged that as co-dependent, weak, or other negative descriptions, but in that moment, I was too weary. Humans can't make complete sense of their lives while on Earth, but in the next dimension, everything would be understood. I had lots of questions for that time.

Danielle said, "You chose to see beyond the patterns and boundaries of this lifetime. That's not weak, it's evolved. That was your journey back to strength. When you made the choice to stay here, you both embraced your inner Light. She had to leave for you to figure this all out. You had to know you must love yourself more, and you made the choice to do differently. You seized the opportunities both when she was here and when she left, and as a result you are able to be where you are now."

I listened.

Danielle continued, "I saw you die, and you came back from that. You said no, it's not over. There's nothing you cannot achieve. There's nothing you can't do. You are unstoppable. Your higher self has grown and changed that. When she thanks you for your healing and the healing you are doing for yourself, you are healing her. She attributes your healing here to her healing there. That's so incredibly powerful what you have done for yourself and what you have done has a couple. Think about where you were and what you have done, and what you are meant to achieve, and that was a choice you made. You can do anything."

After what I'd experienced, I would do anything to move forward. "We did get the love part right this lifetime?"

Danielle answered, "You always got the love part down great. Sometimes we have to repeat and repeat to learn what we need to learn. You were both meant to be here and represent that love as an example for others. You're teachers. It's what you always do."

"We're love teachers?"

"Because of who you were and who you are, just by emanating that energy and sending that frequency, it heals."

"Ahhh. There was a lot of joy in this life. We can do that now?"

"You are doing it now even more so being the two of you. It's the greatest gift two spirits can give. The two of you are so connected to your heart centers and you demonstrate unconditional love. You are meant to bring healing by that energy of loving each other. How beautiful is that? That is why the two of you are here. That was so eye opening to me. It's about being able to transcend and expand your spirit you're so connected to your hearts and to one another's hearts."

I thought how good it felt to be around people who truly love each other, and weren't we all here to do that?

"You chose together to come back into Earth energy, not as punishment, but to continue to be healers and teachers. What she would like to happen for you is to let go more. You've been very angry. The important thing is you've gained more understanding. I understand how you could be really really hurt by her choices. It's important for you to know she didn't make those choices consciously. It's as if we come here to learn unconditional love, but circumstances disconnect us. We are all here to understand and go beyond that and not let anything disconnect us," Danielle said.

Hemitra began, "We are all unique. We all come in with different vibrations and our perception is how we see, and what takes us down different paths. I have always taken things very personally and internalized it and analyzed it. I hung onto things and wasn't even aware of that. You were more aware than I of an easier path. You were always connected to your spirit. I was too, but I didn't listen. I didn't listen and didn't turn on my inner guidance. It was too late. Who we are has been shaped by our Earth experiences, and traumas can disconnect us from source. We forget who we are, and when we incarnate again, it's part of our pattern. We come to change our patterns. We have doubted ourselves for too many lifetimes. No more!!"

Danielle added, "And she said you are doing that. To me, you feel so much lighter. It was good for you to vent. The clarity is coming. You balance each other. You are in the space that you can have the physical and bring in the spirit. You can and do have both. That's what everyone needs to know. She looks at what you've done as a success."

"I'm happy I stayed," I said.

"You have reasons, you really do. The physical aspect and the spiritual are one. You are aware of the body/spirit connection, and the body is a sacred vehicle." Danielle added.

"I had to argue with her to understand."

Danielle said, "She would expect nothing less. You won't always agree. She doesn't look at it as arguing, and you will agree more now. This is not about right or wrong. This is about connecting with who you are. It's so much bigger than you ever imagined, and it has the potential for such growth and healing."

The end of the reading approached, and my head swam with the hard reveal of our deep issues. "Right now, Hemitra, all I care about is that I love you, and we're together. We got the big piece right. I just experienced what it was like to disconnect from us and from everything on Earth and in spirit. I started recreating a lethal life pattern that had to change. I did judge your process, and I have a lot to learn. When you were on Earth, we helped and healed each other. I saw the pain you carried and realized I couldn't help or change you. I was less judgmental when I didn't know our long pattern. I may need all my time here and maybe a few more lifetimes to learn these lessons. By the way, you ARE a lot to handle!"

Danielle said, "She's giving you a really big hug."

Chapter 35

As I realized the deep impact we have on each other and our loved ones on the other side, I wanted to be the best I could be this time around. I thought about Hemitra saying my judgment of her process held us back. I didn't want to hold us back. Judgment? Weren't we born learning how to judge? This was right. That was wrong. That person should act a certain way. In my upbringing, I never heard a teacher, parent or person give the ok to bad behavior because the bad actor was having an Earth experience in order to learn lessons.

The harshest judgments I executed were directed at me. "Not good enough, not perfect," and the stream of criticism flowed. Those judgments probably put up walls in every direction. They came so naturally, I'd never noticed. In fact, I considered them necessary to keep me on track. Our human conditioning ran deep.

Hemitra offered her opinion from the realm of clarity. I would be off thinking less than perfect thoughts about someone or myself, and her voice in my head would say, "Isn't that a judgment?" I would stop and think, and she was right. The awareness she brought allowed me to rewire just a bit and move on. The more it happened the less time I stayed in a criticizing mode. At those times, I felt truly free. The ideal of releasing judgment didn't always happen, but my guide's intervention lightened and enlightened my Earth experience. As time passed, my awareness grew.

The coaching from my spirit guide made me smile, and I at times, I stepped outside of the woman who flung judgmental thoughts and tried to remember that we are all here to learn different lessons, and we're all a little messed up. My loved ones and friends were doing great on their own, and my judgments might have held them back. I was reminded that even the energy of thought was received by the one it was directed toward. I also didn't perfect the lesson.

Since the last reading with Danielle, the issue of abandonment by Hemitra miraculously lost all its charge, and I didn't think about it. I searched my heart, but there didn't seem to be any lingering darkness. I couldn't carry that burden, and it wasn't mine to carry. The obvious truth was that all I could do was my own soul work. Talking as we did from our different dimensions did somehow heal what I had felt wasn't healable. We would still have big talks in the afterlife together.

One of my favorite repeat conversations with Hemitra was when I hit little walls and larger ones or made a blundering mistake and fell into a self-critical place. I would see and hear Hemitra's as she put her arm around me. She would say, "That's so human." It happened often, and I liked her point of view. "Just human." Another time, I would see a vision of her casually looking at her perfectly groomed fingernails, as she counseled me and always brought in the being human reference. That made me step back and know that no matter how good our human intentions were, we would inevitably fall to just being fallible humans. It was fun having a personal genie to coach me. Earth seemed an imperfect design, and I guess, it was designed to be that way. Accepting my screw ups as a human being helped soften me and brought the freedom of forgiveness. I liked that one a lot.

****

Months later, I had one of those quick gut reactions and negative thoughts about someone. There she was. This time the vision flashed as my partner holding out her arms and shrugging her shoulders. She meant the just human thing. She wasn't being critical. It felt like I stepped out of myself and stood with her, as we looked back at the whole human condition. I might have said, "Isn't it something, this being in bodies on Earth?" Of course, she could relate well remembering her own human baggage. We had fun on the Earth plane, and we were still laughing.

In another session with Danielle, she said that I must develop a personal relationship with my other guides and higher ups. She emphasized that the message came up repeatedly, and those contacts would give me the strength I needed. It was important to connect to all the Divine essences around since the spirit world offered vast resources that we all have available. Life on Earth is more than the connection between two souls.

She mentioned a healer guide, who appeared as a woman with butterfly wings. The woman was indigo blue and like a fairy. Danielle said this guide had never incarnated on Earth. I'd been told about the blue fairy guide before, and she had been described exactly like Danielle's vision.

Although Hemitra felt pretty sure she was the only other worldly authority I needed, she was still a new kid in that realm, and I understand there's a hierarchy of help that we all have.

A large a strong Native American man was my protector guide, and I was told he had been my grandfather and the chief of a tribe long ago. I had seen this protector guide and contacted him years before in a meditation.

Danielle brought forth another important guide, a woman dressed in an ancient Greek robe. I was to go to her because she was a teacher guide.

In meditation one day, I took myself on a journey to speak with guides and saw Jesus. Surprised, since I had been raised Christian, but didn't practice organized religion, I asked Danielle. She told me Jesus was a very strong guide for me. It turned out from other journeys to the realm of masters and angels, that Jesus had a very good sense of humor.

It was a relief to know that we always arrived on our Earth assignments with a team of helpers on all levels, and we were not meant to be disconnected from the ongoing lives of our loved ones in spirit. I became increasingly aware of how my life was a co-creation of my thoughts and the help and cooperation from Hemitra and my loved ones in spirit, ancestors, guides and angelic beings.

This was a good beginning, and I became easier toward me. Being human means accepting our light and our dark because that was the human condition. I maintained my humanness and my razor- sharp tongue for special occasions. At the end of this path, I may have made a little progress, but we humans get points for those small steps.

****

The learning continued, and in another session, Danielle began, "Its feels like she's come to a different plane. It's almost like you've both entered a different dimension. She's gotten stronger and learned a lot. She's not so invasive. She's not ringing the bell to tell you she's there with you."

In the first months, Hemitra would tell me I needed to rest, but when I would wake at night, I felt her presence and she would say. "You're not sleeping." Fifteen minutes later, "You're still not sleeping." I responded in a daze that I was really tired. She wanted to share her new life with me just as much as I wanted to know she was present. We had some adjusting to do on both sides.

"You have transitioned too. She is living through you. I want you to know she's sitting there holding your hands. She has evolved further. If you feel a difference in her energy, she's growing. Just as you're learning here, she's learning there. You're learning and growing as individuals and together, and you're both expanding. Even when you're doing your own thing, she's always with you because she can be doing her own thing and be with you. I know that you know she's with you."

I now knew that Hemitra and our loved ones on the other side could be with us, and at the same time, be in a class where they quickly learned to change colors in the aurora borealis or travel to a different universe by a mere thought.

"She told me she's really enjoying the space that you two are sharing."

"I am too."

"It feels so much more peaceful now, and it's not so much of a fight. She feels you've been more accepting of her form, and that's really been helping your relationship. You had bliss here, and you both had that ecstasy, but it's even more now than she could imagine. It's because you are sharing a consciousness. There is no separation, and when she was here you shared so much, but you didn't have this much of an understanding of the oneness." Danielle continued.

"I had clues."

"Yes, you had clues, but it wasn't the melding you have now. You will miss her physical body a long time. Humans grieve the loss of the body."

"Yes, I miss her, and I always will, and our new connection goes far beyond what I could ever imagine."

Danielle commented, "It was so much more than the physical when you were both here, and because it was so, and you were aware of that when she was in an Earth body is why you are able to communicate like you are now."

"It's indescribable." That's the best I could do when I couldn't find words.

Hemitra had changed and grown since her transition, and now I know, when we cross over, we start where we were on Earth. No grade can be skipped, and our evolution was up to us. The next dimension showed a clear picture of what we missed or ignored in our life on Earth.

"She is still here. The only thing she still has to learn is to respect the physical process. You know the physical essence is of importance."

Hemitra said, "I couldn't be in a physical body. The whole point of this Earth experience is to navigate the energy that we have chosen. When we're in a physical system, it seems slow and stagnant. It's a trick. We are here to feel that."

It seemed to me that it was a pretty good trick, as I began to heal my broken spirit and weary body. Learning to respect the physical process was something that happened in a body, and I didn't want to hope or anticipate what Hemitra's process of being in a body again might look like. I could only stay in and care for mine.

"She said she so appreciated the unconditional love from you. She said, she never felt anything like that and just know how grateful she is. To experience that purity, she said is divine energy, and to experience that divine energy is helping each of you elevate your vibration. You're growing and have entered a different vibration. She wants you to truly understand what a gift that is," Danielle continued.

"It took me time, but I appreciate it more than I can say." Hemitra and I shared a beautiful love together on Earth, and as a loved one in spirit, she showed me unconditional love beyond any prior comprehension.

"She is so present in your physical world there's no denying it. She's really proud of the personal work you've been doing and honoring your visions together, and you are honoring yourself more. You're caring much more for yourself and appreciating your body, and you have gratitude for your kids and your life. It's by this gratitude that you elevate your vibration. The love between you is awe inspiring. You are truly an example of unconditional love. You're living goddesses, especially you," Danielle said, and added, "She's in a complimentary mood. You'd better take it.

Danielle continued, "Look what you've taught your kids about unconditional love. For example, what's needed for unconditional love was when you both loved yourselves enough to be together and love each other."

Danielle referred to my choosing a life with Hemitra and dissolving my marriage as a step on the path to unconditional love and an example for my children. It hardly felt like that at the time to the children or to me, but years later, it made sense.

"Understanding there is more than just the physical and the connection to the heart is through daily connection with a spiritual practice, contacting those in spirit, yoga, meditation. There are so many things that challenge our vibration. We will always experience pain and emotion. It's when you don't let it go, it disconnects you. She said she understands that this hasn't been easy, and she's so grateful for you and your tenacity and the power of your spirit. She said you are a warrior, because of what you've overcome. You have chosen life. You have chosen to remain in your body and she is in awe of you spirit, and she is overwhelmed by your will and your Light."

Hemitra constantly expressed loving compliments, and I realized how our loved ones on the other side view us with compassion and total understanding. They know how hard it is sometimes to be veiled in the human condition. Her words flooded my heart. What I experienced from the lessons she taught me changed my entire view of reality. The knowing made me appreciate the impact and importance of everyone's incarnations in a body. Our human lives effect the entire whole more than we know.

After Hemitra's passing, I sank to emotional depth and grief, I didn't know existed. I was blessed by the support from family and friends. A large part of how I emerged from the dark with a deeper understanding of who I was and my strength was because of Hemitra's help and guidance. We did it together. The moments I nearly drowned in that pain, Hemitra intervened and lifted me up with her loving communication, and of course, the commands that I must do this. It wasn't easy for Hemitra to lower her vibration and scoop me out of the dark waters. Grief was part of our human experience, but she made me realize that grief offered me an opportunity to let go into the abyss and leave or break open my heart to a greater knowing of love.

One of the most important lessons of this life would be my natural connection with Hemitra and my loved ones in spirit to help me through the human journey. Unless I used that greater force that guided us, I was lost. Connection by daily spiritual practice was necessary to stay in a positive vibration.

I meditated, went back to yoga, and gratefully connected with my spirit guides, masters and Hemitra. Yes, Sweet One, this was the plan. I hated it, but everything was and is perfect.

Chapter 36

"This is so critical," Danielle had said. "If only one of you discovers enough self-love, it's everything. It will work."

Hemitra had added, "You can't be free if you have low self-esteem", and "I don't want to say it's all up to you, but it's all up to you. Think of the freedom it will give our souls."

Self-worth was the big issue that had surfaced from the past, and it was up to me. It weighed on my mind, since I'd just come through remembering lives that ended in tragedy. The trouble was, I didn't know how to accomplish the job.

When I thought of friends and others I'd gotten to know well, it seemed that no matter how successful or materially abundant they were, at a deep level, self-worth was in question. In the many circles of women over the years, though I saw great vitality and strength in them, they shared inadequate feelings about some part of their being that didn't feel self-worth. Were we humans fundamentally broken?

I knew Hemitra had an early life of pain, and I briefly thought about my childhood, as I tried to figure out my own patterns.

I picked parents who started me with security and glimpses of the mystical missing pieces. My Mom and Dad were well-adjusted, middle class, good parents. Growing up in the country, I thrived in the freedom my parents allowed my brother and me. At age 10, I got a beautiful black quarter horse. She and I spent hours on wooded trails and galloping through flower filled meadows, many times, with my friends who also had horses and shared the journey.

I laughed a lot and usually felt happy. School was fun, and I got good grades, played sports and enjoyed friends. The problems I had as a kid were not getting home from my treks through the woods on time and bringing home grade school report cards with the section for conduct marked with an I or a couple of Ns which stood for improving or needs improvement, but not quite there. I talked too much to friends in class, and I guess I may have stretched boundaries.

My life wasn't perfect. Dad was strict and critical, but he was also busy at work or taking care of our 20 acres. I was grounded a lot for my misdeeds, but that didn't seem to slow me down or dampen my spirits. Dad was different from my friends' dads. He kept honeybees and talked about books he read that explained how our ancient ancestors worshipped the honeybee for her mysteries. He read Henry David Thoreau's *Walden,* out loud to us, taught us to love the Earth and be self-sufficient. Nature became my spiritual foundation.

My friends loved my fun nurturing mom. She and I shared the desire to know what lay beyond the illusions of our cultural limits, and she told me she had read *The Search for Bridey Murphy*, the story of a woman who remembered her past lives and went on to find her senior citizen children in another county. This information made perfect sense to me. My mother and I had a mutual interest in all the realms of parapsychology that we could find in books. We knew what was in plain sight just couldn't be the whole story.

Despite growing up a happy kid, what I experienced in ordinary life fell short of satisfying a deep longing for something more just like everyone else. It seemed now that desire was the struggle to remember the truth inside- the wisdom that cannot be learned or unlearned.

My parents showed me glimpses of life beyond the accepted boundaries of the time. I tasted freedom, and I learned to love and care for our planet. As I grew, the economy grew and prospered, and the world hurtled toward this critical time of the 21st century. I felt grateful for my years of innocence.

I graduated from college and liked teaching middle school English. Jack, my college sweetheart and I, fell in love and married. We had our issues, but we coped with them and lived happily ever after to the extent that such things happen. We became the hub of four generations, including two beautiful daughters, and we lived in a home we loved.

My life with Hemitra, as we both agreed, was and still is magical. Our hearts guided us to each other and to the work we did, as we lived an Earth life and mediated with other celestial dimensions.

With no serious hidden skeletons that I could find in this life, I didn't understand how to find answers. I never doubted the truth of low self-esteem, especially since remembering the tragic endings in many lives with Hemitra.

Of course, I didn't always feel confident, not at all. Lack of self-love remained a dark shadow, since I was told by Hemitra that it was the whole key to "freeing our souls."

I asked intelligent friends. What about this self-worth?

"That's everybody's issue, without question. I see universal self-loathing. It seems to be innate. It's the human condition, and there are no exceptions," my friend Anna Marie stated.

"So how is that corrected?" I asked.

"The only solution is to love yourself. How? I don't know. That's the big question."

Michele commented, "Standards for people are too high. Everyone's under pressure to be successful and keep up in a really complex material world. I see hopelessness in so many people. No one's life is simple anymore."

Life wasn't simple now. Did hopelessness resulted from what we called human progress? The Earth was used as a resource to deplete for profit. We must have more and more things and throw away the stuff we no longer used. The material world was great fun, and we incarnate here to experience that, but the system for any positive future was flawed, and most of the manufactured goods were designed to break far sooner than necessary. Planned obsolescence was a key piece of our science to keep the economy going. What about all that trash?

Rampant consumerism was encouraged and enticed. More and more material piled in more and more landfills. Now, the bioaccumulation of waste of every kind, fouled our water, land, and air and flowed through our blood streams. What about future generations? An end of life on Earth was destined if the course wasn't corrected. The gross selfishness and disrespect for living things had gotten to overwhelming proportions.

"Humans have lost their spiritual knowing that they had in former incarnations. They now have only a materialist image of the world, and that view will kill humanity. Living only in the five senses has a paralyzing, deadening effect. The dying human race needs a life-giving elixir" (Steiner, 1918, pp. 40-41). The statement was made a hundred years ago, and obsessive materialism and its side effects only increased to the present.

I had felt a growing sadness as our kids grew up, and the environment become more and more toxic from chemicals and manufacturing waste. Human immune systems and the immune systems of all life on Earth were weakened.

Childhood cancer, violent school shootings, prejudice, riots, hatred and the monstrous cruelty of human beings against each other became normal. Our population grew emotionally and physically compromised and driven out of balance by the barrage of unnatural everything and the pressure of this complex material world. No system on Earth was exempt from a militant consciousness and organizations that demanded complete control for material gain, and no unkindness was skipped to yield a profit, no matter what was sacrificed to make that happen.

The planet seemed to be filled with lack of self-worth and self-love. If humans had self-worth wouldn't they nurture themselves and the Earth? A world devoid of the natural aspect of itself didn't run smoothly.

Aggressive Yang energy had dominated the Earth for the last 5000 years, and western history was written as if all of the past began at that time. The Gaia cultures and the Yin energy were denied and buried by western historians. They called them myth and primitive. Five thousand years was a short run in comparison with seven or so million years of human existence, and in that time, patriarchy succeeded in bringing Earth to the brink of destruction. Science and material progress replaced the human spirit and the health of the Earth. A rich tapestry of ancient knowing had been lost, ignored and suppressed. Can our science yet explain how the pyramids were built or how we plan to survive the results our behavior of extinction?

Indigenous cultures all over the world had long predicted the return of the Great Mother to human consciousness at this time. She who gives and nurtures life by the power of the feminine must bring balance once again to Earth. Too much Yang energy created overwhelm and stress, society ran on fear and chaos. The Goddess is one but was called by different names for her many manifestations as mother, warrior, teacher, healer, lover. We needed the female aspect now to balance the out-of-control Yang forces. The Divine Feminine resided in us all, and it manifests in acts of kindness, strength, compassion, nurturance, love and forgiveness.

This lifetime, Hemitra and I, and millions of renegades responded to the rising feminine consciousness that marked the beginning of a new era. Brilliant books were written and workshops taught to educate those who were ready to remember their roots and a peaceful Earth honoring time in our world history. Western culture had run amuck for profit, control and domination of absolutely everything. We had arrived at the end of a challenging era in the Earth's history, and the collective hopelessness reflected it.

I felt finished with remembering past lives but returned to the many memories that Hemitra and I lived in the last 5000 years. The knight wore a red cross and killed people in the cruel wars of the Inquisition. I didn't like him much. Countries of the world at that time, focused energies on building armies and the first basic war machines to destroy the enemy. The enemy seemed to be anyone with different ideals, skin color, or the ones who owned useful territory that could be conquered. We had succeeded in creating great weapons, biological, chemical and others to wipe out life. Today, the US alone could destroy the world many times over with the push of a button, and the Holy wars had never stopped.

The judgement I felt about the young widow in England had recently taken me to my knees. I wouldn't pick her as my heroine or an example of self-worth. She lived in the time of an Industrial Revolution in the British Empire and witnessed the cruelty of child labor and unfair class structures that were good for the rich and devastating for the poor, as people were sacrificed for profit. Equality two centuries later hadn't completely happened.

I'd had a brief memory of being burned at the stake. It was possible that I deserved punishment. In Europe from the 1400s to 1700s, about 80,000 were accused of being witches and burned at the stake or hung, and some accounts say the numbers were greater. Witches were almost always women, and the few men named were somehow linked up with the so -called witches. Women who served as herbalists or midwives became targets. Midwives eased the pain and trauma of childbirth, and the thinking, at dark times in history, was that women, as original sinners, should feel that pain. It didn't take much to be accused of being a witch but acted as a convenience to keep women in their place. Female was considered less than male. When women showed their inherent intuition, that was witchcraft. Woman's roll was to do what they were told by husbands, men and the over-arching patriarchal institutions. Intuitive knowing was labeled consorting with the devil. Ancient knowledge of healing must be destroyed.

Today, natural, effective and safe healing methods like classical homeopathy had been suppressed and extinguished whenever possible by the synthetic and profitable world of the chemical lords. Today, the U.S. is a medical industrial complex.

Crimes against women and the Earth raged on. A culture that attacked its female population and destroyed its own home was a civilization on its way to destruction.

I thought about the little I knew of lives before patriarchy. Danielle said, in one of our sessions, that Hemitra and I shared a life in Atlantis, and that was a very positive, powerful life.

"People were very connected to their hearts, and that is what we've forgotten. When you communicate with Hemitra you are bringing forth that heart energy. You are connected to the energy from that time period, and times when we lived in our hearts and were connected to the Earth energies."

The golden age of Atlantis was supposed to exist between 50,000 BC and 30,000 BC. However, according to Plato, it existed 9000 years before him. Some said it had been in the Atlantic Ocean outside the Straits of Gibraltar. Other accounts place Atlantis off the coast of Bimini and Cuba. Legend told that Atlantis was an advanced civilization, and they used crystal technology extensively for all their energy needs. That civilization was taken over by a hostile consciousness, and it ended in corruption and sank into the ocean. Many, or most, believe Atlantis was a myth that Plato created. Myth, to the ancients, existed as our recorded history now exists. Why would the truth seeking, great philosopher and teacher, Plato, make up that tale? Edgar Cayce, the famous intuitive, channeled extensive information on the lost civilization of Atlantis. I felt sure there was much more of Earth's history that lay shrouded in mystery, and if I only limited myself to what I was told by mass consciousness, I would have completely missed the most evolutionary, or sometimes revolutionary, experiences of my life.

Danielle also talked about an Egyptian life which sounded like it was long ago, perhaps at the time of predynastic Egypt. She said she saw Hemitra and me as part of a powerful circle of healers, who served the community. She mentioned a giant healing crystal in the center of our circle, and I saw it as orange with a fire like core. Others were there whom I knew from this life, and we were all equals. A mystical other worldly energy surrounded that life. What Danielle channeled sounded intriguing, but I didn't remember either of the mentioned ancient times. Humans' brains changed a great deal from the time when we could access those mysteries.

When I had asked about Delphi, Danielle and Linda verified that Hemitra and I shared a beautiful happy life. We served together for a lifetime. That lifetime gave Hemitra and me the most comfort, and Hemitra brought forth an amazing healing from the other side not long ago, using the energy of the sacred waters of Delphi. The lives that occurred thousands of years ago were the ones that Danielle spoke of as powerful and happy. Self-love didn't seem to be the issue in our ancient history.

Chapter 37

Hemitra and I always referred to the last 5000 years as the Age of Separation, as we used the term from a wonderful Seneca grandmother and wise woman. The human race had been separated from their essential nature and enslaved to a system that did enormous harm without any thought for the wellbeing of the next generations.

For the many millions of years that humans incarnated here, we made our important decisions based on gut instincts. When we were separated from what was natural, and what we knew deep inside, anxiety and depression resulted. We felt powerless when we were divided from the truth. How can one feel self-worth when we followed what we were told and instinctively knew it wasn't in our highest good? Humans had been seduced and manipulated to believe there were no other options that existed than what we were taught by those in power through time.

My partner and I learned a lot about our history from the remembered lives of the last 5000 years. They seemed to cover many of the possible choices for human existence. Those movies of intrigue, love, adventure, misadventure, and pain needed to be revealed. They were our sacred dramas, and I felt grateful to have reviewed the details of some of our many lives. They were fascinating non-fiction stories, but they were only stories. When we reincarnate into the weight of what we have lived, we could get stuck in our stories and hold on to the pain, fear and guilt of those lives. The challenge was to let go of what no longer served us and remember who we were and why we were here.

We all chose to be here to experience those Earth lives and learn every aspect of being human. For our training, we've lived everything that our free will might conceive, including the most grueling horrors to the most beautiful lives of love here on Earth. We have been female and male, heroines and heroes, victims and villains, as we played on planet. Our purpose on Earth was to experience all of our choices each incarnation and return to wholeness by choosing love in spite of our dualistic existence.

Hemitra helped me put being "just human" in perspective. What I had to do was step back from myself and my Earth life and be a witness to the drama I experienced here in this place of polarities. When we chose times and cultures to take live in, our greatest influence was the consciousness of those cultures, and that was part of the plan. The varied stories I co-created with Hemitra were our way to learn and know what it's like to be fully human. I felt the pain, and it forced me to look at the dance we engaged in for so long and detach from that through love and compassion. I needed to stop judging our stories and get neutral about what we had done. My dear spirit guide prodded me until I saw the truth, and my heart could accept my role here as a human, who lived both the Dark and the Light.

This planet had been designed as a place of contrasting polarities. We came here repeatedly to embody the Light and the Dark. That's what made us human. Our Earthly reality was that we live here in the 3rd dimension. This reality has been called the Maya, the illusion…living behind the veil. And yet here in this dimension, we do exist. Our reality in Earth space was not so much an illusion, as it was simply a slice of an even greater piece, a grander tapestry, of which we were all a part. What we experience in our five senses represented just a strand of that magnificent weaving of creation.

The human body is a miracle, and it's a great gift to live an Earth life. Humans aren't just connected to Earth. Our magnificent bodies are the same elements as the Earth. We are made of the stuff of diamonds and dolphins. Her soil is our flesh, Her rocks our bones, Her oceans our blood. We are one soul, and being human represented just a facet of that whole. That's what we had forgotten. As Hemitra constantly reminded me, we are all part of many dimensions. We are human, we are of the Earth and we are divine. We must stay connected for a meaningful existence.

There were many lessons that could only be learned in the dense physical body on this planet of polarities. Our experiences contributed to the world's evolution, and our loved ones in spirit needed us as we needed them. When we accepted our own divinity and reconnected to the larger whole of who we are, self-love wasn't an issue. We had just forgotten the truth, and that we had a chosen purpose that we agreed to accomplish here.

We can all communicate with the spiritual world and have a loving relationship with our loved ones and the divine. When we connect on a personal level, it changes our perspective, and the veil is lifted. That knowing is inside us. Loving guidance awaited our remembering and connecting.

Hemitra reminded me that "We can do anything. We aren't limited."

One of my greatest and most essential lessons this lifetime was knowing and growing my personal relationship with the world of spirit and my loved ones and guides. I experienced greater strength and confidence, as I partnered once again with Hemitra and my cosmic team.

No progress could be made without that connection, and when we remembered the fullness of who we were in that oneness, we were powerful beyond recognition. At times, when I managed to remember the truth, I felt almost invincible. That also wasn't consistent in my just human state.

"In earlier times, the human soul could still maintain a real connection with the dead." The ancients were in tune with the spiritual world. "It was once natural for a soul to have a living relationship with the dead. Such a bridge must be built again between the living and the dead so that we can learn to view the world with different eyes, because humanity has lost much since ancient times" (Steiner, 1918, p.60).

****

After Hemitra passed, both Hemitra and Danielle told me continually to raise my vibration. A great deal of the time my grief kept me crawling at ground level and below. My new spirit guide enthusiastically tried to set me on course. She used gentle persuasion, tough love and plain ignoring me, until I got the message. I still question that Hemitra actually followed Heaven's guidebook training rules. What's new? It's ok, because raising my vibration was always the most important piece. I could never have communicated with Hemitra if I hadn't gotten into a positive space. No progress was made, while I stayed under the acceptable vibration line, and I put up a good fight to stay stuck.

I needed many reminders to stay upright. One day, I obsessed and raged about an environmental issue. Why was it considered necessary to flood the entire planet from every polar bear to the creatures on the bottom of the deepest ocean with EMFs, as the toxicity levels reached dangerous plus markers everywhere on Earth, and regular unnatural frequencies bombarded everything?

Helpless frustration led to my playing an imaginary scene. Damn! I wanted to get the Winchester, saddle the mare, ride out and form a posse to DO SOMETHING! In my fantasy, I placed the rifle in its slip in her saddle a couple times. I could picture riding out to gather a posse, but then what? Next, Jack's Aunt Mary appeared from the other side. I saw her clearly in my mind. She said, "Your book is really interesting."

Thank you, I answered silently. I'd never talked to Aunt Mary since her passing, years ago. She and Uncle Charles had lived in upstate New York, and visits from them were always a treat. They were lovely and kind with open minds and hearts. Both intelligent and quick to laugh, they were loved by our family. I connected daily to my guides and loved ones in spirit now, and I would address all those who "loved me and had my best interests at heart." I was happy to see Aunt Mary as one of those loved ones.

The vision going on in my head included my horse standing there saddled and ready to go out and form a posse. Mary saw my mind's story and said sweetly and without judgement, "That never really worked, did it?" I laughed and had to agree with her. No, it never did. The visit reinforced the fact that we had no secret thoughts.

The idea wouldn't work, since the mare was dead, I don't have a Winchester, and I hadn't shot anyone this lifetime, not yet anyway. Wasn't I a defender of the Earth? I needed the reminder that this life was about living in the heart, and nothing could be fixed with the same consciousness that caused the problem. I had learned from many lives to fight force with force, but now it was time to evolve with love. Focusing on the problems only gave the problems greater power and weakened me. My very human self-needed messages to raise my vibration, because every choice we all made mattered for the future of humanity. We agreed to be part of a cultural shift that brought the Earth to this point in history. Collectively lifting our vibration to the heart must happen now.

As Betty and Hemitra both agreed that if we did just a little bit of being in a higher vibration, we would make progress. Any kindness counted more that we could imagine. One day, I drove to take some of Hemitra's things to a local donation site. I was hurting, and when I pulled up, a large, strong, middle aged man greeted me.

"Hi, how are you?" the man asked.

"I'm ok," I said as a polite exchange. "How are you?"

I'm wonderful," the man answered in a gentle but strong voice. With the response, his whole being lit up and his eyes shone with a force that caught me off guard.

"I got up this morning. The sun is shining and I'm standing here," the man continued.

I felt the guy had probably overcome a hurdle in his life, and his heart radiated such gratitude that he uplifted my whole day. I will never forget that moment. It's true, we are all incredibly powerful in our hearts. I returned his gaze and said, Thank you very much." He will never know what he did for me that day, and that those few seconds of his open- hearted appreciation were incredibly important. They changed my world at that critical time.

We are powerful beyond our recognition when we speak and act in love and appreciation, as we generate with every thought, emotion, word and action. How can we not love ourselves and feel worthy when we know our power comes from both Heaven and Earth, and we are a physical bridge between the two? We must remember and redevelop self-worth because we affect everything and everyone.

Hemitra repeatedly nudged me to remember the agreement that I initially tried to forget. If we had stayed together on Earth, I wouldn't have learned these primary lessons. I couldn't do it alone. From her celestial state she reminded me of our truest and deepest divine nature in love to help me return to wholeness and self- love.

****

Twelve years ago, Virginia's lovely mother made her transition to spirit, and Virginia received clear messages from her. Hilda had also been a friend of Hemitra's and mine, and one day at our house, I led a meditation to see if the three of us could speak with Hilda. From Virginia's mother, I heard in my mind, "The awareness doesn't end with death. It is much greater now. There are many possibilities, and you are fortunate that you are here for a truly wondrous transformational time."

Hilda wouldn't have talked that way when she still lived in body, but from her clear perspective of all things, she knew what lay in store for the Earth. This next era was unprecedented, and we were in the midst of it.

We now lived in the transition time, and all the fear, chaos and hatred made it obvious that the polarities had reached their extremes. I had to remind myself not to focus my energies there, and it took help to do that.

Unimagined changes were surfacing to catapult us into the next era, as millions of evolved and heart connected humans brought in brilliant solutions from the quantum reality to restore humanity. I recently heard about a well- known scientist who obtained a huge grant, because he found a method to detoxify nuclear waste. How amazing, and so much more to come!

Human hearts were responding and remembering that nurturing compassion and right relationship must once again be forefront on our planet. Sustainable, renewable, green, biodegradable, fair trade, ethical, efficient, organic, recrafted... We must all rise to the heart and enact any possible gesture of love. The future of humanity depended on it.

I understood why Hemitra and I incarnated to help the Earth and join the many millions of renegades and rebels whose purpose was similar. This life and this time to be here was a gift for us to contribute our small love offering, as we all moved forward together toward our ancient future destiny. I wanted to be worthy of this magnificent Earth and the incredible love I'd always received.

Chapter 38

Spring brought new life with the warmth of the sun. The neglected gardens overflowed with weeds. There had been no time for any yard work last spring. I cleaned the area beds, bought flowers, planted, mulched and dug some more. Hemitra advised by my side. I wasn't always aware of her consciously, but she was a split second away when I thought of her.

I dug and planted more, moved rocks, and added rocks to the rock garden. The Earth acted like a healing spa, and I kept working for days. One afternoon, as the sun sat at about 3 p.m., a feeling came over me. Everything stopped, and I was suspended in a blissful place. It was a space of rapture and complete peace. I knew for sure that all was well in the universe, especially in my universe. For certain, I should never have another concern or Earthly care. This was a dream like experience, but I stayed rooted to the Earth and the beauty around me. The feeling may have lasted a minute. I don't know. I remember that part of me questioned how long this euphoria would continue? As soon as I questioned, the incredible moment ended. I'd never experienced anything like it and never felt it again. I had tasted the meeting of Heaven and Earth, and I will always remember that brief interlude of deep connectedness and its truth. What amazing possibilities live in us!

That experience told me that the universe was unfolding exactly the way it should. We're here to hold our hearts open and live as part of Earth and part of Heaven and be a bridge between the two. I experienced the rapture of a moment of that.

****

A few months later, I began to plan a workshop. My heart still hurt, but I was healing, and I needed to move forward. I wanted to share the vital information I'd learned since Hemitra's passing. We had said we would start teaching again after she no longer had to care for her mom. Somewhere in our subconscious, we also knew this time our collaboration would be from two different dimensions.

Weeks before the event, I would see the hexagon shape. We raised honeybees, and I kept noticing and thinking of the perfect six-sided wax cells in their honeycomb, where eggs were laid and honey stored.

All over the ancient world, Melissae, or bee priestesses, worshipped the honeybee for her mysteries. Linda said for many years that we had been part of those sacred bee cults, and I loved and worshipped the honeybee this lifetime also.

The honeybee was said to be the best example of true community on Earth. In a hive, there were female worker bees, male drones and a queen. When the bees needed to make a queen, they feed one of the egg cells royal jelly, which was a product from the bees. The queen developed two plus times as large as the workers and lived for about six years to lay thousands of eggs. The workers were not fed royal jelly and lived six weeks. That's big Earth magic! I used the queen bee as an example of an Earth Goddess who embodied the power of the feminine.

"Bee consciousness is of a very high nature that humans won't attain until we complete our current evolutionary cycle or Earth cycle. The bee has a Venus consciousness, and the groups that worshipped the honeybee were called Apis cults, or Venus cults. The bees and their hive life was based on love, and more than we can imagine, our lives depend on the health of the honeybee" (Steiner & Braatz, 1998, p.170).

All numbers are sacred, but for this new material, I was inspired to use the six, which is the Lovers card in tarot, the number representing Venus-the planet of love, and the Star of David. The number is expansive and signifies moving consciousness from the power center to the heart. The heart would be the center of our focus, because that's where we must live to ensure our planetary survival.

Magic happened with synchronicities that confirmed my path. I opened the computer one day and saw the latest documents I'd used lined up in docs. I didn't recognize the second document and opened it. This paper hadn't been read for years, and I didn't know how it got there. It was part of a doctoral piece that a good friend of ours had written. We met Lynn in Malta and became instant friends. I commented about a beautiful honeybee necklace that she wore, and she explained her paper. She wrote it about the honeybee worshipping cults in ancient Crete, and their importance to the time.

A couple weeks of having the six in my awareness, I saw Danielle and we talked about the workshop and the hexagon shape. Hemitra told us that I was "right on track." Hemitra also said we had been using and meditating with the geometry of the number six, thousands of years ago.

Danielle commented, "You've known and used sacred geometry for many lifetimes. I see you doing that in Greece and in Egypt."

That statement made me think about where our ideas came from? I'd learned that I didn't completely create the thoughts and information that came to me. I simply started with a desire to make our workshop meaningful. Hemitra, guides and loved ones who were always connected to quantum knowledge did their part and created with me. Somehow the memories came to my awareness. I was never alone on my own, and even when I forgot that, it was best to flow with the unfolding ideas and synchronicities that came forth. I would know what felt right.

"All history, all social dynamics, all ethical life, proceed by virtue of cooperation between the so-called living and the so-called dead" (Steiner, 1918), concluded that the 'dire circumstances' the world experienced in 1918, World War I, could have been averted if the human race hadn't forgotten the ancient practice of communicating with those on the other side.

****

The reading continued, and Hemitra complemented my purple top. "You look really beautiful. That's a good color for you."

Danielle began to say something, and Hemitra interrupted with, "If it were up to me, you'd be wearing nothing at all."

I loved that Hemitra often made sexy, enticing comments which reminded me our life together and the memories of all our lives together. What a good partner to bring back our electrically charged relationships through time. What she said made me remember another piece of information earlier in this life, or perhaps she was bringing the information forward for a reason.

I talked to Danielle about using our theater lamp with the color gels as a background for the workshop. For all the years that Hemitra and I taught, we used color and sound as healing tools, and we used a theater lamp for one weekend workshop.

Before I met Hemitra, I was hanging out with my fun crowd who wanted to bring in a new consciousness. A friend from the group recommended an intuitive who was visiting the area. At the time, I studied color healing and worked with Melanie, who was a true master and a great teacher for me. In the reading, I asked the intuitive about ancient color healing. She proceeded to describe the use of light and color long ago, but now the information had grown hazy. She said I worked in the second temple in some part of Egypt using the color. Next, she said, "You healed with sex."

No more information was given, but the statement stood out. I also didn't write that skill on my resume, yet I'd always had a wholesome attitude toward the sacredness of love and sexuality.

I asked Danielle to make a comment on that era in Egypt of healing with color, light and sacred sexuality with Hemitra.

"It has to do with vibration and raising your vibration through the sensuality. That was a temple of learning and healing. What she shows me is that to control your mind in some ways helps you to go to different places and elevate your vibration, and it's so much more," said Danielle. "She's using the word Tantra. You were Tantric priestesses."

Linda also called us Tantric priestesses. She said she remembered being with us in the temple in the Egyptian life, and she placed the time as very ancient Egypt after the fall of Atlantis. She said during the era, women were highly regarded and shared rulership with men. The knowledge of sound and color were important healing modalities.

Hemitra and I had lived the life in Delphi with our sister Linda, and when we created our center, Linda was always the beloved intuitive, a teacher of our program and an eternal friend. It gave me comfort to remember the timelessness of relationships, and this friendship was a journey through eons.

Hemitra and I unconsciously brought that beautiful knowing of a tantric path with us. Our learning from ancient cultures included the sacredness of the body and physical love as a merger with the divine. The body was a portal and path to higher truth. Tantric masters through time said this form of love could cure all ills and teach the true mysteries of the universe. On Earth there were many choices. The opposite of the beauty and power of the body was taught by strict religious sects, who preached that the body was of animal nature and foul. One should use the mind to rise from the baseness of being human. Over time, sexuality had sadly been degraded and diminished along with the feminine and the Earth.

Danielle continued, "You two are completely connected by this cord, and because you were very physical in this lifetime and all the rest, your spirits were able to line up with each other. What Hemitra's saying is that there are great loves between humans, but sometimes they aren't in alignment physically. They don't line up in all ways. You two were in alignment at the same time with your physical selves as well as mentally, emotionally and spiritually, and that created a beyond this dimension reality. What you both experienced is almost something you can't even articulate. It's beyond love, it's beyond the body and beyond this world. That's why you were able to expand easily into other dimensions together."

"Because you were so physical in this lifetime and the rest…" What a beautiful, accurate description of Hemitra's and my relationship! Our ability to travel to other worlds began as soon as we were together in the same room. Simple physical touch brought forth memories of other times. Our life exemplified the body as a powerful vessel to experience the mysteries and divine states available to us all.

In an earlier reading, Hemitra told me, "We always loved each other, but we got better." As we evolve as humans, our relationships evolve and grow, and if we work at it-everything is possible for anyone.

I also thought about Hemitra's having a hard time being in a body. We live in a world of opposites, as we reside in the light and the dark. I knew that when we laughed, loved, lived, worked and played together, Hemitra reveled in her embodiment. It's not possible to be happy and sad at the same time. She's right. Her Earth life proved to be a great success.

I mentioned to Danielle that months after Hemitra's transition, I took a workshop with Lisa Schrader, called "Awakening Shakti." Lisa described Shakti as the divine feminine power that existed in women and men. Awakening this universal life force energy represented a sacred sensual path to life and happiness. I felt embraced by Lisa's sincerity and warmth, as I joined the community of like-minded women in the course.

"Everything gets easier when you tap into your authentic feminine power." Lisa's statement sounded as if every woman on planet could use this shot of female vitality, as we were graciously invited to welcome in the magnetic and receptive qualities of our true feminine selves to heal from the 'hypermasculine' mode of constant action and stress.

How do we awaken the frequencies of more pleasure in our bodies and cultivate the healing qualities of happiness and laughter? How do we keep our hearts open and live life in wholeness and beauty, as we unite body, heart and soul? How do we act as a channel for the Goddess energy to embody and live our Shakti, the source of one's greatest gift as a woman? We must connect to the emotional intelligence of the feminine despite the wounding and challenge with sexuality in our culture and embrace our sexual sensual energy as our creative power.

"For the hope of humanity, we must wake up to who we are, and women lead the way." Lisa's teachings echoed what fueled Hemitra's and my enthusiasm to teach and create our center as well as live our lives. She embodied her own awakened Shakti and feminine radiance, and she taught with caring and passion. Lisa's workshop proved to be an oasis of healing on my difficult journey, as she skillfully offered the beauty of ancient knowing to the group.

Hemitra told Danielle and me that she had brought Lisa's workshop to me, because I needed the healing. I'm sure she did. I could never explain exactly how that happened, but I did receive a lovely healing on my journey to reawaken and live again.

****

As I created or co-created the workshop with Hemitra, I visualized the three -dimensional hexagon in gold lines and lay it over the house. My friend, Damini, helped me create a hexagon poster with all the interior lines of that shape for our altar at the class.

Through Danielle, Hemitra told me to put a dove on the altar. It was to represent peace and freedom. The most important idea to stress was that we were all so much more than our miraculous bodies, and we naturally lived and functioned in different dimensions. We must free ourselves from the barriers and constraints that we put on ourselves by thinking that this is the only reality. By breaking from those illusionary boundaries we'd learned, we gained peace and freedom.

"Initiates of ancient humanity were trained to set themselves free of the grasp of Earth alone and awaken forces within their souls that allowed them to develop relationships with those who had passed to the other side. Those relationships would allow humans to access the whole cosmos" (Steiner, 1918, p. 206).

In preparation for the workshop, I gathered materials. Where was the music? I found some, and other pieces remained hidden. By now, I knew better than to frantically search, and I asked my partner for help. Then, I'd simply feel the way. I would walk into a room, and without thinking, move to a drawer or cabinet, and suddenly, whatever I looked for was in my hand. This was great! Thanks, Honey. Hemitra made comments, as I prepared. At one point in the late afternoon, she said I should get the color gels laid out. I didn't do that until after dark. Some of the colors needed double gels to be correct. They didn't translate in artificial light. "See," said the voice in my head. I laughed. No, I couldn't see. The colors all looked like mud. You were right Hemitra. I finished in the morning.

Three lovely women joined me in this life, and life after life, workshop of the heart and soul. It proved a small and perfect restart for us. Denyse had done our classes, and we'd been friends for years. Deb, another woman, was also a dear friend, and Andrea, the new woman, fit right in. Denyse said she could feel Hemitra's presence as soon as she drove in the driveway. Hemitra had said through Danielle, that her essence would not be missed.

****

In two weeks, the after-event comments from Hemitra followed through Danielle.

Danielle started the reading, "She wants to talk about the workshop. She loved it."

"We loved it!" I added. "It was about love. It was about the heart and other dimensions. It was us just like before, and we actively included loved ones in spirit."

"Hemitra said, we were back. It was perfect!"

Danielle commented. "There was no difference between you and her. You were one. There was no separation. You would have a thought, she would have a thought. It was seamless. You did it together."

Hemitra added, "Is it really you or me or is it us? That's what we always had. It's not you or me, it's collective energy. The reality is us."

"Yes, we did." I didn't always know who had those thoughts. Sometimes, I clearly heard or saw Hemitra. Our guides give us words and thoughts, even though we think they are our own thoughts.

Danielle continued, "It had a lot to do with Goddess energy and connecting to that Goddess within each of us and recognizing it. She is so excited. You must have been working with Earth energy. The structure of the honeycomb was important in helping people connect with the frequency, and what you were teaching. The Goddess is coming through strongly. You both come back to help and serve the Earth. It's a strong purpose for you and always has been. What you taught and are teaching is the way back to the heart, and what you both demonstrated was that there are no boundaries. That is your mission."

I loved our mission.

"The three women were very special."

"Yes," said Danielle. "Very very special, and it's not the first time their paths have crossed."

That statement made me think how we incarnate in soul groups and the perfection in what seemed an imperfect world.

Danielle observed, "A lot times she's spunky, but she's very cuddly now. She's in a nurturing place. She's got her arm around you and there's incredible sweetness. She just adores you."

Hemitra said, "Look how perfect she is! Look how beautiful she is! I can't get over it. Look how cute she is."

Her comments touched me deeply, but I felt my exhaustion and hardly attractive.

Danielle said, "She's in a complimentary mood. She wants you to know how special you are, and she's making a point. Make sure she hears this. Make sure she listens. Make sure she knows that, 'You are the best thing that's ever happened to me. You are my life, you are my love, you are my soul. Know that! My experience, my journey where I am, is better because we are connected. Your soul lifts me up.'"

"Just know she loves you, and she's always with you. She is smiling from ear to ear. She says she couldn't love anyone more.

Chapter 39

Danielle counseled that I was to take the memories of ancient Greece and bring them here and incorporate them. She said, "Hemitra is bringing Delphi forward," and she reminded me that we could all communicate telepathically in that life. It was a high energy lifetime.

"That was a beautiful life," Danielle repeated.

I wanted to know more. From our files, I located the transcription of a past life reading that was done the year of Hemitra's illness. It was with Jan, an intuitive hypnotherapist we met while we were studying with William Bengston at Lilydale. I had scheduled a reading for me, while Hemitra rested. I wanted to go back to the time Hemitra and I shared in Delphi, in what I believed was pre-Hellenic Greece, just as the tide was turning and the classical Greek period was beginning. We had started to write our book on past lives and this would be more research.

The reading took place at Jan's home. That day, Jan guided me into hypnosis and the Grecian life long ago. The first thing I felt was a powerful awareness from the land around me. It overwhelmed me with such love and comfort that I cried. The rushes and realization of the Earth and Her presence stayed with me the entire reading and the tears continued.

I said, "It's perfect and peaceful here. I see a group of women. They feel very loving. I'm young."

Jan asked, "How long were you there?"

"I don't know. I see a rough looking man. I think he was my father. Maybe it was when I was brought to the temple. I see rocks and a wall and there are mountains. The women are cooking. There's a community feeling."

Jan asked, "Was Hemitra always there?"

"Yes. I'm watching the group, and I'm watching her. I belong with her. Now she's playing with my hair. I'm laughing with her."

Jan questioned, "How long were you together?"

"I've known her for a while. This has been my home. It seems that I'm in training. They like what I do. I work with nature, and I like them. The group is serious and focused. They help the people who live in the villages around here. I see the world going on beyond these mountains. There may be a war somewhere. We're safe in our community. I can feel the mountains, and I love them. There's a special energy from the Earth, and that's why we're here. We're isolated from the world. I see that we're doing something for the people from the villages. Someone is carrying a child. We're healers. I feel drawn to the child, as if I'm a healer. I love the land and really connect with it."

Jan: "How do you heal?"

"I see myself and others picking herbs. I'm on a hillside and notice that the grass is dry, as I look for some plant. I'm not sure all the ways we heal."

Jan: "Are you happy?"

"Yes!"

Jan: "Is Hemitra happy?"

"Yes! We love it here, and we're dedicated to our work. It's really a sacred place- a place unto itself. It's protected, but it's being noticed."

Jan asked, "Who protects this place?"

"It's sacred. It's palpable. Everyone knows that."

Jan: "You are lovers?"

"Yes. We're very happy together. I see us walking arm and arm and snuggling. I feel honored to do this work and be together."

Jan: "Where's Hemitra?"

"She's right here."

Jan told me to move ahead.

"Time has passed. I'm drawn to the place where the gas comes from the ground. I see a spring. I'm not allowed to be one to use the gases, but I'm close. I see myself taking care of Hemitra because she's been doing that work, and it's draining. I gave her something to drink. Some women are older."

Jan: "Are there other women lovers?"

"I don't know."

Jan told me to move on in time.

"I've gone to the next level, and there's a training. I see a fire and I'm in a training or conducting a training. My heart is happy. We're dedicated to the work."

"Move ahead," said Jane.

"I feel sad now. There's something different. I don't feel as comfortable. There are lots of people coming from the rest of the world. I see more men, important men. Something's changed. We're older. We're together. It's still great. There's the overwhelming feeling of the land. The sun shines brighter here, and the place is such a draw. Many come here for healing.

The whole land mass.... It's Heaven on Earth. There's so much goodness in this place."
Jan: "Is Hemitra still a prophetess?"

"Yes."

Jan: "Are you too?"

"Yes. We take it seriously. I keep going back to the rocks and the water. There was amazing energy there coming from the Earth. It wasn't just the gases."

Jan said, "What's the next event? What has changed?"

"I'm alone. She's gone, but I see her here."

Jan: "Where's Hemitra?"

"On the other side, and I see her standing beside me. I'm watching her. I've withdrawn from what's happening. I see goats and people gathering things. There are buildings being constructed."

Jan said, "Go to the last day of that lifetime."

"I'm dressed and lying somewhere. It's peaceful."

Jan: "What's wrong with you?"

"I'm just leaving. It's not a big deal. You go easily. There are kids around. They're dressed like the pictures of ancient Greece. I'm grateful for the lifetime. It was good. I feel solid with the universe. I feel connected to everything. I remember the food. There was such vitality in it and in everything… Now I don't see myself there. The lifetime was a gift to be there with her."

"She's with me now. We're together on the other side. People are talking about us. We did good work. We're laughing and saying it was wonderful. This was a preplanned lifetime. We did everything we wanted to do, and we planned to be there together. I see us dancing around and just being happy."

"Hemitra's saying the water that ran under the Earth was very sacred. It really was. We could see the nature spirits, and I felt tremendous power there. It was a lifetime of connectedness. We were honored. It was easier then, and it was powerful to be together. We had to be really clean mentally and spiritually. There weren't many challenges, except change."

Jan asked, "Why did you choose it?"

"To be in a higher place. It was an opportunity to grow. I see a heart. People liked us. It was such a gift at that time, and the world was being drawn there. It was such a strong clean spiritual place, and we worshiped the Earth. That life stayed with us forever. I feel like I could stay there forever. In spirit, I saw us taking another look around."

Jan guided me back from hypnosis, and we talked.

"She said, you and Hemitra shared a great love that lifetime, and it set the platform for this lifetime."

I wanted to know more about what that meant.

****

Chapter 40

I thought about the reading and even questioned. I knew facts about Delphi before Jan's hypnosis session. Linda had done the first reading for us long ago. Did I make things up, because I was influenced by previous information and impressions? Even with the past intuitive readings and my memories, the regression and the spirit trip to Delphi with Jan took me to spaces and depths I'd never known. I felt incredibly alive and clear. My sense of the whole land mass took over most of my perception, and everything else was secondary. When I realized Hemitra left her body, I accepted it and still saw her with me. Something profound and important to understand unearthed itself in that regression.

What I felt in the past life session to ancient Greece perfectly matched the initial memory that surfaced when Hemitra and I sat together that June day in the summer long ago. It felt like we'd stepped into ancient Greece, and it all started. Though we had no idea what lay ahead, we had landed together again as two women. I remembered the bliss of that innocent moment with more of an understanding of the euphoria we both experienced.

Almost immediately, Hemitra and I paired up and began to be a teaching team. She brought her passion, skills and conviction regarding the ancient Goddess culture and women's mysteries. I offered what I had learned from my teachers and experienced over the years on color healing and chakras, Native American wisdom, herbs, homeopathy, and communication with plants, animals, and nature spirits.

We started a six-weekend program for women that went on for 15 years. Again, we were the Gaia worshipping twosome, as we lived our passion for the Earth. Throughout the years, women nicknamed us the "Lighthearted Temple Sisters" without knowing about the memories of Delphi. They also called us the "Good Time Suburban Goddesses." The joy of being and the sweetness of our relationship, the humor and laughter, sharing the work we treasured—did it repeat from thousands of years before? What we love and who we are in our Earth lives continues in the afterlife and future lifetimes in different formats, and sometimes the same theme repeats with the same soul in a different body.

Some of our happiest memories were those times with our women's groups as we searched the meadow and woods behind our house, and we foraged for wild plants to make medicinal tinctures and salves. The women experienced their own keen intuition as we sat in meditation talking to violets and other intelligent plant beings, nature spirits, and the elementals of air, fire, earth and water. We guided them on inner journeys to find their animal guides or went back in trance time to receive messages from ancient ancestors.

During our weekend on the Goddess, we studied many faces of the divine feminine, remembering our deep connection to Gaia, and the way we once nurtured and cared for our Earth. Evidence of Gaia cultures around the world dated back thousands of years before recorded history and were part of the ancient creation myths. However, without written records, the evidence showed itself from archeological digs which unearthed a myriad of female figures and animal statues around the globe. In these early societies, there were no signs of war or fortification. Both men and women were equal parts of this culture. We explored what it might have been like to be female in a society other than patriarchy, that invested thousands of years naming women as the lesser sex? Every account of the earliest history of Delphi speaks of that same Gaia worship and reverence for the female and the feminine body of the Earth. We were teaching what we had lived in the past.

The last weekend of our training was called "Masks of Transformation," the conclusion of our work together, and with each group, it proved emotional and profound. We made molds of the women's faces and they decorated them. The masks they made looked amazing covered with artwork and sacred symbols, feathers, bones, shells and other creative selections. We then did a process in pairs- the purpose was to deeply feel and witness the inner self as reflected by a partner.

All our offerings were designed to reconnect to our inner knowing, and what was rightfully ours.

In our first reading on Delphi with Linda, she mentioned caves in the area where rituals were performed, and that she saw us wearing animal masks in those cave rituals. The Corycian, a famous cave is nestled seven miles up the winding slopes of Mount Parnassos from the Delphic center. The cave has amazing high ceilings and deep interior filled with large stalactites and stalagmites, and it's one of the Earth's great caves. History tells that in this famous cave, religious rites were performed for thousands of years. Bones and ritual objects were found that date back to Paleolithic times. There are other caves tucked in places on the mountain, and these places were sacred and holy to the early inhabitants (Sahellarion, 2018). We did our mask rituals again in this current century. The giant cave was missing, and that would have been a nice touch.

The sacred Castalian Spring and the most sacred Kassotis spring were two of five springs at Delphi close to where the women did prophecy. Before doing the work, the priestess always washed in the Castalian spring, and all who came for healing or an audience with the oracle had to cleanse their bodies there. Throughout the long reign of the Delphic oracle (Hart, 1985), the water of the springs was considered sacred. It was said that water nymphs, the Naiads, presided over the springs at Delphi and imparted magical healing qualities to the pure water.

Shortly after Hemitra's passing, when I was driving home from the county courthouse after probating her will and breaking apart from the grief, I asked for help. In that moment, as I felt the water and saw Hemitra, my emotional pain miraculously disappeared, and I thought I'd lost my mind. Linda and my girlfriend set me straight, "See it believe it," Hemitra demanded from her place as my new guide. I was clinging desperately to the edge, but in that devastating moment, the energy of the water of one of the sacred springs of Delphi magically healed me in this life. I had received divine assistance from the Naiads and Hemitra from another time and dimension.

Six months later in a reading with Danielle, Hemitra reinforced the power of those sacred waters, no longer in this time, when she said, "Remember the water essences will heal you. Connect to the water and that energy source in Delphi and bring it here. Imagine you are in that realm and imagine the waters of Delphi pouring over you. You are rebuilding your cells."

In the regression with Jan, I clearly saw that Hemitra stayed by my side even though she left her body and went to spirit before me. I don't remember any grief. She was with me, and then in spirit and still with me. I also regarded my own passing with no fear or trauma. It would have helped to have been sure of those things this lifetime. How different the feeling at that time! My memory suggested that we still had the power of knowing we were Heaven and we were Earth at once, and that our relationships with our loved ones were eternal? It was my hardest lesson now.

Humanity has lost much since ancient times. Ancient initiates of the mystery trainings were taught to awaken "cosmic memories" and communicate with the spirit world for vital information and deeply moving experiences… "Heaven and Earth work together to create a unity" (Steiner, 1918, pp. 205-206).

The facts I uncovered about Delphi, a place and time thousands of years ago, now further explained the unbreakable bond between Hemitra and me, and why we did the work we did, and why we shared the same passions.

Chapter 41

Another time I felt bliss similar to my past life experience at Delphi was when Hemitra and I co- lead a sacred site tour to Malta a few years before her mom's illness. In preparation for our trip, we researched the temples and ancient history of Malta, which dated all the way back to Paleolithic, then Neolithic civilizations. Like the Egyptian pyramids, researchers couldn't understand the high scientific knowledge of the architectural construction of the 50 ancient temples on the island.

In Malta, we visited the famous Hypogeum, a large underground multi chambered labyrinth with halls, and stairs. This archeological wonder, built 5000-6000 years ago, served as a sacred birth and burial chamber. In certain areas, the ceiling had been painted with red ochre designs-hexagons, hexagons with spirals within them, and honeybees.

Some records say the bones of several thousand humans were found there, which indicated a long history. Our guide led us to a chamber called the 'Holiest of Holies.' It was carefully designed for light shafts to come through on Summer Solstice. All over the world without any modern communication, our ancient ancestors spoke the same language and honored the seasons with elaborate astrological observations and used the same sacred geometry symbols—spirals, triangles hexagons, and animal art.

Underground in this holy place, we all felt deep respect for the consciousness of the ancestors with their mathematical and engineering sophistication, and their connectedness to the Earth and the Heavens. Like Delphi, this space was one of Earth's many sacred sites.

On one of our day trips in Malta, we visited Mnajdra by the sea. This small structure yards from the Mediterranean Sea was thought to have been used for astronomical observation and was a calendar for the equinox and solstices. Throughout the ancient world, temples, pyramids and rock formations were specially constructed to catch the sun's rays on the days of summer and winter solstice. The light would come through and cascade into these special constructions. This was an advanced knowledge of the celestial alignments that marked the change of seasons.

On a sunny, bright day, our group walked down the sandy slope to the temple. As I stepped across the threshold of this ancient ruin, my heart filled with a flood of emotion. The Earth there held enormous energy.

I'd read about ley lines, invisible energy pathways all over the earth. The sacred sites of the ancients, stone circles and temples of all kinds spread over the planet were constructed on powerful ley lines. Our ancient ancestors were in tune with their location and effect. That may have been part of what some of us felt that day at the temple on the shore of the Mediterranean.

The site of a dowser, who used dowsing rods to test the ley lines at Delphi, wrote that a major ley line is said to run right under the Oracle site at Delphi, and it runs from Skellig St. Michael in Ireland to Armageddon in Turkey and beyond. This long ley line has been called the Apollo-Athena Line where it is in Delphi (Hedge, 2013).

Where and when did the oracle of Delphi originate? Gayle Randall's research focused on both archeology and mythology to trace the oracle's beginnings. She used material from many ancient writers including Homer, Herodotus and Plutarch to name a few.

The search for the Delphic oracle's beginnings can be traced by myth to the Neanderthal Era (70,000-8000 BCE), and this is much earlier than most accounts. Myth tells that the oracle was Gaia herself. With no timeline, "It appears the Oracle had always been there." Ancient Delphi was an established community center of prophecy and most likely focused on family and local problems many centuries before Classical Greece (Randall).

Oracles were common to our distant ancestors, and there were many oracular sites in the ancient world, but none was more revered or more powerful than the oracles of Delphi. This temple sanctuary is located beneath the "Shining Rocks" of Mount Parnassus in central Greece. Some historians say it was in prominence for 1200 years of recorded history. The Delphic oracle's recorded history started in the 9th century BCE, and "oral tradition dated the power of the oracle way back through the Mycenaean era 1600 BCE to 1100 BCE." There were no written records going back that far. The Greeks believed that the oracle existed since the dawn of time (Hart, 1985).

As Delphi became a famous religious sanctuary, one early story of Delphi, was that Greek historian Diodoros Siculus of the 1st century BCE, wrote that long ago a goat herder who came upon the gases that seeped from the ground in Delphi, "became inspired," saw the future, and felt a "tremendous upliftment." The goats would jump about and sometimes fall into ravines around that site (Hart, 1985).

I searched excitedly for the distant beginnings of the Delphic oracle. From my reading with Jan and Linda's comments, it could be that Hemitra and I lived our life in Delphi at the end of the Mycenaean era, as the Golden Age of Greece dawned. We were Gaia worshippers and life seemed simple, rural and humble. We did prophecy, and we were healers and teachers. The men I remembered, as we grew older, could have taken over at the time when the God Apollo slayed the She Snake, the Python. The Python, to the Delphi inhabitants was the Goddess. It represented the wisdom, power, and divinity of the Earth. Serpents in many ancient cultures represented Mother nature, the Great Goddess. The priestesses of Delphi were called Pythia.

Apollo's mythical slaying of the python symbolized the suppression of the ancient Earth worshipping cultures that dated back to prerecorded history. Apollo's brutal act brought the end closer for the Gaia cultures and the matriarchal traditions that had been sustained in Greece for so long. Coexistence with the Earth was gradually replaced by a male dominated patriarchy, as separation and power over the wisdom of the Earth and the feminine became the cultural paradigm, which rules today.

In Linda's initial channeling, she said that Hemitra and I in our elder years, resented what was happening at Delphi. Did we experience the beginning of the end of Goddess worship that had stretched far back through the mists of time?

I found that many millions of articles had been written on the Delphi oracle and this ancient mysticism. It was repeatedly said that the thousands of years of the oracles' prophetic reign positively affected Greek civilization.

The Oracles inspired all of Greece with their high standards. For many centuries they were a "sisterhood of mystics"" who seemed to have "superhuman powers" (Broad, 2007, p. 1).

The 1200 years of history, that most writer's emphasis as the most important time of the oracle at Delphi, the sun god Apollo was supreme and his priestesses were the Pythia. Her prophetic messages were said to be channeled from Apollo and not from the Earth Mother.

The Pythia were initiates of a mystery training. This ongoing community of dedicated women passed down their secrets from generation to generation. There are no accounts of how they trained since it was knowledge held by the women. To be a Delphic oracle, it is said that they had to undergo strict moral, psychological, mental training, and purification. They lived lives of dedicated service and passed that valuable model down through generations (Hart, 1985).

At first, young women served as oracles, but later the women chosen were over 50, and it's thought that the women lived in the local area. The process of divination took place in the adyton, a small room in the lower underground level part of the temple of Apollo where a sweet-smelling gas arose from a fissure in the rocks. Two faults cross directly under the oracle chamber in Delphi where the gas seeped through into the oracle chamber (Hart, 1985).

Before she began her work, the oracle purified herself in the Castaglian spring. She and two other women, her support, then approached the temple. Next, she drank from the Kassotis spring which came up into the adyon and ran into a basin inside. This water was thought to be sacred, magical and healing, and the priestesses drank for "divine inspiration" (Hart, 1985).

In the adyton lay the Omphalos, a large conical shaped stone. Omphalos means navel or center. Delphi became known as "the center of the world and the place where Heaven met Earth" (Pinterest.com, 2018, Aug. 7).

The oracle sat on a tripod and held a sprig of laurel leaves and a shell filled with the sacred spring water. She breathed the gas and went into a trance state. The gas was said to smell like a sweet perfume. Plutarch believed the Oracle received divine inspiration and could only receive the inspiration safely when she was trained and prepared (Hart, 1985).

The oracles reputation remained excellent for all the hundreds of years that the woman served. Plutarch always wrote about the integrity of the priestesses and the vapors she used. The oracle was credited with the great success of Athens and Sparta because she "encouraged democratic ideals" (Broad, 2007, pp. 67-69).

Aristotle, Socrates and Plato, and many other famous Greeks were associated with the Delphic oracle, interacted with and gave her long lasting respect. Socrates, considered a great thinker and teacher asked his students to contemplate one of the famous sayings from the Oracle, to 'Know Thyself.' The Delphic oracle was the most prestigious and authoritative oracle among the Greeks, and she was among the most powerful women of the classical world.

As the oracle's fame spread, the sanctuary at Delphi became one of the wealthiest places in the world, filled with gold, silver and grand statues. A Delphic coin was issued in 480 BCE. The oracles continued to give practical grounded advice about governing. The Oracles continued to teach ethical values to the leaders of Greece.

It was a great life for the oracles since Greek men were extremely chauvinistic and women had few options in life. The oracle women enjoyed their own homes, no taxation and respect and reverence from the entire world. The height of the Oracles fame was between the 6th and 4th century BCE.

The golden age of Greece and the oracle site at Delphi both began their decline by the time of Aristotle's death in 322 BCE. The oracle continued through Roman domination, but her powerful hold had waned, and her counsel was more for local reasons. The last Roman to seek counsel at Delphi was told by the oracle, "Tell the king, the fair-wrought house has fallen. No shelter has Apollo, no sacred laurel leaves. The fountains now are silent, the voice is stilled. It is finished" (Pinterest.com, Popular Quotes).

After the birth of Christ, the Christians demonized the oracle, called Apollo the devil, and began to rid the world of such evil pagan darkness. History was now written by patriarchal organizations whose base purpose was control and domination.

Michelangelo painted the Oracle on the Sistine Chapel's ceiling between 1508 and 1512. He honored the Oracle priestesses because one of the mystic women had predicted the birth of Christ (Michelangelo).

In 1893, a group of French archaeologists searched the area of Delphi and found no geology that supported the possibility of a gas there or a fissure where it would seep through the rocks. They assumed the entire history was a myth, and the oracle of Delphi's worldwide fame fell (Wikipedia).

In 1920, again the French explored and found a limestone with holes that would have supported a tripod. They also found the Omphalos, the sacred rounded stone sculpture in the adyton where the priestesses did prophecy (Wikipedia).

In 1981, Jelle De Boer and John Hale found evidence of ethylene gas and a fissure that crossed under the sanctuary. Delphi often experienced earthquakes which had changed the underground structure enough to mask the truth of the past.

The ancient scholars had it right. De Boer and Hale's research reclaimed the legendary history of Delphi. They found that small doses of the ethylene gas that had been at the site produced a state of euphoria, and mental elation (De Boer & Hale, 2000).

However, after de Boer's (2007) long study of Delphi, he concluded that the gases the priestesses used were simply a stimulus and an inspiration to those women who had intense spiritual training, and a devotion to serve. "The influence of the oracle on a society that began much of what we judge to be Western Civilization, could never be explained simply by inhaling ethylene gas because her messages still stand as timeless wisdom and integrity."

As a priest of Delphi for many years, Plutarch's quote showed his reverence and first- hand knowledge of the priestesses.

The prophetic priestesses are moved (by the god) each in accordance with her natural facilities...(Plutarch, 1962).

As a matter of fact, the voice is not that of a god, nor the utterance of it, nor the diction, nor the metre, but all these are the woman's; He (Apollo) puts into her mind only the visions and creates a light in her soul in regard to the future; for inspiration is precisely this."

"Delphi will be forever one of the most sacred seats of the life of the human race" (Broad, 2007, p. 80).

I repeated Danielle's words in my mind. "It was a wonderful life for you and Hemitra. I see you both in white Grecian robes. Beautiful. Happy, very very, happy, and yes, there's a strong connection to this lifetime."

Chapter 42

When I returned from hypnosis in the past life regression with Jan, the skin on my face was tight from my salty tears. The powerful presence I had rushing through me was the force field of that ancient timeless sacred site of Delphi. I knew the truth in my heart. The research on Delphi and the Oracle confirmed in my mind that for such an important, long enduring phenomena to occur, the oracle priestesses lived in oneness with the Great Mother Gaia, and her inspirations. The visions I saw in regression and remembering gave me a deep feeling level of the sacred. The information search continued.

Hemitra stayed with me, and I felt her enthusiasm, as I made discoveries. In a conversation with Linda, she reported that Hemitra paced back and forth. She was helping me. Hemitra and my writing guides created the synchronicity to find the perfect articles. I was the initiator, and I asked for the help. It was also my fingers, mind and body carrying out the task. It's always humbling as a human to realize how much we receive from our loved ones in spirit, guides and angels, but some things can only be accomplished here in a body, and I had to turn on and use the computer.

Making this conscious contact with divine forces and the ability to travel through time and space felt right, and my psychic link up with Delphi and a lifetime when we were all connected to Heaven and Earth, was again helping to heal my heart. My personal subjective experience of that life in ancient Greece gained more solid footing when I found a website by Martin Gray, a National Geographic photographer whose life had been inspired by his travel experiences to 600 sacred sites in 80 countries over a 20 -year period.

Gray observed, "Ancient legends and modern-day reports tell of extraordinary experiences that people have had while visiting these holy magical places. Different sacred sites have the power to heal the body, enlighten the mind, increase creativity, develop psychic abilities, and awaken the soul to knowing its true purpose in life" (Gray, 2007).

Martin Gray concluded there were four things that create the power and magic of these sacred areas:

1. There were many Earth influences: Places such as caves, mountains, rock formations, underground fault systems, springs, waterfalls and forest groves are ancient sacred sites, and they can be explained by magnetism, thermal energy, faults and seismic activity, mineral ores, and other geophysical factors. The power factors of the ancient sites were like a magnet, creating an energy in and around it.

2. The movement of the sun, stars and planets. The ancients knew and lived by the information available from the Heavens.

3. The structure and artifacts at sacred sites. Temples, pyramids and ancient architecture were created with spiritual purpose and mystical knowledge as well as for shelter or worship.

4. The power of human intention in cocreation with the divine and the spiritual activity that occurred at sacred sites over time (Gray, 2007).

Our ancient ancestors revered the Earth and had a direct relationship with Her consciousness. They sensed these special sites, lived with and utilized the other worldly energies at mystical sites as the source for healing, worship, and inspiration. Delphi was only one of the many sacred sites on the Earth.

Respect and nurturance of our planet is imperative at this time when the pendulum has swung so far from reverence for the Earth to dominance and disregard for Her, the factor which has brought us into our current ecological crisis. "Human beings are out of touch with themselves, their fellow humans, and the Earth they live upon. Contact with these sacred sites can assist in the awakening and transformation of human consciousness and thereby in the healing of the Earth" (Gray, 2007).

Gray lamented the fact that the mysticism of sacred sites hadn't received much understanding from mainstream social anthropologists, geographers or religious historians. This "journey through mystic realms and witnessing of things that can be felt but not measured, are disregarded by most of the mainstream." Disregard for ancient myths was a big mistake considering that in these places around the world, "extraordinary phenomenon" repeatedly occurred. "These holy places and their mysterious spiritual magnetism contain deep meaning for us all, in fact, contain a knowledge of vital importance to the well -being of humanity and the planet we live upon" (Gray, 2007).

Hemitra and I and many millions of others shared Martin Gray's passion and belief in the essential nature of remembering the sacredness of the Earth for our survival as humans. Since the time of Apollo, a new consciousness replaced the unquestionable wisdom of Gaia. Whoever took power from war or aggression made the rules according to what served them. The rational mind and five senses dominated to the exclusion of heart and intuition, science verses nature, materialism revered, mysticism feared.

"Man's inner life of the soul has undergone change. Prior to 800BC man was still united with nature." After that time, humans separated from the intelligence of the natural world and soul forces or 'supersensible' perceptions that arose from an unconscious knowing. Humans became focused on the external, material and the left brain conscious mind. From the 15th century there was much progress made in the world of science, but the exclusive focus on science, mind, and the external world only would "leave mankind's spirit mechanized, man's soul vegetative and man's body animalized" (Steiner, 1918).

A "new perception" is about to enter our materialist world which will revive human's relationship to Earth and Spirit. "Even in these dark and sad times we shall not lose hope- the hope of reawakening in a new form, of the spiritual life of mankind, that we are perhaps destined to have just in this time of greatest need" (Steiner, 1918).

Our separateness from the Earth and from spirit deteriorates our morality, our very humanness and leaves us in a state of ego and self-doubt. We were never designed to be disconnected from the essential parts of ourselves and stuck in the limits of only our five senses.

The result of our arrogant and historically long disregard in caring for the Earth and honoring Her wisdom must end and we must shift our thinking. "These legendary places have the mysterious capacity to awaken and catalyze within visitors the qualities of compassion, wisdom, peace of mind, and respect for the Earth" (Gray, 2007).

Mystical influences abounded at the holy site of Delphi. Mt. Parnassus was considered a sacred mountain and Delphi was nestled at her base. Pilgrims endured a difficult journey to get to Delphi, allowing it to remain secluded and pristine through the centuries. Five sacred springs bubbled forth from under the ground, the domain of the magical Naiads who inspired the oracles and imparted their healing and magical gifts. Caves in the area were used for ritual purposes. There were periodic earthquakes and seismic activity in the area. The famous underground faults where the ethylene gas flowed upward into the adyton highlighted Delphi for thousands of years. The land, the women, the many frequencies, elementals, ley lines, dedication, love, joy, pure intention, and the unbreakable connection with it all passed through generations and made the Delphic oracle a world renown phenomenon.

The priestesses' mystery training must have included the secrets from those powerful hidden dimensions that served as guides and healers for the women for the thousands of years that they, and the natural forces they embraced, counseled and comforted all of ancient Greece and the known world at the time. In that long era, the priestesses and also the priests at a later time, lived impeccable lives and embraced an unwavering code of ethics like the pure natural forces that supported them.

Nature is the most powerful force on Earth. Elementals and humans were the original stewards and co-creators of the natural world. The spirits of nature partnered with our ancient ancestors and want to now, but we have ignored them for centuries, even demonized them. Our relationship with our Earth was one of nurturing stewardship, as humans counseled with the subtle energies of air, earth, air, fire and water and all the unseen beings in co-creating their lives. They knew the invisible world was as real as the physical world. We lived connected to the Earth and to Heaven, to the seen, and the unseen. The subtle world was now waiting for the physical world to wake up.

****

In the Grecian life reading with Jan, I felt a deep sense of ethics and unwavering commitment as well as joy with Hemitra and our purpose. Danielle and I talked about the fact that when one was connected to their heart center, with the Earth, and to spirit, it would be impossible to do harm to this Earthly home. The women I'd just researched were one with the Earth, had 'impeccable' reputations and were dedicated to their work. I remained convinced that the power of intention and the Earth there created that long standing phenomenon. All of our connections to Earth's sacredness and Heaven taught us how to live our best, kindest and most loving lives. We were connected to our hearts, and we knew there was no separation between Heaven and Earth.

Today, many people were reawakening to the awareness of our interdependence and oneness with the Earth. Hemitra and I loved our work helping women remember the love and power of Gaia and reclaim their connection to Her. The lifetime thousands of years ago did set a template for this lifetime, and it felt right that we chose to come back together at the end of this long era of history, at the beginning of a new and necessary way of thinking.

Chapter 43

When a loved one leaves their Earth life, we face our biggest challenge, and this mythic, but inevitable initiation can provide our greatest gifts. In the months and years after Hemitra made her transition, it was an opportunity to realize at a deeper level of who we were as individuals and together.

When one of our friends and former students, Jacqueline, learned of Hemitra's passing, she sent me a condolence note. "I never saw two people so happy together. You thought alike, and everyone could feel how close you two were. I love you both because you always lived in a different dimension and you brought all of us there. You changed my life."

I was sure now that it was the joy and laughter that lit us up. All the close girl- and boyfriends in my life had a great sense of humor. Laughter and fun made life worthwhile, and Hemitra and I excelled at fun. I found a hand-written letter from a student who had taken many of our classes.

Heart of the Goddess

"They laugh. They play. They hug. They argue- sometimes. They love each other like kids do; they share, constantly. What they share is something children have shared since time immemorial; the moment, their fantasies, themselves, all these essential things that we try so hard to forget the minute we decide we should become grownups. They also work very hard, but you'd never know it, because here they are having so much fun. It's very confusing for somebody like me, a solid by-product of the puritanical work ethic.

What was I doing the first time I went there, listening to these two women who seemed to have nothing better to do than poke jokes at each other and talk about rocks as if they were alive? How come I was not leaving, asking for my money back? I came here for serious stuff.

Some psychic I had connected with told me to look these ladies up. When I asked her why, she simply said, "I have no idea, it just felt like I should tell you. They do important work, and they're not fools like a lot of these New Age people. They know what's going on and what they are doing.".

Something extremely feminine emanated from Sue and Hemitra. It was soothing. I liked that. As they spoke and laughed, I began to notice they seemed to genuinely care about each of us as individuals. I felt very welcome, totally accepted for whoever I was at the time.

We studied three minerals each evening. First, we drank their energies mixed with water. Then, lying on a thick carpet and wrapped up in blankets and sheep skins, our eyes closed, we listened to Sue and Hemitra take us on a journey through these rocks.

I realized that at 38, I did not love myself. It made me cry. There were monsters in me, they were waiting for me deep in a lake inside the blue agate, and I was appalled at the size of those things. They were "my" monsters. It was my birth, it was my guilt, and all these fears collected over the years, and maybe also, lifetimes. I managed to dislodge them and send them away forever. By the time the visualization was over, I was exhausted, but I was freed.

It's amazing what can happen to you inside a rock, or when you play with honeysuckle in a meadow with Hemitra and Sue or when you draw a picture of yourself with crayons fit for toddlers, or when they have you dancing with jungle music.

I was in therapy for two years twice a week with a lady I had a great deal of respect for. We did a lot of healthy work together. It wasn't a lot of fun, talking and talking half the time you don't know where you are or whether you are making progress. It's a slow process, all verbal, and it becomes quite expensive.

Hemitra and Sue show us how to play again, how to be light and happy and childlike. They make it all fun, and you do so much work, and so fast. You run into past lives, stumble on huge anxiety, and can deal with it immediately and free yourself of it forever. Their secret? The atmosphere of trust that they create, their nurturing, their kindness toward their students, their joy and simplicity, and their deep understanding of how things really work.

Sue and Hemitra, Hemitra and Sue, an amazing pair.

June 25, 1989
Christine Duval

The warm flickering candlelight created an air of magic in Hemitra's living room. Covered by a silk cloth, the glass coffee table glistened with Earth treasures; shimmering amethyst geodes, clear quartz clusters, luscious turquoise, mysterious indigo lapis, deep rich orange carnelian, soft pink rose quartz, cool green aventurine, and a long list of others, nestled among the candles.

Once a week, the class studied three rock specimens. We made essences of each by putting the minerals or crystals in pure water for a week then taking the water and adding a small amount of vodka or brandy as a preservative. Before each meditation, the women drank a dropper full of the potion, and we played appropriate music, as Hemitra and I took turns guiding the trance journeys through the misty realms of rock consciousness.

After the meditation, we shared our journeys and then discussed the properties of the crystal we were studying. The women intuitively knew the crystal's quality as it was presented in its purest homeopathic form by the crystal itself. They received healing and information- rocks speak clearly and the women understood. Amethyst soothed the chatter of the conscious mind and allowed inner calm to guide one to higher realms and deeper understanding, rose quartz affected the heart and encouraged self-love—sometimes bringing up tears, and emotional release.

Our relationship with rocks made us all better, more aware, and more compassionate. The quality and message of each of the crystals was constant, unchanging, unadulterated by negative human emotions, existing in their healing perfection, steady and trustworthy. As we honored these sacred jewels and merged consciousness with their purity and wisdom we learned and we became more.

****

We studied everything available about crystals and crystal healing. Though non-traditional, rock medicine worked. In fact, crystal healing dated back thousands of years. Many believed that our ancient ancestors knew extensive ways to harness the power and wisdom of the crystals, and that knowledge had been lost in time. Today's technology used quartz crystals in computers, cameras, watches and other devices. Those who worked with crystals followed a path that had been created by wise ones long ago. They were remembering.

Nikola Tesla, the brilliant scientist, referred to crystals as "living beings, and the secrets of the universe are found in energy, frequency, and vibration."

"The sacred geometry of crystals is the key to ancient knowledge to raise the consciousness of the planet... They are the geometric blueprints of creation."

At the beginning, making a living was forefront in our minds. It would have been easy if I'd gone back to teach in the classroom and Hemitra had continued in sales. Although that practical need concerned us, as we struggled in the start -up, Hemitra and I, in all our lives, seemed to function outside the borders of convention. Also, the incredible joy of being together was the plan. Those mineral treasures created a path.

Everyone who took our classes wanted to buy the beautiful crystals and minerals. We filed for a wholesale license, and when we opened our 2000 sq ft center the year after, it included a 600 sq ft gift shop with crystals, gemstones and other jewelry, and a long list of inventory.

Memories that had been untapped for years appeared, vividly reviewing the details of our life together. This happened from the beginning after Hemitra's passing, as she helped to bring them forth.

Another folder contained copies of our feature article in the magazine section of a prominent Philadelphia newspaper. We'd been in business a few years and attracted enough attention to draw it in. When we got publicity, we remained in the mode of being 'business partners' and 'housemates,' carefully skirting our couple status.

We lived and worked in suburbia, 30 minutes outside Philadelphia. It made sense to us that opening a place called Heart of the Goddess in 1990 was enough for the residents to take in. Being a woman couple might invite homophobia. We had great customers-women and men who shopped for women. We didn't care who they slept with, and they didn't need additional information about us.

Matthew, the news writer, arrived for an initial interview, while author Vicki Nobel's second of three weekend long shamanic workshops was in process. It was Friday evening, and a circle of 50 plus women and a few men gathered in the large workshop room. Matthew joined us, taking note of what was said and done as the sound of drums beat and the smell of incense wafted everywhere. He painted an accurate picture of the shamanic workshop, quoting our facilitator and some circle participants, mentioning it on the first page of his article and comparing the evening to the essence of Woodstock. Fair enough. He also wrote about some of our offerings: Shamanic Healing, Aromatherapy, Past Life Regression, Homeopathy, and our six weekend Woman Wisdom to name only a few. All were described in his article as workshops 'ahead of the curve.'

He was personable and had an excellent reputation as a writer. He asked lots of questions, with particular interest in us personally. Where did we live?

"Oh, you live together, you work together?" Nothing offensive, and he did a great job, but clearly, he was interested in the details.

The article started with a description of our building and location; the dull outside and the contrast of the interior where gentle music played, incense burned and a water fountain bubbled. The attractive store displayed models of Goddess statues across cultures and before written history, well placed crystals everywhere, a large case of silver and gold jewelry, clothing, drums, windchimes and books.

"It was a place inspired by the Goddess movement, yet much more eclectic," the author surmised.

I liked Matthew's description of the women and men who attended our workshop and shopped in the store—all manner of dress, all ages, backgrounds, and philosophies. I was tense as the writer dug into our backgrounds, and our life together. He wrote about our meeting at the fabulous Summer Solstice party in my backyard, complete with the Lenape Nation chief, maypole, and sweat lodge.

Matthew called our personalities and backgrounds as different as different can be, though seeking the same thing. Hemitra, a debutant who attended college to become an actress and had a short acting career, did modeling, sales, then learned Transcendental Meditation and became a long time Transcendental Meditation teacher. We met after the point in her life that called her to the Goddess.

I was Mrs. Natural everything, raised in the PA countryside on horseback, schoolteacher, and traditional role as a wife who stayed home with the kids. I also followed a non-traditional role talking to plants and animals and receiving answers back. He wrote that I was into deeper ecology, and that my divorce "startled everyone." Hummmm.

It took hours to set us up with props for the two -page color photo spread. In the upstairs workshop room, our large purple cloth was laid on the floor first, then the large turquoise silk fabric woven around the purple. In the center, the photographer placed a three-foot diameter gold plaster wall sculpture of Artemis from the store. Above Artemis to the right, Matthew chose to position a hand painted leather frame drum. The image on the drum was two snakes in a circle. Around the drum, a dozen lit votive candles burned, and around the cloth were small round hanging sculptures of the moon, stars and sun.

The photographer posed Hemitra and me on the floor reclining next to Artemis, with elbows on small green silk pillows. Of course, we wore glamorous earrings and jewelry from our inventory. We were grateful for the publicity, even if tentative about the questioning. We were also grateful to end the photo shoot.

Matthew had interviewed some of the women in our group. One of the questions he posed to a current student, "How many women here are lesbians?"

She looked puzzled, shrugged and said, "I don't know."

Our purpose was to serve the public, teach what we felt passionately, and not focus on issues from a society that bristled in fear of differences. I suppose I could have deepened the story by telling him that when Hemitra and I met, I remembered our past lives, that falling in love again was a given- we always did that. I should have also mentioned that Linda, our best and most loved intuitive reader, was a priestess of Delphi with us in a past life, and isn't it amazing how we all ended up here together? I waited until now to tell that tale.

Matthew's well written clever article was syndicated in several cities around the country and whoever read it, it gave them something to talk about.

As I replayed the memories of our wild, sweet life together, which we still shared, I imagined the time when my well-worn body had reached its expiration date. After moving through the tunnel and into the great beauty of the Light, I'd join my loved ones at a not to be described in words party. By then, my kids and grandkids will be well versed on the rules of engagement with loved ones in spirit. No doubt, they will best like the fact that I'll be there for them and offer counsel only if they ask for my opinion, and I can't interfere with their free will.

Hemitra and I will exchange a lot of hugs and a Heavenly high five, perhaps saying, "Hey, that was a good one! We did it. We arrived on Earth to live our lives to the fullest together and apart. We came to love each other and serve Gaia, the Mother

Goddess, and we came to laugh. We made enough errors and backward steps to experience our full humanness, and we can claim that we gave our small love contribution to add to all the other delicious pieces that make up the whole. We made a little progress."

We'll be able to instantly share all the memories of our favorite Earth scenes. I'm going to pick those perfect June days in the late 20th century or the early 21st century. In all the years of teaching the last weekend of our women's group, the sun shone, and the gift of perfect weather was ours. That first day we invited the elementals to join us and co-create our class. The elementals were always ready to join in and play with unconditional love and acceptance. These powerful beings were the Sylphs, the elemental consciousness of the air, the Undines, the beings that rule the waters, the Salamanders that grace us with the wonder of the fire, and the Gnomes who keep vigil on the Earth body.

Here we stepped out of time and space and went beyond the boundaries of our conditioning as the women naturally received messages from these intelligences and deciphered how this information related to their own hearts and souls. Each of the elements represented one of the four directions— east, west, north and south.

Hemitra and I talked about the elements one by one, and we lead a meditation before the women walked the corresponding direction of each element and connected with the wisdom of those powerful energies. With each elemental we gave an exercise.

For our communion with the hardworking Gnomes, the women took trowels, and we asked them to go to the garden and dig in the rich ground. They dug into the loamy Earth and encountered the perfect chemistry of the topsoil that gave life to all Earth beings. They were silent, as they held the Earth in their hands, caressed it, or held it close to their faces, as they took in the heavy scent of the sacred ground.

Hemitra and I chanted and sang, "The Earth, the Air, the Fire, the Water, return return, return, return." In harmony we softly beat our frame drums, walking around each woman and repeating, "I am you, you are me, we are one, I am you, you are me, we are one," as they focused on the life-giving Earth. The blood ran hot in our veins with passion and purpose, as the women once again merged soul and soil, some moved to tears at the depth of their innate understanding of our collective oneness. We were home.

Return, return, return, return, we must.

****

Dear Precious Humans,

It's true. This is a pinnacle lifetime-for you, for me and for our Mother, the Earth. This is the one that decides them all, and the universe is watching. This is the era that's been whispered about, written about, and known by indigenous cultures for millennium. We are in the time of the Great Shift-the time of the greatest spiritual evolution the Earth has ever experienced. Now the plan for healing and regeneration unfolds, as Gaia returns. You've come here to get it done. There is no way to emphasize strongly enough that every one of your thoughts and actions effects Everything!! It's critical that you remember who you are, and why you are here at this moment in the Earth's history.

You are being tested now by difficult times, as we personally and collectively make this gigantic spiritual leap from the era of power over and domination to living from your heart center. You are needed. We are all needed now!

You chose this incarnation and your exciting assignment. You were born for these times, and you're trained and ready. You arrived with many varied stories and dramas from lives that span all of history. They are your learning treasures, and you needed all those priceless experiences to help you grow and learn, but you are vastly more than those stories and much more than you ever imagined.

Let your heart accept the dark and light of your humanity in order to rise to a divine understanding of your role here. Break those limits! You are part of Earth and part of Heaven, and you are connected to the entire benevolent universe. It's all inside, and you're here to remember that you are a multi-dimensional super star.

There's no greater classroom or vehicle for your evolution than being in a body, but you are much more than your body. Take radical good care of yourself. It hurts others when you don't, and it benefits you, your loved ones, and everyone when you practice self-love and cultivate self-worth. It all begins with extreme care of your priceless body, which is the home of your spirit. It's a lot of work, but the rewards are amazing, and without that, nothing else matters.

265

You came to this place of polarities in human form. That's why legends of angels, guides and loved ones kneel at your feet, as you experience Earth, feel heartbreaking emotions, witness unthinkable events, and know amazing bliss as you break through the false boundaries that have kept you feeling diminished and held you and the world in an illusion of separateness. You are adored.

Love yourself. That's the first step to freedom and the foundation of everything else. Be yourself. That's better than good enough. Connect, connect, connect with Heaven and Earth. Once you remember who you really are, self-love and self-worth are easy.

Chose a path filled with ease, humor, joy and pleasure. We forget that we're here to find happiness, to dance, make love, create music and art, and play with our friends. You always have the answers available from the spirits of nature and your loved ones, guides and angels in the next dimension. You're just human living the human condition. Let them figure out the hard stuff. Just ask and learn to receive.

Any small act of kindness or love from the heart toward yourself or another is exponentially powerful compared to acts of violence and hatred. The heart is mighty beyond imagination.

If you only make a small positive step, it counts, it's a success. Some days that may not happen. You build your soul with those steps, and they multiple over and over. They are eternal.

We're in the finals, and the stakes are high. We don't want to say it's all up to you, but it's all up to you, all of us! This is the one that's going to decide everything! This is your chance to change everything. You can do this. You have to, you must! Let's get it done now. Think of the freedom it will give our souls!

If we want our species to survive, if we want to find meaning in our lives, if we want to save the Earth and every life form on Her, love is the one and only answer!

Shine On, You Crazy Diamonds!!

Love and Blessings,
Sue & Hemitra

References

Bengston, W. & Fraser, S. (2010) *The Energy Cure: Unraveling the Mystery of Hands-On Healing*. Boulder, CO: Sounds True, Inc.

Broad W. (2007). *The Oracle, Ancient Delphi and the Science Behind It's Lost Secrets*. Penguin Books.

Dass, R. (1971). *Be Here Now*. San Cristobal, New Mexica: Lama Foundation

De Boer, J. Z. & Hale, J.R. (2000). *The Geological Origins of the Oracle at Delphi, Greece*. https://sp.lyellcollection.org/content/171/1/399

Destinations Greece. (2018, August 17). https://www.Pinterest.com

Dinshah, D. (1999). *Let There Be Light*. Dinshah Health Society

Gray, M. (2007). *Sacred Earth: Places of Peace and Power*. https://sacredsites.com/martin_gray/biography.html

Hart, E. (1985, Oct/Nov). *The Delphi Oracle*. Sunrise Magazine, Oct/Nov 1985.

Hedge Druid, The. www.hedgedruid.com/2013/03/delphi-the- apollo-and-athena-ley-line/

Jain. *Sacred Geometry*. https://jain108academy.com

Landry, P. (1993, July 4). *Drums Across the Main Line*. In Ladies Who Incant.

Michelangelo. http://www.michelangelo.net/delphic-sibyl/

Nicola Tesla Association. *Genius for the Future*.
http://www.unt-genius.hr/EN/

Parsintl.com/publication/the-philadelphia-inquirer/

Plutarch M. (1962). "The Oracles of Delphi" V, 397 from
The Delphic Oracle by E. Hart.
https://sites.google.com/site/eloisewritings/home/the-delphic-oracle

Pontiac, R. (2012, May 15) *Attention is Existence:
Instruction from the Invisibles*. Newtopia Magazine.

Popular quotes www.pinterest.com

Pythia. https://en.wikipedia.org/wiki/Pythia

Randall, G. *The Delphic Oracle, A History*.
https//independent.academia.edu/GayleRandall

Sahellarion, K. (2018, Oct.13). *Mystical Beauty and Sacred
Sites around the Oracle of Delphi*. Home/Travel/Cultural
Travel.

Startistics. http://startistics.com/2011/06/8-the serpent/

Steiner R. (1918). *The Dead are with Us: A Lecture by
Rudolf Steiner*. Nuremberg, February 10, 1918.
Bibliographic Survey, Vol. 182, 1961.

Steiner, R. & Bamford, C. (Compiler) (1999). *Staying
Connected: How to Continue Your Relationships with Those
Who Have Died*. Hudson, N.Y.: Anthroposophic Press.

Steiner, R. & Braatz R. (Translator) (1998). *Bees*. Hudson,
N.Y.: Anthroposophic Press.

Unt-genius.hr/EN/quotes.html the Nicola Tesla Association-
Genius for the Future

White, S. (1988). *Across the Unknown*. Columbus, Ohio:
Ariel Press.

White, S. (1988). *The Betty Book*. Columbus, Ohio: Ariel Press.

White, S. (2010). *The Unobstructed Universe*. Columbus, Ohio: Ariel Press.

About the Author

Suzanne King is a teacher and author and is Certified in Past-Life Regression from the Weiss Institute, a Certified Hypnotist, and a member of the National Guild of Hypnotists.

For 15 years, she was co-owner of Heart of the Goddess, a Holistic Learning Center, and was the co-creator of Woman Wisdom® Training, a series of workshops that forged a path for women to honor the Divine Feminine.

Suzanne offers decades of teaching experience, both in the traditional classroom and in the creation and teaching of programs for women and children.

Other work includes *Sacred Animal Wisdom, A Handbook for the Human Heart* and *We Love Honeybees*, a DVD for kids.

She lives in a suburb outside of Philadelphia, Pennsylvania.

Suzanne may be contacted at:
suzannerking.com
suzanneking@verizon.net

Made in the USA
Middletown, DE
21 September 2021